CREATIVITY WITHOUT LAW

Creativity without Law

Challenging the Assumptions of Intellectual Property

Edited by
Kate Darling and Aaron Perzanowski

NEW YORK UNIVERSITY PRESS
New York

NEW YORK UNIVERSITY PRESS
New York
www.nyupress.org

© 2017 by New York University
All rights reserved

References to Internet websites (URLs) were accurate at the time of writing. Neither the author nor New York University Press is responsible for URLs that may have expired or changed since the manuscript was prepared.

ISBN: 978-1-4798-4193-6 (hardback)
ISBN: 978-1-4798-5624-4 (paperback)

For Library of Congress Cataloging-in-Publication data, please contact the Library of Congress.

CONTENTS

Introduction

AARON PERZANOWSKI AND KATE DARLING

In an economy increasingly sustained by information, creativity and innovation are key drivers of public policy. From immigration to taxation, policymakers evaluate new laws and regulations, in part, on the basis of their power to foster or thwart innovation. In no area are these considerations more salient than in intellectual property (IP) law. Indeed, spurring innovation is at the core of IP policy. But the central narrative of IP law, that legal protection against copying is necessary in order to promote creative behavior, has been subjected to surprisingly little scrutiny. The theory certainly has intuitive appeal, and for many innovators, the conventional wisdom appears to hold true. Without some assurances against widespread copying, for example, it is difficult to imagine sufficient private investment to finance the latest pharmaceutical breakthrough or Hollywood summer blockbuster. But an increasing number of creators challenge the prevailing narrative by thriving outside of traditional IP law. This book collects some of their stories and considers what they mean for the IP system and our innovation economy more generally.

Intellectual property law is not premised on any single theory or justification. The foundations of IP law incorporate both labor theory—the notion that the effort spent inventing, authoring, or composing demands the reward of property rights—and personality theory—the notion that one's creations are a manifestation of the self and control over them is necessary for self-realization. These theoretical underpinnings sometimes play a prominent role in IP systems outside of the United States, particularly in the continental European tradition. But despite the debts it owes to John Locke and Georg Hegel, the dominant justification for IP law in the United States is a utilitarian one. We grant patents and copyrights in order to encourage authors and inventors to engage in the socially valuable but sometimes costly enterprise of creating something new.

Because information can be copied easily and cheaply, we worry that would-be innovators will be reluctant to invest their time, effort, and capital in creating and disseminating new technologies and expressive works. In a world without IP law—the thinking goes—innovators would be powerless to stop unscrupulous competitors from appropriating their ideas and undercutting their prices. These free-riding competitors, after all, have no up-front investment to recoup. In such a world, policymakers fear that the next great inventor or artist will instead opt for a safe and reliable career in dentistry or accounting, depriving us of their genius.

IP law hopes to avoid this outcome by granting innovators and creators the legal power to exclude others from their work, enabling them to capture the full value of their contributions and secure a tidy return on their investment. But intellectual property rights are not costless; the IP system embodies an unavoidable tradeoff between incentives and access. By creating limited statutory monopolies, IP results in higher prices and decreased public access to creative works. We are willing to tolerate those costs, however, on the assumption that exclusive rights are the unavoidable price we pay to secure a steady supply of creative output.

By revealing the on-the-ground practices of a range of previously ignored creators and innovators, the studies in this book challenge this intellectual property orthodoxy. The communities these studies uncover force us to rethink the assumptions underlying IP law: that creativity cannot thrive without legal rights of exclusion, that widespread copying is inevitable without legal intervention, and that law dictates the way the public interacts with creative works. Collectively, these studies reveal that, despite its deep preoccupation with incentives, IP policy has embraced legal exclusivity without a careful examination of the conditions and motivations that define the creative environment.[1] As a consequence, IP law displays a troubling insensitivity to the specific needs of particular creative communities, and it has historically disregarded non-legal regulatory tools that enable more granular, and potentially more effective, management of creative incentives.

While IP is a crucial tool for maintaining creative incentives in some industries, scholars of creativity already understand that the assumptions underlying the IP system largely ignore the range of powerful non-economic motivations that compel creative efforts. From painters to open source developers, many artists and inventors are moved to create, not by the hope for monetary return, but by innate urges that are often quite resistant to financial considerations.[2] Although some of our case studies reinforce this point, the communities we highlight offer a new set of insights. Specifically, they reveal that the assumptions behind IP law overlook the capacity of creative industries for self-governance and dynamic social and market responses to the appropriation of information.

Some of these communities are forced to operate without IP protection because current law does not reach or explicitly excludes their creative output. Others could assert IP in theory, but in practice they choose to opt out of the formal legal system and rely on informal social norms to govern their creative behavior. And still other creators take copying as a given and route around its harmful effects through nimble marketplace strategy. From tattoo artists to physicians, Nigerian filmmakers to roller derby players, the communities illustrated in this book demonstrate that creativity can thrive without legal incentives, and perhaps more strikingly, that some creative communities prefer self-regulation to law.

Perhaps not surprisingly, IP law demonstrates something of a blind spot for non-legal means of regulation. For lawyers, judges, and legislators, legal prohibitions are the most obvious means of changing human behavior. By creating civil or criminal liability for disfavored actions, the law harnesses the immense power of the state to influence how we act. Law is undoubtedly a powerful tool. But it is not the only means of regulation, nor is it always the most effective.

In addition to law, we can think about three other general approaches to regulating behavior: architecture, norms, and markets.[3] For any real or perceived social ill, we can deploy one or more of these modes of regulation with varying success. Take for example the scourge of cell phone use at movie theaters. No longer limited to the poorly timed ringing phone, distractions from the cinematic experience now include texting, email, and brazen games of Candy Crush. How do we curtail this growing menace? We could of course pass a law that locks up unrepentant phone users. But the legal solution imposes costs on law enforcement and the judicial system. And it may seem to many of us something of an overreaction. Other tools can be subtler, less expensive, and have the appearance of greater legitimacy.

We might, for example, rely on architecture to reduce cell phone use. Architecture here refers not just to the design of our buildings but to all of the features of the physical environment, both natural and built, that shape our behavior. For example, speed bumps help regulate our driving habits by altering road conditions. A more contentious deployment of regulation through architecture can be found in the use by famed urban planner Robert Moses of overpasses too low to accommodate buses in order to promote racial segregation.[4] If our comparatively innocuous goal is eliminating cell phone use, we could install wireless jamming technology in movie theaters or build them from materials that impede wireless reception. After all, if your neighbor's phone receives no signal, she is less likely to disturb your viewing experience.

We might also rely on social norms to reduce cell phone use. Social norms are obligations to engage in or refrain from certain behaviors enforced through private interactions rather than by the state. They regulate through the pressure of social disapproval. Sometimes that disapproval is expressed by others when we violate a norm; other times it is expressed internally through our own sense of guilt when we fail to meet the expectations of our community. If a community objects to a behavior and holds in contempt those who disregard prevailing expectations, it can leverage our sensitivity to social judgment and isolation to alter behavior. Disapproving looks, impatient sighs, and frustrated shushing all communicate the violation of movie theater norms and, for at least some cell phone users, discourage such behavior in the future. These social norms often emerge organically, but they can also be reinforced through deliberate efforts. Consider the pre-feature public service announcements at the Alamo Drafthouse, a popular movie theater in Austin, Texas.[5] One short clip featured a voicemail message left by an irate customer who was thrown out by theater management after repeatedly texting during a film and tauntingly concluded by thanking the customer for never returning. The announcement served the dual purpose of informing patrons of the relevant norms and shaming a violator.

Finally, we could discourage cell phone use through market mechanisms. Regulation via the market relies on the simple insight that by making undesirable behavior more expensive, fewer people will engage in it. Consider fuel economy. In the United States, we rely on legally mandated fuel economy standards to increase the average miles per gallon of our vehicles. But the market can be used to achieve a similar outcome. In countries with higher fuel costs, consumer demand drives greater fuel efficiency. So to return to our cell phone example, if mobile carriers imposed additional fees for calls and texts within one hundred yards of a movie theater, we would expect cell phone use during movies to decrease, at least among less affluent users. Or perhaps movie theaters sell more expensive tickets that entitle patrons to sit in a designated Smart Phone Zone. In either case, the theory is that forcing cell phone users to bear additional costs for their actions will reduce phone use in theaters.

As even these simple examples suggest, these four modes of regulation are not entirely independent. They interact, complementing and opposing one another to create the overall regulatory environment that shapes our behavior. Often, these separate regulatory approaches bolster each other. The architectural regulation of the speed bump reinforces the legal regulation of the speed limit. And the norm system of the Alamo Drafthouse leverages the legal regime of trespass law when it removes norm violators. But in some cases, they work in opposition, and their effectiveness is reduced as a result. The posted speed limit on the freeway might be 70 miles per hour, but the norm, enforced through tailgating and horn honking, might strongly suggest a faster rate of travel. To take an example we will return to in another chapter, copyright law prohibits the unauthorized reproduction and distribution of protected works. But that legal rule is less powerful in an architectural environment, like the Internet, that enables widespread, low-cost, anonymous sharing of information.

The dominant narrative of IP largely overlooks the role that social norms, marketplace strategy, and architectural changes can play in shaping an environment hospitable to creativity. Instead, it overemphasizes legal regulation, approaching the problem of maintaining creative incentives as simply a challenge to design the right set of laws. But optimizing legal regulation requires some understanding of the other factors that influence creators. In part, the reluctance of IP policymakers to engage with these other regulatory tools reflects the considerable variability among creative industries and communities. With few exceptions,

IP law in the United States emphasizes uniformity.[6] Although the law draws rough divisions between the copyright, patent, trademark, and trade secret regimes, IP law does not generally draw distinctions between industries. The same copyright rules apply to book publishers, recording artists, movie studios, fine artists, and software developers. And the patent rules that govern the biotech sector are the same as those that apply to the aerospace, consumer electronics, and financial services industries. But as the research collected here reveals, the social norms and market conditions that prevail across creative communities are anything but uniform. The picture that emerges from these studies is a complex set of factors that contribute to creative incentives. This understanding simultaneously undermines the accepted wisdom of IP law and explains the tendency of lawmakers to retreat to uniform legal regulation in the face of the untidy industry-specific facts of creativity in the real world.

This collection of studies offers important insights for IP policy—not despite their messiness, but because of it. For these creators, the degree of available IP protection is rarely determinative in their creative decision-making. As these studies demonstrate, markets for information goods can function despite the absence of meaningful intellectual property protection. Some creative communities rely on social sanctions to prevent copying. Others accept copying as inevitable and focus their efforts on marketplace strategies to recoup their investments nonetheless. And while our focus will be on norms and marketplace strategy, we will see that nearly every community is deeply influenced by the physical and technological architecture in which it is situated.

Within these communities, we see both common features shared across a range of industries and highly individualized, industry-specific responses. In communities that rely on social norms, for example, an expectation of attribution—crediting the contributions of others—is nearly universal. So are rules that preserve the building blocks and stock elements necessary for future creativity. And for communities that rely on marketplace strategies, a focus on selling services and experiences rather than easily copied products is widespread. But these case studies also reveal considerable variation along a number of dimensions: what kinds of creativity are valued and promoted; the relationship between creators and consumers; how ownership is determined and apportioned among creators; what exceptions to the general rule against copying are deemed appropriate or necessary. Through both their shared features and their points of departure, these case studies reveal how particular communities of creators, situated within a social and market context, develop sustainable creative practices without relying on formal IP law.

We cannot prove, nor do we claim, that communities that rely on social norms or market-based responses to address information appropriation produce an optimal balance of incentives and costs. But the same is true of the case for strong IP protection. In part, this question remains unanswered because it involves inescapable value judgments about the socially desirable quantity and quality of creative and innovative output. How many films should we produce in a year and of what sort? How many inventions are ideal and what unmet needs should they address? But in part, the answer eludes us because IP policy has paid insufficient attention to isolating and measuring the incentives at the core of the justification for the IP system. Not until we distinguish the backdrop of non-legal incentives from those that depend on law can we engage in the kind of clear-eyed assessment necessary to transform incentives from a rhetorical tool or article of faith to an empirically grounded basis for public policy.[7]

This book is divided into three parts. The first explores the surprisingly intertwined arts of food, drink, and medicine. For good reason, we naturally associate the culinary and mixological arts. But it turns out that pharmaceuticals and cocktails are distant cousins whose point of genealogical separation is closely tied to IP protection. Both food and drink are unlikely candidates for such protection. They are unable to satisfy patent law's requirements of novelty and non-obviousness, and likewise run headlong into limits on copyright protection. Drugs and medical procedures, on the other hand, are more appropriate subjects for patent protection, but for many decades the medical community strongly discouraged their patenting. In the absence of IP, innovative communities of chefs, bartenders, and medical practitioners have developed either social norms or market responses to regulate the creation and use of those works.

While the creations of many chefs are undoubtedly innovative, not all valuable creativity finds a home in the IP system. Copyright law has been reluctant to embrace culinary creations, considering them unprotectable methods or processes, or perhaps useful articles—items with intrinsic utilitarian functions. As presented in chapter 1, Emmanuelle Fauchart and Eric von Hippel's research documents the system of social norms among a sample of accomplished French chefs. Recognizing the value of the recipes they create and their limited legal recourse against copying, these chefs have developed and enforced a set of strong implicit social norms that enhance their private economic returns from their recipe-related creations and maintain strong incentives for innovation in the kitchen despite the unavailability of legal exclusivity.

Next in chapter 2, Matt Schruers demonstrates that from their earliest days as delivery mechanisms for medicines, to the era of patent elixirs, to today's resurgence of craft cocktails, alcoholic beverages have been fruitful ground for innovation. Although cocktail recipes are unprotected by copyright or patent law, new libations are far from scarce, despite the fact that these inventions can be freely copied and used by competitors. While culinary creations are regulated through informal norms, innovation in the mixological arts is driven by market strategies, in particular by cross-financing the investments made in easily copied information. Cocktails are often devised and sold as services, rather than products, as well as promotion for the spirits they contain. As this chapter colorfully illustrates, classic intellectual property theory often fails to account for market-based innovation incentives.

In chapter 3, Kathy Strandburg looks at the field of medicine, which has a long history of opposition to patents. She tracks the historical evolution of user innovation among physicians, with particular focus on ether anesthesia, a medical breakthrough that started out as a nineteenth-century party drug. User innovator communities often eschew patenting, relying instead on reputation-based reward systems and sharing norms. But while virtually all medical innovation was once the province of user innovator physicians, this is no longer the case. The ethical norms against patenting drugs and devices are no longer observed today, yet the norm against patenting medical procedures has remained surprisingly robust. This chapter argues that physician patenting norms have evolved to track changes in the role physicians play in medical innovation. This story helps illustrate the interplay between social norms and law, showing how they can influence each other and shift over time.

In Part II, we consider three communities for whom IP protection is available that nevertheless reject formal law in favor of social norms.

Though they share an outsider's skepticism of the legal system, creators in the worlds of tattoos, graffiti, and roller derby are motivated by overlapping yet distinct concerns. For some, the IP system leads to unwanted outcomes that are inconsistent with their creative priorities. In other instances, the act of self-regulation reflects and reinforces deep cultural commitments that go beyond creativity. And for others, the economics of self-regulation are more appealing than those of legal enforcement. Taken together, these case studies show that for some creators, social norms are not merely a second-best alternative to the legal system; they are the preferred means of regulating and promoting creativity.

Aaron Perzanowski's research on the tattoo industry, discussed in chapter 4, provides one illustration of this phenomenon. Despite generating billions of dollars in annual revenue, the tattoo industry rarely relies on formal assertions of legal rights in disputes over copying or ownership of creative works. Instead, tattooing is governed by a set of nuanced, overlapping, and occasionally contradictory social norms enforced through informal sanctions. But tattoo artists opt for self-governance despite the fact that their creations fit comfortably within the scope of copyright protection. This chapter offers a descriptive account, drawn from qualitative interview data, of the social norms that have overshadowed formal law within the tattoo community. It also provides a set of complementary cultural and economic explanations for the development of those norms.

Graffiti artists face a different set of concerns. Although graffiti images are copyright eligible in the abstract, the inherently illicit act of spray painting private property without permission complicates efforts to rely on formal law. As presented in chapter 5, Marta Iljadica's empirical research on the graffiti subculture in London demonstrates that despite its illegality, graffiti writing has rules. Those rules address questions of subject matter, originality, and copying common to any expressive work. But they also extend to concerns unique to the graffiti context. Because graffiti is inextricably tied to the physical environment, it raises questions of placement: which structures are appropriate canvases for graffiti writings and which are off-limits? And because available real estate is limited, graffiti writers must confront scarcity: under what conditions is it permissible to cover another artist's work with your own? So although the rules of graffiti writing parallel those of formal copyright law in some ways, they also go beyond it to confront a set of problems graffiti writers are themselves best suited to address.

The flexibility of social norms in building and maintaining a community is demonstrated by the shifting efforts at self-regulation undertaken by roller derby athletes. Dave Fagundes explains in chapter 6 how roller derby skaters once guaranteed exclusive use of the pseudonyms under which they compete. Roller derby names were initially a central part of this countercultural, all-girl sport. Despite the availability of trademark protection, skaters developed an elaborate rule structure, registration system, and governance regime to protect the uniqueness of their pseudonyms. When the norms around name exclusivity changed over time, so did the governance regime. This suggests that regardless of law, communities can develop and evolve norms systems if they are close-knit and the norms are welfare-maximizing. Communities are especially likely to rely on self-regulatory approaches, even formal ones that require substantial investment, when membership is closely linked to individual identity.

A skeptical reader might be tempted to discount the case studies presented in the first two parts as outliers that bear little resemblance to traditional IP-intensive industries in terms of their output and structure. In Part III, we turn to creative practices that—while still unfamiliar to most readers—exhibit many of the hallmarks of typical IP-reliant industries and nonetheless subvert expectations about the role of legal regulation. From vibrant and productive fan fiction communities, to online pornography, to the Nigerian film industry, all of the examples in this part offer strong parallels to the industries that drive copyright policy. They illustrate that some content industries will create despite the absence of copyright incentives and will innovate around the need for IP enforcement. Some of their success relies on special market characteristics like fast-paced product cycles, optimally low production costs, and sometimes the nature of the creative process itself. But whether driven by inherent motivation or clever business models, these markets are able to sustain content production even in the absence of law or norms.

Fan fiction, a practice that sometimes attracts the ire of copyright holders, but can often lay a strong claim to fair use, is neither clearly lawful nor unlawful. Untroubled by the legal status of their creations, fans write stories, draw pictures, make movies, remix existing content, and share their works with the broader community. This practice is as communal as it is creative, and requires spaces where fan fiction authors can come together to disseminate works, connect, and collaborate. In chapter 7, Rebecca Tushnet demonstrates the importance of architecture in fostering online communities. Despite being touched by copyright law, media fandom is low-IP and generally governed by the norms of its community. Their concepts of right and wrong, often subject to debate, are increasingly built into the architecture of online platforms. And those platforms, in turn, exert a significant impact on creativity without relying on law.

A notoriously innovative industry, adult entertainment has survived and thrived through every technological disruption. Kate Darling discusses in chapter 8 how the copying and sharing of digital files over the Internet has posed new challenges for content producers, effectively eliminating their copyright protection. But rather than destroy all incentive for production, this change has driven companies to reinvent their business models. Amidst some struggles, the U.S. industry has quickly shifted toward selling services and interactive experience goods, while continuing to create traditional content as a loss leader.

Across the globe, we find another industry that deals in low-cost entertainment products. Nollywood, the Nigerian film industry, is the top producer of digital video films in the world. Funmi Arewa argues in chapter 9 that Nigeria is an unlikely locale for the development of a major film industry given its lack of robust intellectual property enforcement. She demonstrates how Nollywood constitutes a natural experiment for creativity in the relative absence of IP protection, in which the intertwined actions of creators, entrepreneurs, and infringers all contribute to the market's growth. Because the viral spread of Nollywood films has been a key element of success, content producers can adopt business strategies that actually harness copyright infringement by monetizing wide-reaching distribution networks.

Finally, Chris Sprigman concludes with a discussion of IP's "negative space." Each of the studies in this book explores creative communities and industries that could theoretically be governed by IP law, but instead exist in a space outside of it. Together, this body of scholarship challenges the canonical justification that IP incentives are central to innovation and creativity. Drawing on his previous work on the fashion industry and stand-up comedy, Sprigman argues that the type of creation incentivized by IP is inherently limited. A lesson he distills from our growing but still incomplete understanding of creativity without law is a need to shift our focus from a preoccupation with intellectual property to a more inclusive inquiry into innovation and its many drivers, broadening our horizon and the tools at our disposal to create effective policy.

Criticism of the IP system is nothing new. IP scholarship has frequently questioned the theory behind our laws, arguing that creators have diverse motivations and that the chosen regulatory tools are an economic burden to society. But it is only recently that IP scholars have begun to conduct empirical research in an attempt to explore and test these arguments. The growing body of industry-specific studies presented here should serve as a catalyst to quantify the assumptions in what has been largely a theoretical discussion. The ideological debate between those who would maximize IP protection and those who would abolish it has proven predictable and unproductive. Evidence-based IP policymaking is the best way to cut through the rehashing of familiar arguments. The case studies collected here do not prove that IP is unnecessary or unwise. Indeed, in some industries IP law is the most effective strategy for managing creative incentives. But these case studies do suggest that the received wisdom about incentives is too simple a story. Creativity on the ground is messy and complicated. And IP policy should take into account the full range of factors that influence creation, copying, and use. These studies also show that the conditions for incentives and investment are often industry-specific in ways that would be nearly impossible to predict without a deep understanding of the community in which they operate. If we hope to optimize innovation law and policy, we must take seriously the possibility of shifting away from the monoculture of uniform regulation that defines the current IP system.

NOTES

1 When Congress asked economist Fritz Machlup to evaluate the patent system in the 1950s, he found the evidence supporting the incentive theory inconclusive. In his estimation, if we had no patent system, the evidence could not justify its creation, nor could it justify the elimination of the existing system. Subcomm. On Patents, Trademarks, and Copyrights of the Senate Comm. on the Judiciary, 85th Congress, An Economic Review of the Patent System, Study No. 15, at 80

(1958). In recent years, scholars have devoted significant attention to empirical assessments of the operation and underlying justifications of the IP system. But we are no closer to vindicating the hunches that motivate copyright and patent law. And, perhaps more troublingly, the work of IP scholars has gone largely unnoticed among policymakers who should be keenly interested in evidence-based decision-making.

2 Jessica Silbey, *The Eureka Myth: Creators, Innovators and Everyday Intellectual Property* (Stanford: Stanford Law Books, 2015).

3 Lawrence Lessig, "The New Chicago School," 27 *Journal of Legal Studies* 661, 662–63 (1998).

4 Sarah Schindler, "Architectural Exclusion: Discrimination and Segregation Through Physical Design of the Built Environment," 124 *Yale Law Journal* 1836 (2015).

5 Alamo Drafthouse, #DontTalk Collection, https://goo.gl/c43nh4.

6 Michael W. Carroll, "One for All: The Problem of Uniformity Cost in Intellectual Property Law," 55 *American University Law Review* 845 (2006): 856.

7 Mark Lemley, "Faith-Based Intellectual Property," 62 *UCLA Law Review* 1328 (2015).

PART I

Cuisine and Curatives

1

Norms-Based Intellectual Property Systems

The Case of French Chefs

EMMANUELLE FAUCHART AND ERIC VON HIPPEL

When one thinks of intellectual property (IP) rights, one tends to think of rights encoded in law like patent grants, copyright, trade secrecy, and trademarks. In these law-based IP systems, detailed bodies of legislation and case law spell out the rights an owner can claim to specific types of IP and the procedures by which these rights can be claimed. The law of contracts then specifies how the rights can be licensed and bought or sold. Claimed violations of IP rights and contracts can be adjudicated and compensation determined via private legal actions in the courts.

In this chapter we propose that norms-based IP systems also exist and are important in at least some fields. Norms-based IP systems, as we define them, function within a group to provide group members with IP rights based on social norms only. Such systems must provide the basic functions of law-based IP systems, but may provide these by different means. Thus, both types of IP systems must grant innovators valuable monopoly rights over their innovations. Both must also enforce these rights, but may use different means to do so. In the case of law-based systems, for example, possible IP violations are adjudicated by courts. Court-mandated sanctions for confirmed violations then may include financial payments and prohibitions of further violations. In the case of norms-based systems, possible IP violations are assessed by informal community consensus. Sanctions for confirmed violations are applied by community members and may include shaming, loss of status within the community, and reduced future access to valuable community resources such as information.

Our research is related to and draws on work by laws and norms scholars who have explored the roles of laws relative to norms in several arenas.[1] We also build on work by Merges related to private IP systems.[2] Our major contribution in this chapter is to provide an existence proof for norms-based IP systems—a documentation of a present-day IP system based solely on norms. We do this by exploring how accomplished French chefs currently protect the new recipes they develop. Accomplished chefs consider their recipes to be a very valuable form of IP. After all, professional reputations and customer patronage at restaurants can be built around successful recipes. At the same time, recipes are not a form of innovation that is effectively covered by current law-based IP systems. Recipes are rarely patentable, and combinations of ingredients cannot be copyrighted. Legal protections are potentially available via trade secrecy laws, but, as we will see, chefs very seldom use them.

In brief overview, we find that an IP system based on implicit social norms and offering functionality quite similar to law-based systems does operate among accomplished French chefs. Via grounded research, we identify three strong implicit social norms held by all chefs we interviewed. First, a chef must not copy another chef's recipe innovation exactly. This norm has a very important role in creating a norms-based analog to important functions of law-based IP systems. The functional effect is analogous to patenting in that the community acknowledges the right of a recipe inventor to exclude others from practicing his invention, even if all the information required to do so is publicly available. The effect is also analogous to copyright in its regulation of the right to copy a particular "form of material expression" of an idea.

A second norm mandates that, if a chef reveals recipe-related secret information to a colleague, that chef must not pass on the information to others without permission. This norm gives a chef a property right similar to that attainable via a contract under trade secrecy law: Protected by this norm, a chef can selectively reveal his or her secret information to another without fearing that as a result, the information will become generally known. A third norm is that colleagues must credit developers of significant recipes as the authors of that information. This gives an additional property right to a chef who may choose to selectively or publicly reveal information about his innovation without jeopardizing the valuable related property right of acknowledged authorship.

Via quantitative research, we next show that accomplished chefs are significantly more likely to deny requested information to colleagues whom they believe may violate the three social norms just described. This selective denial of information is behavioral evidence that a functioning norms-based IP system exists: It shows that three implicit norms that together offer functionality similar to that of law-based IP systems are being enforced in the community we studied. As one accomplished chef said, "If another chef copies a recipe exactly we are very furious; we will not talk to this chef anymore, and we won't communicate information to him in the future." We conclude that information not afforded the protection of IP law may nonetheless be controlled by an effective IP regime based entirely on implicit norms.

Our findings introduce the likelihood that norms-based and law-based IP systems are both functioning in the world today. The potential effects of norms-based IP systems will add a new dimension to current scholarly research and debate on the economics of IP systems. At present, much of that debate involves the possibility that extant law-based IP systems may be constraining rather than supporting innovative progress.[3] Modification or elimination of these systems is sometimes proposed, with the implicit assumption that the law-based IP systems under discussion are the only ones at issue. Our findings indicate that, in at least some fields, the situation is different. Modification or elimination of law-based IP coverage of a field may simply reveal, or even induce communities to newly create, a norms-based IP protection system in that field.

As we learn more about norms-based systems, we will learn how each type can be most usefully understood and applied. We will then be in a position to more deeply explore how mixed norms and law-based systems can best function and serve the intended social and private purposes of creating, defending, and diffusing IP.

In this chapter, we first review social norms, law-based IP rights, and norms-based rights systems. Then, we discuss the methods used in our case study and present our grounded research findings on the recipe hiding, trading, and revealing choices made by French chefs. We conclude that norms-based IP systems exist, can be effective, and should be further explored.

Social Norms

Social norms are pervasive and powerful structural characteristics of groups that summarize and simplify group influence processes. They are enforced by a group among its members and generally are developed only for behaviors that are viewed as important by most group members.[4] Social norms can be advantageous for groups.[5] Social norms have traditionally been viewed by sociologists as rarely written down or explicitly discussed.[6] In such cases, evidence that a norm is in place can be seen if any departure of real behavior from the norm is followed by some punishment.[7] Social norms can deal with matters that both do and do not have important economic consequences for the group.[8] For example, workplace norms such as output restrictions directly address the economic concerns of a group. Thus, a "rate buster" who produces significantly more than the average worker in a production group could induce management to lower piece-rate pay for all workers in the group—a matter with significant economic implications for those workers. In contrast, social norms regulating such matters as mode of dress, manners at the table, and so forth may but need not have important economic significance for group members.

Norms are enforceable when groups control stimuli that are valued (or disvalued) by the target person. The more an individual has a personal need for a social reward controlled by the group, the more he or she conforms. Group members who do not need or care about such social rewards (e.g., very high-status members or very low-status members not committed to remaining in the group) often conform less than other group members.[9]

Bendor and Swistak use evolutionary game theory to test the conditions under which social norms are stable.[10] The stability of a social norm, they find, is maintained when all are treated as supporting the norm unless they actually transgress—the "nice" element of a "nice but retaliatory" strategy. However, all participants must punish one who does transgress and also punish those who do not join in punishing him—the "retaliatory" element of the strategy. In other words, if a social norm is violated, the obligation to impose punishment must not be restricted to those who were hurt by the initial transgression; the obligation must be extended to third parties if the norm is to remain stable. The "if you are not my friend then you are my foe" element of the nice but retaliatory strategy ensures that it is in the private interest of third parties to participate in punishment of transgressions. Although participation may involve a cost to these parties, they must participate or face the presumably greater cost of being punished, too. The net result—assuming that the transgression is not engaged in by too many simultaneously—is that a norm remains stable.

Law-Based IP Rights Systems

There are three distinct types of law-based IP rights systems in most countries: the patent grant, the copyright, and the right to protect trade secrets. Each of these systems covers different categories of IP and has different characteristics. In this section we briefly review the subject matter coverage and characteristics of each system. We also note why each has little or no applicability at present to the subject of our case study—novel recipes.

The most general form of patent is the utility patent. In the United States, utility patents may be granted for inventions related to composition of matter and/or a method and/or a use. They may not be granted for ideas per se, mathematical formulas, laws of nature, or anything repugnant to morals and public policy. Within subject matter potentially protectable by patent, protection will be granted only when the IP meets additional criteria of usefulness, novelty, and nonobviousness to those skilled in the relevant art. (The tests for whether these criteria have been met are based on judgment. When a low threshold is used, patents are easier to get, and vice versa.[11]) Within their sphere and duration of coverage, patent grants give inventors exclusive rights to the invention claimed. No one else may use or make that invention without a license from the patent owner—even if they independently develop it. Unlike novel industrial food recipes for a high-protein tortilla, for example, novel haute cuisine recipes today seldom fulfill the three criteria necessary for claiming a patent: usefulness, novelty, and nonobviousness. (This may change in the future, if and as haute cuisine chefs move toward recipe innovations involving novel science such as sous vide—cooking at low temperatures under vacuum—and molecular gastronomy.)

Copyright is a low-cost and immediate form of legal protection that applies to original writings and images ranging from novels to software code to movies. Authors need not apply for copyright protection; it is automatic under present law. Only the specific expression of an idea is protected, not—as in the case of patents—the underlying invention or idea itself. The crucial novel information in a new recipe—the list of ingredients, the proportions used, and the processing methods used—cannot currently be protected by copyright. However, original writings and images related to presenting a recipe in a cookbook or other medium can be copyrighted. (Buccafusco argues that copyright may be appropriately extended to cover novel dishes, although courts have not yet chosen to do this. It is the dish itself, he argues, rather than the recipe, that can be reasonably seen as a creative and potentially copyrightable work of authorship.[12])

Trade secrets are applicable to any information not generally known in an industry and of demonstrable economic value to a firm possessing the secret. Trade secret law protects only information that can be kept secret by a firm while being commercially exploited. Employees and others can be legally bound by contract to not reveal a firm's trade secrets. A possessor of a trade secret may take legal steps to prevent its use by others if he can show that those others have discovered the secret through unfair and dishonest means, such as theft or breach of a contract promising to keep it secret. However, the holder of a trade secret cannot exclude anyone who independently discovers that secret or who legally acquires it by such means as accidental disclosure or reverse engineering.

In practice, trade secrets have proven to be effective only with regard to product innovations incorporating various technological barriers to analysis and process innovations that can be hidden from public view. Aspects of recipe ingredients and preparation techniques that can be effectively hidden in a restaurant's kitchen can therefore in principle be protected as trade secrets. For example, a chef may legally require as a condition of employment that employees sign a labor contract binding them to not disclose recipe-related trade secrets. However, as we will see in grounded research findings presented later, chefs in our sample seldom take the steps required to legally defend the status of their recipe-related IP as trade secrets. This is because, as chef interviewees told us, they think that the benefits of doing so are unlikely to outweigh the costs.

Owners of IP rights under all three of these systems can keep their rights entirely to themselves or license or sell all or aspects of their rights to others. For example, a patent owner can grant rights to another individual to use his patent for any purpose, or only for a specific type of application. Similarly, the holder of a trade secret can make legally binding contracts with others in which all or only aspects of the secret are revealed in exchange for a fee or other consideration along with a commitment to not diffuse the secret further. Violations to such agreements can be brought to a court of law for adjudication.

Norms-Based Rights Systems

Findings of laws and norms studies make it quite plausible that effective IP systems based only on social norms might exist today. These studies explore the role that norms play in a range of fields traditionally assumed by legal scholars to be the exclusive province of law. For example, private methods of contract enforcement independent of law have been explored.[13]

Greif describes how a coalition of Maghribi traders successfully enforced contracts with their agents in distant lands by privately established rules.[14] For example, the community of traders had a norm that none would hire an agent who had fallen short of his obligations to any trader. Ostrom and others have documented the quite elaborate community practices that enable communities to successfully share resources held in common, such as commonly accessible fisheries.[15] Methods by which neighbors settle disputes without recourse to the law have been studied by Ellickson and others.[16]

Often in these studies, implicit norms are found to play a dominant role. Thus, Ellickson, in exploring how rural neighbors allocated the costs of maintaining the fences that separated their properties and herds of cattle, found that essentially none was aware of Section 841, the California statute that specifies how boundary-fence costs are to be allocated. He therefore sought to identify "the norms to which [adjacent rural property owners] were dancing."

Although rural residents could quickly resolve simple hypothetical fence-cost disputes posed to them, they never articulated general principles of fence-cost allocation. Their statements and practices revealed, however, that they tend to follow a norm of proportionality. This norm calls for adjoining landowners to share fencing costs in rough proportion to the average density of livestock present on the respective sides of the boundary line.[17]

A second norm is that ranchers (i.e., large landowners) will never ask for a contribution to fencing costs from owners of ranchettes (i.e., small landowners), even though the law would sanction it.[18] In other words, Ellickson found that the boundary-fence maintenance norms actually followed by rural neighbors differed in a number of respects from the law.

Ellickson argues that law is often unimportant relative to norms in shaping many types of social interactions: "I didn't appreciate how unimportant law can be when I embarked upon this project." His book, he says, "seeks to demonstrate that people frequently resolve their dispute in cooperative fashion without paying any attention to the laws that apply to those disputes."[19]

Studies of IP-related norms have been conducted by a number of scholars, including many in this book. An earlier example is research on scientific communities. These norms generally involve restrictions on the claiming of IP rights by scientists. Thus, Merton documented the existence of a "communitarian" norm in such communities, mandating the open sharing of the "intellectual property" of scientific research results and research methods used to obtain them.[20] Others have explored the detailed workings of this norm and how it is limited in some circumstances by implicit or explicit assertion of property rights by scientists and their employers.[21]

Case Study Context and Methods

Our case study explores the operation of a social norms–based IP system among accomplished haute cuisine chefs working in France. Specifically, we focus on norms-based IP related to recipes developed by these chefs. We have selected this arena for study because it combines two characteristics useful for our purposes.

First, IP in the form of novel recipes has high economic importance to accomplished chefs. Second, as we saw above, extant law-based IP systems today are not applicable and/or are little used to protect this form of IP. As a result, we expect that chefs will rely largely on a norm-based IP system to protect their recipe-related IP if and as this is feasible for them. In turn this will—we hope—simplify our task of understanding the operation and effects of an IP system of this type.

Our study proceeded in two major phases. First, we conducted grounded field research to identify important social norms dealing with recipe-related IP. Second, we conducted a quantitative, questionnaire-based study to determine whether innovators deployed these norms to gain private economic advantage and whether violators of the norms were in fact sanctioned by accomplished haute cuisine chefs.

Our samples for both studies consisted of the chefs de cuisine in restaurants that had received "stars" and/or "forks" from the Michelin guide as a sign of culinary excellence. The Michelin guide is an independent evaluation agency for restaurants. The award of stars by the guide is a major honor. Forks are also prestigious, but less so than stars. (Forks are given to "good gastronomic restaurants" that also have a good balance between gastronomic level and price of the meal. Awards can range from 1 to 5 forks.) In the 2005 Michelin guide there are 26 three-star, 70 two-star, and 405 one-star restaurants in France. Michelin stars are given to restaurants and not to chefs de cuisine. However, the award is mainly based on factors related to the performance of the chef de cuisine. Hence, when a chef de cuisine leaves a restaurant, the stars are "suspended" until the next examination by the Michelin experts.

A major criterion for awarding stars or forks to a restaurant is "renewal"—the ability to offer creative and new recipes on a regular basis. By focusing on the chefs de cuisine who have actually created these recipes, we are focusing on those who presumably regard innovation as important to their professional and economic success. Typical comments by awardees and others support this expectation. Thus, Thierry Thiercelin said after gaining his first star: "Now there is no room for error anymore; I must be at 100% of my capabilities and able to answer my customers' expectations for innovative and renewed recipes."[22]

Losing or gaining a star has substantial economic consequences. Johnson et al. report that the loss of a star is catastrophic—causing [restaurant] sales to drop as much as 50% in some cases.[23] Chefs who have been responsible for winning stars for restaurants are often in a position to profit from increased restaurant sales and have other opportunities to benefit financially as well. There is demand for chefs believed able to help an establishment gain a star; in particular, luxury hotels in Paris seek such chefs. Also, enhanced reputation may enable a chef to profit from lines of prepared food bearing his label in food stores, or through consulting to agribusiness firms, consulting to restaurants in foreign countries, participating in TV shows, increased book sales. An anonymous gastronomy expert summed up the situation nicely for the *Nouvel Observateur*: "Gaining a Michelin star ensures that your banker will be kind to you."[24]

In our grounded research we interviewed ten accomplished chefs with places of business near Paris and so could be conveniently visited by the first author of this chapter. Requests for a meeting were made to twelve chefs, and ten responded positively. Seven of these were interviewed face to face, and three were interviewed by email. Seven of the ten chefs interviewed had Michelin stars. Three had no stars but were listed in the Michelin guide as chefs de cuisine in "good gastronomic restaurants."

In the quantitative phase of our study, we again focused on obtaining information from very accomplished chefs. We therefore distributed our questionnaire to chefs who had been recognized in the Michelin guide. These included chefs holding stars, "rising stars," and chefs holding from two to five forks. (Rising stars are chefs listed in the guide as likely to receive their first star within the next year.) Questionnaires were mailed to all sample members at their places of business, and respondents were asked to return them by mail. No follow-up was done to increase the rate of response: We did not want to annoy the chefs and decided to take non-response as a "no." Of 485 questionnaires sent, 104 were returned, a response rate of 21.4%. Of these, ten contained essentially no data and so were not included in our analyses. The 94 analyzable questionnaires were reasonably well distributed across the expertise categories in the Michelin guide: 7% came from two-star chefs, 62% from one-star chefs, 3% from rising stars, and 28% from chefs awarded forks.

Those chefs who filled out our questionnaires tended to do so quite completely. However, some questions solicited responses only under some conditions. (For example, "Please only answer the following additional questions about action X if you did do action X.") For this reason, the sample size given in our tables is significantly less than 94 in some analyses.

Grounded Research Findings

Chefs interviewed in our grounded research phase told us without exception that the development of novel haute cuisine recipes is a very important activity for them and for similarly accomplished chefs. We also learned that these chefs and their colleagues seldom attempted to gain legal protection for their recipe IP. As was noted earlier, recipes seldom rise to the level of novelty required to qualify for a patent grant, and copyright is not applicable to the content of recipes, so it is reasonable that chefs would not attempt to apply these forms of protection. However, aspects of recipes can be kept secret even when a recipe is in use at a restaurant—for example, food preparation techniques not visible to diners and secret ingredients. This recipe-related IP can in principle be protected by trade secrecy law. Interviewees stated that accomplished chefs sometimes send a written notice to those hiring a former employee saying that that person is prohibited from revealing trade secrets learned from his former employer. However, we were told that if such a trade secret is revealed by a former employee or by some other means, chefs who suspect their legal rights have been violated will very rarely seek redress through the courts. Probably instances of turning to the courts do exist, but our interviewees could not recall any such case. This is generally regarded as too difficult and too expensive to be worth attempting.

When we raised the issue of whether or how rights to recipes could be protected given the absence of applicable and effective laws, we were given examples and stories of "proper professional behavior" in this regard. Applicable social norms that appear in these stories have not been clearly codified or written down by chefs—they are implicit. However, three major norms consistently emerged in all our interviews. First, it is not honorable for chefs to exactly copy recipes developed by other chefs. Chefs were vehement about how very wrong it was to copy the recipe of a colleague. One interviewee said, "If another chef copies a recipe exactly, we are very furious: We will not talk to this chef anymore, and we won't communicate information to him in the future." It is, however, acceptable to develop creative variations on recipes developed by others. How different a new recipe should be to avoid the prohibition against exact copying is not precisely specifiable, but chefs think they know a too-close copy when they see it. This anti-copy norm seems to us to offer IP protection similar to that offered by a patent grant or a copyright. As we will see later, accomplished chefs could duplicate many of the valuable recipes developed by colleagues using only public, legally unprotected information—but the norm prevents them from doing this. The anti-copy norm benefits innovating chefs whose restaurants might well lose sales and profits if their novel recipes were copied by others.

The second important norm that emerged in our interviews is that a chef who asks for and is given proprietary information by a colleague will not pass on that information to others without permission. This norm applies only to information that can be kept as a trade secret if not revealed. The requirement to not pass it on is important but is generally not stated when information is transferred in response to a request—it is implicit. As one of our interviewees said, "If I give information to another chef, I trust him to not pass it on. I do not have to say this."

This norm gives holders of proprietary information the freedom to selectively reveal aspects of what they know. That is, a chef can choose to reveal information to colleague A and at the same time feel confident that A will not tell others. Freedom to selectively and conditionally reveal information seems to us to offer functionality similar to legal contracting related to trade secrets: One can contract to reveal a trade secret to A with the stipulation that A will not pass on that information to others.

Often, as we will see in our quantitative data, chefs selectively reveal secret information to colleagues with the expectation that they will not pass it on and that the information recipients will be more likely to reciprocate by revealing valuable information in return. This is informal information trading, and has been documented by several scholars.[25] Informal information trading has been shown to increase participants' profits under some conditions. The basic argument is that revealing a unit of secret information to another reduces the monopoly profits that an innovator can obtain from its information—because now a rival is also using it. However, a trade will nonetheless pay whenever that reduction in monopoly profits is more than offset by the increase in profits gained by receiving in reciprocation a new unit of secret information from the trading partner. When this happens, it has been shown that information trading fits the conditions for a prisoner's dilemma.[26] Given repeated plays, cooperation will be the most profitable long-term strategy for those engaged in the practice.[27]

The third norm involved the right to be acknowledged as the author of a recipe one has created. This applies to a recipe that one may observe at a creator's restaurant or ask the developer about; it also applies when the innovator publicly reveals his recipe by, for example, publishing it in a cookbook or a magazine or describing it on TV. This norm offers a functionality offered by copyright and by law on the "moral rights" of authors and artists to have the paternity of their work acknowledged.[28]

A chef who presents the recipe of another as his own is considered not honorable. For example, consider an excerpt from a letter of reproach written by a famous chef to a former employee who presented one of the chef's recipes on TV without proper attribution. The chef also distributed his letter to a number of his colleagues, so that the community as a whole would learn of his former employee's violation of an important norm. A copy, written in French, was given to us by an interviewee, and we translate a portion of it as follows:

> Sir: First, I must tell you that seeing on TV a former employee showing things I have taught him is a real pleasure.
>
> Unfortunately this pleasure was brief, as your presentation has revealed a rare ingratitude. Never did I hear you say what you owe to the master I have been for you. You should admit that presenting recipes that are mine and that I taught you without referring to my name constitutes an unacceptable indelicacy. . . . I hope that in your future presentations you will repair these errors and shall credit me with what I have taught to you. Only after this honest acknowledgement will I be happy that you receive a share of my notoriety.

The norm requiring acknowledgment of authorship enables chefs to profit more than free riders even when they reveal their innovations to all. Given known authorship, a chef can use free revealing to raise his reputation with the general public and thus, for example, increase his profit from selling cookbooks and/or from increased traffic to his restaurant. Chefs often select their more important and interesting recipes to reveal in this public way, reasoning that their reputations will be more effectively enhanced by revealing major rather than minor innovations.

Chefs interviewed clearly thought that adherence to the norms described above was very important: "[If someone were to violate an important norm], . . . my esteem for the guy becomes very low. I think the chef has no self-esteem, and does not respect the code of honor." Transgressions of the three norms we identified—and presumably of any additional norms that may also exist in this community—are, we were told, punished by negative gossip within the community, by a related lowering of a violator's reputation, and by a decreased likelihood that additional requests for information will be answered by community members. Famous chefs do not necessarily need to take personal action to ensure that transgressions are noticed and appropriately punished by their community. As one interviewee said, "The community knows my style and can recognize when someone is copying me. Therefore, I do not need to intervene in any way."

Note that our interviews did not necessarily evoke a complete set of IP-related norms. We could have missed an important norm simply because our questions did not trigger stories related to it from our interviewees. (By way of analogy, we could learn about the norm "thou shalt not kill" from interviewees without necessarily triggering any discussion of the norm "thou shalt not steal.") Fortunately, completeness is not necessary to our present purpose. We simply want to understand whether some social norms exist that can serve to at least partially protect the IP of recipe developers.

Note also that chefs' IP-related strategies are complex, and further work will be required to map and understand them fully. For example, an interviewee told us that chefs who publicly reveal a recipe may not necessarily reveal all the information required to exactly reproduce it. "Usually, a chef does not disclose everything when publishing a recipe in a cookbook. The published version may exclude important 'tricks' (elements of technique), and may even omit some ingredients." Interviewees also say that some cookbooks they write are intended for an audience of primarily peers rather than for home cooks. One important function of these books is to convey information about priority. If an imitator publishes a recipe that a famous chef developed, that chef may later publish the same recipe in a professional cookbook of his own. In this way he signals to colleagues that he believes that he, rather than the first to publish, has priority.

Chefs often use the various IP strategies available to them in sequence or as required by events to maximize their private returns. Thus, they often choose to keep exclusivity on new recipes served in their restaurants for a period of time before publishing them in a cookbook.

Findings from Quantitative Research

In overview, our quantitative research is designed to explore two matters: (1) whether the norms that we identified via grounded research are actually being enforced by chefs, and (2) whether chefs are enforcing the norms in a way likely to increase their private innovation-related profits. Our test of the first matter draws on patterns of selective information revealing in our sample of chefs. We first determine whether some of our respondents' recipe-related information is secret—and is thus potential subject matter to be selectively revealed at the discretion of our respondent chefs. We then test whether chefs selectively deny requested information to colleagues they think are likely violators of the three IP-related norms. If they do this, we have evidence that the norms are being enforced. Our test of the second matter involves determining whether patterns in the selective and free revealing of IP can increase chefs' innovation-related profits—the goal of law-based IP systems. If both of these elements can be seen, we think it is reasonable to conclude that a functioning norms-based IP system exists in the field of recipes.

Chefs in our quantitative sample judged that novel recipes were very important to their professional success. When asked about the "importance your customers place upon finding original recipes (your own creations) on your menu," the average importance ranking given by our respondents was 4.52 out of 5 (std dev: 0.72), where 5 was "very important." Chefs also reported that a significant fraction of the recipes they develop would be difficult for others to reproduce without their help (table 1.1). This means that chefs do have recipe-related IP that can be kept secret for some period of time unless they choose to reveal it.

TABLE 1.1 Many Recipes Are Difficult to Reproduce without Help from the Innovator

Percentage of your recipes that another chef would find it difficult to reproduce without your help (%)	Percentage of chefs in total of respondent chefs who ticked this category (%)
0	10.5
25	39.5
50	29
75	5.2
100	0
Do not know	15.8
n	94

IP that can be kept secret by innovators can also be revealed if innovators elect to do so. In the case of accomplished chefs, an opportunity to make such a decision occurs when colleagues working in other restaurants request specific items of recipe-related information. As shown in table 1.2, this happens often. Of the chefs in our sample, 90% report being asked for such information at least once in the past year, and 28% report being asked at least six times.

TABLE 1.2 Most Chefs Receive Recipe-Related Information Requests from Colleagues

How many times did you receive recipe-related information requests from colleagues in the past year?	
Never	10.2
1–5 times	61.4
6–10 times	14.8
More than 10 times	13.6
No answer	3
n	94

Recall from our grounded research discussion that French chef interviewees said that norms violations were punished by negative gossip within the community, by a related lowering of a violator's reputation, and by a decreased likelihood that additional requests for information will be answered by community members. Via our questionnaire, therefore, we sought to determine whether chefs' decisions to reveal their information to a specific requester were related to expectations that the requester was a likely norms violator. This approach had the advantage of linking expectations of norms violations to a type of punishment reported by our interviewees, i.e., selective denial of requested information.

Our research strategy was to ask each respondent to tell us about two cases where he had been asked for recipe-related information. First, we asked a number of questions about the most recent case in which a chef had been asked for information and had provided it. Second, we asked the same questions about the most recent case where a chef had been asked for information and had not provided it. We then analyzed the chefs' responses to see if there is an association between expected adherence to the three norms described earlier and willingness to provide secret IP.

As table 1.3 indicates, we found that IP holders were significantly more likely to deny secret IP to requesters they thought likely to violate each of the three social norms. We also found that this association was strongest when information of high value was being requested. Note that the decision to withhold proprietary information from a colleague judged likely to not adhere to community IP-related norms may be intended as norms enforcement and/or it may be a private attempt to protect IP likely to be at risk if revealed to that person. Either way, the behavior serves to enforce community norms: Access to requested information is selectively denied by community members to individuals with past or anticipated norms violations.

TABLE 1.3 Chefs Are Significantly More Likely to Give Information to Chefs They Think Will Adhere to IP-Related Community Social Norms

I expect that the person who requested recipe-related information from me:	Relationship between information holder's expectations that information requester will adhere to norms and his decision to provide Information[a]	(n)
1. Will NOT copy my recipe exactly.[c]	P < 0 0035	61
2. Will ask my permission before passing on the information I gave him to another.[b]	P < 0 063	65
3. Will credit me as author. [b, d]	P < 0 014	72

a Marginal homogeneity test, paired samples, one-tailed.
b 5-point Likert scale.
c Respondents chose one option from three descriptions of increasingly exact copying behaviors.
d Recall that our qualitative field research identified a norm requiring acknowledgment of authorship for recipe-related information that was privately or publicly revealed. However, our questionnaire asks information providers only about their expectations that a specific information requestor will adhere to that norm in the case of proprietary information selectively revealed to him as an individual.

Note also that there is some possibility that this finding reflects post hoc cognitive dissonance reduction on the part of the chefs rather than norm-related choice making. That is, when answering our questions, a chef could simply be thinking: "I did refuse to give this person information. I would only have done this if he is a bad person or undeserving in some way—so I will respond to the questionnaire accordingly." To reduce the risk of this type of occurrence, nothing in our letter of introduction to chefs or in our questionnaire indicated that we were interested in studying social norms. In addition, we scattered our norms-related questions among others, did not identify questions as norm related, and asked the questions in a non-value-laden way. We simply asked, for example, how likely the chef thought it was that the specific chef who had requested information from him would exactly copy the recipe he was asking about. Finally, we should point out that we know nothing about the actual norms-related behaviors of information seekers because we did not obtain information from information recipients—only providers. However, this does not affect the validity of our finding. The decision to provide or withhold IP is in the hands of the chef holding that IP and is related to his or her perceptions of the attributes of the information seeker, not to the actual attributes of that person.

Although social norms do not always have to do with the economic advantage of individual group members or the group as a whole, IP law is specifically designed to enhance innovators' likely private economic returns from innovation, and so to increase their incentives to innovate. In this section we explore whether norms-related patterns in the information-revealing and -hiding behavior of the chefs in our sample are consistent with a goal of increasing innovators' economic returns from their innovations. If so, we have evidence that a norms-based IP system exists in this community.

We first see that chefs who selectively reveal recipe-related information to a colleague appear to be engaging in informal information trading rather than altruism. As table 1.4 shows, they expect their decision will affect the likelihood that the information seeker will reciprocate in the future. As discussed earlier in the chapter, informal information trading can increase profits for participants, assuming that there is reciprocity and assuming also that information recipients adhere to the norm of not passing on the secret that has been shared with them.

TABLE 1.4 Chefs Feel Their Decision Whether to Reveal or Refuse to Supply Information Requested by a Colleague Will Affect the Likelihood of Getting Information from That Individual in the Future

Expected change in willingness of requester to provide information in the future	Decrease	No change[a]	Increase
Chef provided requested information	4	42	22
Chef refused to provide requested information	23	43	2
Chi-square = 32.472		p = 0.000	

a "No change" was in most cases chosen when chef and requester had shared information equally in the past. In such cases there was already a trading relationship between the partners involving reciprocity. Under these conditions, there would be no reason for an information provider to expect that a particular exchange in a series would materially affect a recipient's willingness to provide information in the future.

We asked chefs about the value of the information that they would be willing to freely reveal in two contrasting ways: (1) free revealing "to everyone at once" in a public forum, and (2) sequential, person-to-person revealing to "anyone who asks." Chefs were more likely to present high-value recipe information in a public forum. In sharp contrast, they were significantly more likely to reveal low-value information privately to anyone who asked (table 1.5). This makes sense to us as an economically reasonable strategy: Increased reputation is likely to result from publicly revealing a recipe only if something valuable and interesting is revealed. In contrast, private but nonselective revealing of information ("to anyone who asks") may not yield the reciprocity benefits associated with more selective revealing of information.

TABLE 1.5 Value of Recipe Information Revealed Privately "To Anyone Who Asks" vs. Revealed to All in a Public Forum

Decision to	High-value information[a] (%)	Low-value information[a] (%)
Reveal in a public forum	78	22
Privately reveal to "anyone who asks"	26	74
Chi-square		p < 0 000

a The value of the information is an index: High-value information is information related to a recipe that is both a "must" on the chef's menu and is "unique among direct competitors" (rated 4 or 5 on a scale of 5 for both items).

Finally, we asked chefs why they would reveal some of their recipes to the public at large (table 1.6). Although we did not offer a complete list of possible motives in our questionnaire, respondents tended to agree with the motives we listed that clearly involved direct personal gain in the form of increased restaurant sales and enhanced personal reputations. In an open response section in the questionnaire, some chefs provided additional motivations for revealing recipes in a public forum; most of these also involved increasing private profits. Chefs wrote that they were motivated to present their IP to the public at large because doing so would enhance their personal reputation, generate publicity for their restaurant, inform potential patrons about what is offered in their restaurant, enable them to claim the "innovation space" before another chef got a related idea, be an enjoyable experience for them, increase likelihood they would receive information requests from chefs they appreciate, or be an opportunity to promote regional products.

TABLE 1.6 Motivations for Publicly Revealing Recipes

Motivations	Mean[a]	Std. dev.	Percentage of high agreement[b]
Attract more customers in your restaurant	3.86	1.12	80
Increase your reputation	3.91	0.90	80
Increase the reputation of French gastronomy	3.58	0.96	64

a Scale: 1 (totally wrong) to 5 (totally right).
b High agreement means a choice of 4 or 5 on a scale from 1 to 5.

In summation, it appears that chefs' behaviors regarding protecting and revealing recipe-related information are consistent with efforts to increase private benefit from their recipe innovations.

Discussion

We have now documented that accomplished French chefs both espouse and enforce IP-related norms. Given these empirical findings, can we conclude that a norms-based IP system worthy of the name really exists among these French chefs?

Although norms-based IP systems clearly have characteristics very different from law-based IP systems, both systems enable innovators to establish and enforce rights to some types of IP to their economic advantage. So we think it reasonable to dignify norms-based IP systems as "real" IP systems worthy of consideration along with their law-based counterparts.

Norms-based systems appear to have some major advantages over law-based IP systems. Recall that social norms are developed by communities to deal with matters of importance to that community. Getting final resolution of a complaint via a law-based system costs on average millions of dollars and can take years—at least in the United States.[29] Indeed, given these high costs, one may wonder what proportion of IP violations nominally covered by law-based systems are actually being adjudicated on the merits by those systems. Kesan and Ball find that only 5% of all cases filed are eventually adjudicated on the merits—the rest are settled before adjudication.[30] This low figure, the authors reason, is because it is often cheaper for both sides to settle than it is to complete a very expensive legal contest. The associated loss to social welfare is that the validity of contested—and often very questionable—patent claims is seldom judicially established.

In contrast, a complaint can be brought in a social norms–based system by simply bringing the matter to the attention of influential members of the community. If these members view the case as having merit, explanations may be requested of the apparent violator of the norm, and/or sanctions can be applied very quickly.

As an example of rapid community norms enforcement among chefs, consider the recent community judgment that Chef Robin (Robin Wickens, owner and chef of the Interlude Restaurant in Melbourne, Australia) had violated an anti-copying norm. The discussion took place in an online forum hosted on eGullet.com, a website for chefs and other serious "foodies." The entire episode, from the discovery of the violation to the close of case-specific discussion on the forum, took only five days.

In March 2006, Forum participant tb86 reported apparent recipe copying by "Chef Robin" (March 14, 2006, 4:02 p.m.). "I am an Australian chef in NY and was looking at the Interlude [a Sydney restaurant] website and realized that a lot of the food has been copied identically from some of the top chefs here." In his message, tb86 provided links to Interlude restaurant food photos, and also those of famous U.S. restaurants showing apparently identical presentations of identical recipes.

The Interlude chef, Chef Robin, quickly took down the incriminating photos from his restaurant website. He then replied (March 15, 2006, 4:53 p.m.): "Thought I should post my reply. My trip to America and staging [working as an intern] at Alinea [a famous Chicago restaurant] gave me ideas and I saw new techniques that after cooking for over ten years in some pretty good restaurants I had seen before. . . . Of course people are going to imitate it and evolve it."

Many eGullet members quickly posted responses, with the great majority condemning Chef Robin's behavior in strong terms. Excerpts from three responses convey the flavor: "The 'evolution' part might be where you are coming up short" (Willie Lee, March 14, 2006, 7:17 p.m.). "Why don't you also check out the menus at Cru and Guilt restaurants in NY for some more 'evolutionary' ideas for your next menu. . . . Why were the links to the photos removed in the last 24 hours? New York is watching you" (Aussiechef76, March 14, 2006, 9:31 p.m.). "Great . . . . thanks to this my plans for ripping off Sandra Lee's Ranch Dressing and puke covered Frito Lay chips is never gonna come to fruition" (peteswanson, March 15, 2006, 3:37 p.m.). Things continued in this vein for five days, at which point the site managers closed the discussion.[31]

Reports of the controversy quickly spread to other news media. For example:

> Among Melbourne diners, the food at Robin Wickens' two-hatted Fitzroy restaurant, Interlude, has inspired such breathless adjectives as "whimsical," "daring," and "arch." But in recent days, a harsher term has been suggested: "plagiarised." The storm began 10 days ago on specialist Internet forum eGullet, after it was revealed that among Wickens' offerings was, in fact, a replica of a dish first "invented" at New York's famed WD-50. . . . Editorial staff from eGullet have since posted pictures of four other dishes by the 2005 Age Good Food Guide young chef of the year [Robin Wickens], which emulate creations by Grant Achatz, of Chicago's Alinea, including a dessert served in a test tube.
>
> There is no question of legal action against Wickens: recipes, no matter how unique, cannot be protected by copyright, nor have they ever been successfully patented. But chefs and diners have questioned whether Wickens' conduct in replicating dishes—right down to the plating—is poor form. The question is pertinent in the world of top-end modern

restaurants, where creativity, not simply fine flavour and execution, is often demanded.

Writing on the eGullet forum, Alinea co-owner Nick Kokonas said he agreed that there was no intellectual property case here. "In my mind, there is something greater—'intellectual integrity,'" he wrote. Wickens has sent letters of apology to Achatz and WD-50's Wylie Dufresne for failing to give credit to them.[32]

Of course, norms-based IP systems also have major disadvantages relative to law-based systems. Communities may punish whistleblowers along with violators; communities have no power to award monetary compensation to an injured party, and so on. Also, recall that norms-based IP systems are only effective in controlling behaviors ". . . when groups control stimuli that are valued (or disvalued) by the target person."[33] In contrast, law-based systems have access to a type of sanction—confiscation of financial resources—that presumably would be of concern to all would-be violators within a particular law's zone of jurisdiction. This may mean that norms-based IP systems apply to a more limited scope of actors than do law-based systems.

For example, consider the case of high-fashion clothing design. Just as with recipes, law-based IP systems do not protect clothing designs. Cox and Jenkins note that, unconstrained by law-based IP, mass merchandisers are quick to "knock off" many novel clothing designs created by high-fashion designers.[34] Mass merchandisers presumably do not consider themselves to be part of the high-fashion designer community and so would not be constrained by any IP-related social norms held by that group.

Of course, it is another question whether the limited reach of norms-based IP systems actually reduces innovators' profits. Thus, when yesterday's high-fashion items become today's mass market items, high-end buyers may no longer value the versions they purchased—because they are no longer exclusive.[35] A likely consequence of rapid copying is therefore an acceleration of the obsolescence cycle in high-fashion clothing designs, as high-end fashion buyers more rapidly move on to the next new thing. Knockoffs, as Raustiala and Sprigman point out, might therefore increase rather than reduce the profits of innovating high-fashion designers.[36]

Conclusion

Our research and the work of others in this book demonstrate that norms-based IP systems are indeed effective and common in today's economies. We think it would be very useful to further determine the ubiquity and economic importance of norms-based IP systems, and to understand the extent to which the norms that underlie such systems are similar. There appear to be interesting differences as well as similarities. One example of a difference: Recall that the first norm we documented among accomplished chefs de cuisine was dishonor in exactly copying recipes developed by other chefs. It is likely that this norm is not found among scientists. After all, exact replication of experiments (with proper attribution) to check the accuracy of reported findings is a valued activity in science. In contrast, the second and third social norms we identified among chefs do seem similar to information exchange norms reported among scientists.[37]

As a second example of a likely difference in IP-related norms among fields, recall that the third important norm we encountered among our sample of chefs was the right to be acknowledged as the author of a recipe. This norm was essential to chefs who wanted to profit from reputation-related gains by freely revealing their proprietary recipe information on, for example, a television program. However, it is not obvious that this third norm is always present in norms-based IP systems that include free revealing, because free revealing can produce private gains for one who reveals via mechanisms that are both dependent on and independent of the recipient's knowing the identity of the donor. Gains that depend on knowing the identity of the donor generally relate to reputational gains, for example: "I am more likely to offer X a job because I know he is an innovator."[38] Mechanisms for private gains by innovators who freely reveal that are not dependent on knowing the identity of the donor include network effects, for example: "If I freely reveal how to build telephones, more telephones will be built and used. The more telephones that are in use, the more benefit I gain from my telephone—because I can connect to more people."[39]

Norms that seem similar on first inspection may in fact differ in important ways. For example, anti-copying norms clearly create monopoly power for innovating chefs. As mentioned earlier, this power is similar to that endowed by a patent grant or a copyright: Chefs may be technically able to copy some recipe innovations using only public information—but the anti-copying norm prohibits them from doing it. However, closer examination may show the monopoly powers granted by community anti-copying norms to be more or less extensive or flexible than those granted by patent. Thus, chefs apparently do not sell the rights to produce exact copies of their recipes to other chefs. Yet this is common practice among owners of patents in other fields. Further investigation is needed to show whether this difference is a matter of what IP-related norms permit—or what chefs choose to do in exploiting their norms-sanctioned rights.

It will also be useful to more deeply explore whether one system tends to dominate the other when both are present. (For example, as noted earlier, Ellickson found that extant laws addressed how border fencing costs should be allocated between neighbors—but he also found that the affected people ignored these laws in favor of a system of norms of their own devising.[40]) Or it may be that norms- and law-based IP systems are often complementary. For example, as Sitkin points out in the context of corporate management, an increased reliance on formal rules and procedures rather than on informal norms can sometimes enhance trust on the part of system users, indicating that these two system types can complement one another.[41]

In sum, in the research reported here, we demonstrate by example that norms-based IP systems exist in the present-day world. We propose that it will be useful to study norms-based IP systems further and to learn how they can most usefully be applied to serve both innovators and society.

NOTES

This chapter was adapted from Emmanuelle Fauchart and Eric Von Hippel, "Norms-based intellectual property systems: The case of French chefs." *Organization Science* 19.2 (2008): 187–201.

1 E.g., Elinor Ostrom, *Governing the Commons* (Cambridge, UK: Cambridge University Press, 1990); Robert C. Ellickson, *Order Without Law: How Neighbors Settle Disputes* (Cambridge, MA: Harvard University Press, 1991); Arti K. Rai, "Regulating scientific research: Intellectual property rights and the norms of science," 94 *Northwestern University Law Review* 77 (1999).

2 Robert P. Merges, "Property rights and the commons: The case of scientific research," 13 *Society Philosophy Policy* (1996): 145–153; Robert P. Merges, "From medieval guilds to open source software: Informal norms, appropriability institutions, and innovation," *University of Wisconsin Law School Institute for Legal Studies Conference on Legal History of Intellectual Property* (November 13, 2004).

3 E.g., Adam B. Jaffe and Josh Lerner, *Innovation and Its Discontents: How Our Broken Patent System Is Endangering Innovation and Progress and What to Do About It* (Princeton, NJ: Princeton University Press, 2004); Yochai Benkler, *The Wealth of Networks* (New Haven, CT: Yale University Press, 2006); James Bessen and Michael J. Meurer, *Patent Failure: How Judges, Bureaucrats, and Lawyers Put Innovators at Risk* (Princeton, NJ: Princeton University Press, 2008); Katherine J. Strandburg, "Users as innovators: Implications for patent doctrine," 79 *University of Colorado Law Review* 46 (2008).

4 Richard J. Hackman, "Group influences on individuals," in *Handbook of Industrial and Organizational Psychology*, Marvin Dunnette, ed. (Chicago: Rand McNally, 1976), 1455–1525.

5 Robert Axlerod, "An evolutionary approach to norms," 80 *American Political Science Review* 1095 (1986).

6 Daniel C. Feldman, "The development and enforcement of group norms," 9 *Academy of Management Review* 47 (1984); Jack P. Gibbs, "Norms: The problem of definition and classification," 70 *American Journal of Sociology* 586 (1965).

7 Jonathan Bendor and Piotr Swistak, "The evolution of norms," 106 *American Journal of Sociology* 1493 (2001); Rajiv Rimal and Kevin Real, "Understanding the influence of perceived norms on behaviors," 13 *Communications Theory* 184 (2003).

8 Jon Elster, "Social norms and economic theory," 3 *Journal of Economic Perspectives* 99 (1989).

9 Hackman, "Group influences on individuals," 1506.

10 Bendor and Swistak, "The evolution of norms," n.p.

11 Bronwyn Hall and Dietmar Harhoff, "Post grant review systems at the U.S. patent office: Design parameters and expected impact," 19 *Berkeley Law and Technology Journal* 1 (2004).

12 Christopher J. Buccafusco, "On the legal consequences of sauces: Should Thomas Keller's recipes be per se copyrightable?" 24 *Cardozo Arts & Entertainment Law Journal* 1121 (2007).

13 E.g., Stewart Macaulay, "Non-contractual relations in business: A preliminary study," 28 *American Sociology Review* (1963); Lisa Bernstein, "Opting out of the legal system: Extralegal contractual relations in the diamond industry," 21 *Journal of Legal Studies* 115 (1992); Avner Greif, "Contract enforceability and economic institutions in early trade: The Maghribi traders' coalition," 83 *American Economic Review* 525 (1993); Kevin Zheng Zhou and Laura Poppo, "Relational contracts in China: Relational governance and contractual assurance," *Institutional Mechanisms for Industry Self-Regulation Program, Working paper.* (Virginia Polytechnic Institute and State University, Blacksburg, 2005).

14 Greif, "Contract enforceability," n.p.

15 Ostrom, *Governing the Commons.*

16 Ellickson, *Order Without Law.*

17 Ibid., 71.

18 Ibid., 71–75.

19 Ibid., vii.

20 Robert K. Merton, *The Sociology of Science: Theoretical and Empirical Investigations* (Chicago: University of Chicago Press, 1973).

21 E.g., Dasgupta Partha and Paul A. David, "Toward a new economics of science," 23 *Research Policy* 487 (1994); Rai, "Regulating scientific research"; Robert Merges, "Contracting into liability rules: Intellectual property rights and collective rights organizations," 84 *California Law Review* 1293 (1996).

22 Unpublished interview.

23 Colin Johnson et al., "Behind the stars: A concise typology of Michelin restaurants in Europe," 46 *Cornell Hotel Restaurant Administration Quarterly* 170 (2005).

24 *Nouvel Observateur*, "Michelin 2005: 3 étoiles pour Régis Marcon" (2005).

25 Eric von Hippel, "Cooperation between rivals: Informal know-how trading," 16 *Research Policy* 291 (1987); Stephan Schrader, "Informal technology transfer between firms: Cooperation through information trading," 20 *Research Policy* 153 (1991); Kristian Kreiner and Majken Schultz, "Informal collaboration in R&D. The formation of networks across organizations," 14 *Organizational Studies* 189 (1993); Isabelle Bouty, "Interpersonal and interaction influences on informal resource exchanges between R&D researchers across organizational boundaries," 43 *Academy of Management Journal* 50 (2000).

26 von Hippel, "Cooperation between rivals," n.p.

27 Robert Axelrod, *The Evolution of Cooperation* (New York: Basic Books, 1984).

28 Henry Hansmann and Marina Santilli, "Authors and artists moral rights: A comparative legal and economic analysis," 26 *Journal of Legal Studies* 95 (1997).

29 AIPLA, *Report of the Economic Survey*, American Intellectual Property Association Law Practice Management Committee (Arlington, VA, 2005); Bessen and Meurer, *Patent Failure.*

30 Jay P. Kesan and Gwendolyn G. Ball, "How are patent cases resolved? An empirical examination of the adjudication and settlement of patent disputes," 84 *Washington University Law Review* 237 (2006).

31 eGForums, The eGullet Society for Culinary Arts and Letters, http://forums.egullet.org/.

32 Kenneth Nguyen, "The good feud guide," *TheAge.com.au* (March 26, 2006), http://www.theage.com.au/.

33 Hackman, "Group influences on individuals," 1506.

34 Christine Cox and Jennifer Jenkins, "Between the seams, a fertile commons: An overview of the relationship between fashion and intellectual property," Norman Lear Center Publication, Duke University Law School, Durham, NC, 4 (2005).

35 Thorstein Veblen, *The Theory of the Leisure Class*, Republished in Penguin 20th Century Classics (New York: Penguin Books, 1994, 1899).

36 Kal Raustiala and Christopher Sprigman, "The piracy paradox: Innovation and intellectual property in fashion design," 92 *Virginia Law Review* 1687 (2006).

37 Bouty, "Interpersonal and interaction influences"; Kreiner and Schultz, "Informal collaboration in R&D; Merges, "Contracting into liability rules."

38 Josh Lerner and Jean Tirole, "Some simple economics of open source," 50 *Journal of Industrial Economics* 197 (2002).

39 Harhoff et al., "Profiting from voluntary information spillovers: How users benefit by freely revealing their innovations," *Research Policy* 32 (10) 1753–1769 (2003). Eric von Hippel, *Democratizing Innovation* (Cambridge, MA: MIT Press, 2005).

40 Ellickson, *Order Without Law.*

41 Sim B. Sitkin, "On the positive effect of the legalization of trust," in *Research on Negotiation in Organizations*, Robert J. Bies et al., eds., vol. 5 (Greenwich, CT: JAI Press, 1995), 185–217.

2

An IP Lawyer Walks Into a Bar

Observations on Creativity in Cocktails

MATTHEW SCHRUERS

> Three measures of Gordon's, one of vodka, half a measure of Kina Lillet.
> Shake it very well until it's ice-cold, then add a large thin slice of lemon
> peel. . . . This drink's my own invention. I'm going to patent it when I can
> think of a good name.

So announces James Bond, having just made the acquaintance of CIA
agent Felix Leiter, in Ian Fleming's inaugural Bond novel, *Casino Royale*.[1]
While volumes could be filled debating whether or not Bond is wrong
for shaking his martinis instead of stirring them, there's no doubt that
he was wrong about the prospects of his intellectual creation. To the
pleasure of cocktail-thieving supervillains everywhere, Mr. Bond is not
going to be patenting anything. (Insert diabolical laughter here.) And
it is not because for a spy, Bond seems to be terrible at keeping secrets,
having disclosed his unprotected formula to his bartender and some foreign agent he only just met. No, he was out of luck in any event. Culinary
recipes, and cocktails in particular, are one of various "negative" spaces
of federal intellectual property law, where little statutory protection is
available.[2]

Bond's particular innovation here may have been inspired by his *mis-
conception* of the law, but the fact is that countless bartenders ("mixologists" being a more modern term) have been innovating for well over
200 years, producing new and interesting cocktail recipes over which
they have no intellectual control. The orthodox theory of American intellectual property law struggles to explain this.[3]

Where protection is unavailable, the orthodox theory suggests that
we ought to encounter an under-supply in the market. But we don't. A

growing abundance of recipes in print and online extends beyond the kitchen, to the bar. The last two decades have seen a renewed enthusiasm for cocktails, and much like "foodie culture" has lifted the restaurant sector, a wave of interest in craft cocktails has transformed the spirits industry. This includes a boom in cocktail recipes, both old and new. This resurgence has occurred notwithstanding the fact that the initial application of IP theory would suggest that it shouldn't be the case.

This chapter explores why creativity occurs behind the bar, even in the absence of exclusive rights. It observes that the roots of modern cocktails can be found in medicine, a field readily associated with IP, and further, that IP is quite robust in other segments of the cocktail commodity chain, but that cocktails themselves are inherently unsuited for IP protection. It concludes by noting how different business models, incentives, and the mere fact of necessity have succeeded in driving cocktail innovation to where it is today.

The Absence of Intellectual Property in Cocktails

One of the justifications for copyright and patent (and to a lesser degree, trademark) is the notion that ideas are public goods, distinguished by two characteristics: "non-rivalrousness" and "non-excludability." The former term describes the fact that the good itself can be consumed in a non-competitive way—my use of a recipe doesn't impair your ability to prepare the same thing. The latter term describes the fact that you cannot prevent others from possessing information once they know it. These aren't new observations, of course. Thomas Jefferson noted them in his correspondence more than 200 years ago, and legal scholarship has acknowledged the public goods nature of ideas for decades.[4]

In short, the difficulty of fencing in an idea complicates a creator's effort to fully appropriate the value of his intangible creation. Since everyone can free-ride once the creation is disclosed, the incentives to develop them are diminished, and the market would therefore be expected to under-supply intellectual endeavor. Thus, intellectual property rights to the rescue.

Yet in the case of recipes, intellectual property falls short. Federal courts, the U.S. Copyright Office, and copyright scholars have long interpreted section 102(b) of the Copyright Act, which prohibits copyrights on a "procedure" or "process," to foreclose protection for lists of ingredients and steps. As the Copyright Office explains, protection may "extend to substantial literary expression—a description, explanation, or illustration, for example—that accompanies a recipe or formula or to a combination of recipes, as in a cookbook."[5] Thus, a sufficiently literary narration for mixing a Manhattan may well acquire copyright protection, but the protection extends only to that specific written expression and not the steps it embodies.

Similarly, one might register a trademark for a particular cocktail's name, but those rights extend only to the name in commerce, not the recipe to which it is applied. This Gosling's Ltd. has done with respect to the phrase "Dark 'N Stormy." (According to the International Bartender's Association, a Dark 'N Stormy consists of 6 cl dark rum topped with 10 cl ginger beer, served over ice in a highball glass and garnished with lime.[6])

When Gosling's sought to enforce its mark, it produced no small amount of confusion in the media. Due to a poorly worded 2009 *New York Times* article, a wholly baffled article in *The Atlantic*, and a correspondingly muddled Wikipedia entry, it is frequently and incorrectly stated that Gosling's has "trademarked the recipe." It hasn't. In fact, Gosling's rights under the Lanham Act are quite limited. It can neither compel bartenders to call Gosling's and ginger beer a "Dark 'N Stormy," nor can it foreclose others from serving other dark rums and ginger beer under another name.[7] At most, the registration—provided the mark hasn't already gone generic—enables Gosling's to restrict use of the phrase "Dark 'N Stormy" in commerce.[8]

Gosling's was not even a pioneer in seeking trademark protection for arbitrary cocktail names. As early as 1896, G.F. Heublin & Brothers secured a registration for the mark "Club Cocktails" in relation to its bottled beverages, and defended the mark vigorously in several legal tussles in the following years. It is worth noting that, like Gosling's Dark 'N Stormy registrations, Heublin's mark appeared to contemplate premixed, *bottled* concoctions, rather than freshly prepared cocktails. This suggests that these actions are a garden-variety application of consumer protection law: A buyer should be able to predict what is in the bottle.[9]

But, assuming that rum consumers also expect a *fresh* Dark 'N Stormy to necessarily contain Gosling's rum, and not some imposter, there is some basis in trademark law for protecting that expectation too. In fact, just such a case was brought before the courts in 1936, *Compania Ron Bacardi S.A. v. Wivel Restaurant*, in which the distiller Bacardi sued New York hotel operators for serving Bacardi Cocktails that did not contain Bacardi's rum.[10] The rum producer argued that consumers expected its brand in the eponymous cocktail, whereas the defendants furnished affidavits from numerous bartenders, testifying that in their years of experience, a variety of rums were used in preparing a Bacardi Cocktail. Bacardi ultimately prevailed, with the court labeling a Bacardi-less Bacardi as "a subterfuge and a fraud."[11] Years later the company prevailed again in similar actions in Illinois.[12] And more recently, energy drink vendor Red Bull reportedly brought several successful actions against bars that used less expensive energy drinks when serving customers who requested a Red Bull and vodka.[13]

Arguably, the success of Bacardi and Red Bull as plaintiffs may be attributed to the fact they sued on their consumers' behalf as much as their own. These cases do not concern the *authorship* of the beverage, but rather its pedigree. Unlike the creator-oriented protections of copyright and patent, the direct beneficiaries of Bacardi's and Red Bull's trademark rights are the imbibing public. Gosling's efforts involving the Dark 'N Stormy are not entirely different; it was not interested in restricting use of the recipe, only in maintaining the association between its own spirit and the cocktail's name. Protecting a bar patron's expectations as to what goes in his glass is what a consumer protection statute should do. The outcomes in the few cases involving cocktail recipes are thus unsurprising, and are quite different from "recipe rights" as they protect consumers, not inventors.

So if neither copyright nor trademark grants rights over what one chooses to put in the glass, what might? To the extent one seeks exclusive rights in methods, processes, and procedures, that is the province of *patent* law. As it turns out, the U.S. Patent and Trademark Office classification system devotes an entire class of patents, Class 426, to "food" and (just to cover all the bases) "edible material." Nevertheless, the USPTO's website notes that "one of the most common questions the Office of Innovation Development receives is whether or not food recipes can be patented," and goes on to caution that most recipes will not rise to the level of novelty and non-obviousness required to secure a patent.[14] Like the Copyright Office, the USPTO rains on the aspiring cocktail patentee's parade. Nowhere will federal law provide such rights.

Of course, an inventive mixologist might avail herself of *state* law protections for trade secrets (there being no federal private cause of action for trade secret misappropriation at the time of this writing). But most states that implement the Uniform Trade Secrets Act (UTSA) limit trade secret protection to that which is the "subject of efforts that are reasonable under the circumstances to maintain its secrecy."[15] And trade secret law "does not offer protection against discovery by fair and honest means, such as by independent invention, accidental disclosure, or by so-called reverse engineering."[16] Nor, as commentary to the UTSA observes, does trade secret law protect against a competitor observing the public use or public display of the secret,[17] which is particularly problematic for the practicing mixologist when many (if not most) cocktails are prepared for clientele and the world to see.

Picking up where federal law leaves off, the publishers of *Bartender Magazine* will issue you a "CocktailRight"™ certificate for a mere $30. These certificates are offered online via a site urging readers to "copyright your original drink recipe."[18] Needless to say, bragging rights that you were taken for $30 are not the same as enforceable legal rights, but the availability of this dubious offer suggests that interest in exclusive cocktail rights exists.

The IP-Centric History and Industry of the Cocktail

The absence of IP in cocktails is more notable than other zones of IP negative space for two reasons. First, since its medicinal roots, mixology has long been associated with the pursuit of exclusive rights; there are numerous examples of inventors seeking exclusive rights for mixed alcoholic products in the "pre-history" of cocktails. Second, the cocktail commodity chain is actually very robust with IP. It is only once one gets to the preparation stage that the protections end. This is not accidental. In spite of the history of mixed beverages and the pervasiveness of IP in getting cocktails from the fermentation process to your glass, the product itself is not only without protection, but in fact is inherently inhospitable to modern principles of IP.

The first reason that cocktails are an odd example of the IP's negative space is that the roots of cocktails may be found in what is today considered to be one of intellectual property's poster children: *pharmacology*.

While cocktail historians have pegged the birth of the word "cocktail" itself somewhere around the early 1800s,[19] the roots of the beverage go much further back, to the prescription of compound-bearing alcohols for restorative or medicinal purposes. This practice pre-dates the modern cocktail by well over 200 years,[20] to—according to one author—"a time when the boundaries between medicine and culture were more flexible and more porous."[21] As it turns out, these porous boundaries may have set medicine back, but not without considerably advancing the bibulous arts.

Ironically, one conspicuous example of the practice of administering blended alcohols as medicine is for the treatment of gout—arthritic inflammation caused by the deposit of uric acid in joints. Even in the seventeenth century, gout was recognized as being associated with a rich diet and alcohol consumption, which were largely luxuries at the time. Certain translations of a 1683 treatise on gout by the prominent seventeenth-century physician Thomas Sydenham (at times described as "the English Hippocrates") associate gout with lifestyles of "ease, voluptuousness, high living, and too free an use of wine and other spirituous liquors."[22]

For treatment, Sydenham's treatise prescribed a complex medicine prepared from an exotic range of plant matter and consumed by the patient. Of two recommended vehicles—an electuary, or ingredients mashed with alcohol into a paste, and a distilled liquid—the latter proved far more popular, and was widely emulated.[23] Over time, the astringent qualities of many such concoctions lent themselves to the name "bitters," and this characteristic is also likely the cause for another alcohol—often brandy or sherry—being adopted as a favored delivery vehicle (but not a very prudent one, at least for gout patients). Brandies and wines not only have the effect of masking astringency, but also have the effect of inviting patients to self-medicate.

Given that the prevailing medical alternatives at the time likely involved bleeding, the elite of the era might well have been willing to pay a premium for such a pleasing and non-invasive treatment. By the late seventeenth century, it was not uncommon to see apothecaries and self-styled "doctors" hawking a variety of oils and elixirs to the public.[24] These products were not immune from passing-off by the competition; in 1680 the producer of another, unpatented medicine known as Daffy's advertised to the public that it should beware of "diverse Persons" counterfeiting his product.[25]

These apothecary pirates likely compelled one Richard Stoughton to obtain a letter patent for his "Elixir Magnum Stomachii, or the Great Cordial Elixir," in 1712.[26] As with many other patents at the time, no formula for the elixir was furnished in a specification, suggesting that challenges with enablement are not new to the patent system. Stoughton's was so popular that even its trade dress acquired distinctiveness, with the phrase "stodgy as a Stoughton bottle" entering common parlance.[27] But whatever promotional value was furnished by Stoughton's royal patent, it seems to have provided limited utility in the way of intellectual property protection. Purported recipes for the elixir soon appeared in print, including one in the 1739 *Compleat Housewife* located under "All Sorts of Cordial Waters," in the company of "Dr. Burgel's Antidote against the Plague" and "A Method to cure the Jaundice, which has been try'd with great Success."[28]

In spite of, or perhaps due to widespread infringement, Stoughton's product became one of the earliest recorded "patent medicines," from which a long and distinctive tradition of quackery blossomed, tarnishing the name of patents in the process. Stoughton's was likely popular insofar as it urged the patient to liberally self-administer, suggesting a substantial quantity mixed with water or wine, sugar, and brandy, "as often as you please."[29] While the word "cocktail" was not applied, Stoughton's prescribed combination of sugar, water, and bitters with a spirit meet the conventional definition for a cocktail.[30] Stoughton's prescription for his patent medicine is thus an *ur*-cocktail, straddling the boundary between eras when one tipped a glass for health, versus a tipple "for health."

Following Stoughton's lead, patent medicines purporting to cure a diverse array of afflictions and dispositions proliferated on both sides of the Atlantic, until they were largely killed off by the food safety movement of the early twentieth century.[31] The purportedly medicinal properties of bitters were touted right up to the Pure Food and Drug Act of 1906. The labels for an impostor version of Angostura Aromatic bitters, for example, claimed to be "a cure for Liver Complaint, Dyspepsia, Fever and Ague, Billious, Intermittent, and Remittent Fevers," and, for good measure, "Asiatic Cholera and Yellow Fever." These exaggerations ultimately caught up with the infringer, however, when the Second Circuit Court of Appeals ruled against them, citing unclean hands.[32]

Snake oils and quackery alone did not advance the cocktail. The practice of using potable alcohol as a medicine delivery vehicle gained additional prominence as the British Empire expanded. When British citizens abroad took to dissolving their bitter anti-malarial quinine powder in gin, they were planting the roots for the modern gin and quinine-bearing tonic.[33] The patented roots of the gin and tonic would not be complete without a lime, and the use of lime can also be linked to medicinal purposes. Citrus was long known to be useful in combating scurvy; it was popularized by medical trials conducted by naval surgeon James Lind in a 1753 treatise, but even Sydenham advocated the use of "anti-scorbutics" for gout sufferers in the hopes of alleviating joint pain.[34]

In December 1867 a Scottish merchant by the name of Lauchlan Rose secured Patent #3499, for "an improved mode of preserving vegetable juices,"[35] and marketed what is today known as Rose's West Indies Lime Juice. Although perhaps intended for the domestic market, Rose's patented process produced a shelf-stable, alcohol-free anti-scorbutic. Coincidentally, that same year the British government had mandated lime juice in merchant sailors' daily rations, extending to civilian sailors a practice long followed by the navy.[36]

For policy reasons, Britain had for some time favored limes sourced from the British West Indies, instead of lemons from Europe. This preference for limes over lemons, and mandated rations for both civilian and naval sailors, cemented the use of the term "limey" to refer to British sailors. More importantly for our purposes, it ensured that mariners would mix their daily rum rations with lime juice. It also likely played a role in the fact that limes reigned in the rum and gin cocktails of the following era, including the Gimlet, which is customarily prepared with Rose's Lime Juice. The choice of limes over lemons was less inspired from a medical perspective, however: as the lime contains a smaller quantity of ascorbic acid, scurvy reappeared on British ships in the late 1800s.[37]

In addition to the patent-driven origins of modern cocktails, those engaged in cocktail innovation might have looked to intellectual property to protect their creations for another reason: Most of a mixologist's inputs used in crafting a cocktail are themselves distinguished by various types of IP protection.

Base ingredients benefit from multiple types of protection. Whereas patents were once used to convey the imprimatur of the state upon the often-spurious quality of patent medicines, today's alcoholic products rely upon a mix of trademarks, collective marks, and, particularly in Europe, regulated geographical indications (GIs). Closely associated with the concept of *terroir*, GIs are recognized under both EU law and the TRIPS Agreement.[38] Plymouth gin, for example, until recently held both a trademark and geographical indication status. While the owners of the Plymouth, England-based Black Friars Distillery declined to renew the geographical indication in late 2014 due to the certification costs, this coexistence illustrates the considerable overlap that the two systems of protection provide. Internationally protected GIs are of relatively recent vintage, and before that time distillers and spirits vendors relied heavily on trademark. Long before the Lanham Act, for example, the manufacturer of Angostura was bringing infringement actions in multiple jurisdictions—as early as the 1870s.[39]

Further down the commodity chain, the many devices and utensils of the bartender's trade are or were similarly protected by a wealth of (now expired) patents for their innovations. In short, a bartender today works with ingredients protected by a range of marks, GIs, and certifications, using barware (once) protected by a variety of patents, and yet the actual product of his craft itself receives no protection.

This is particularly interesting given how differently the separate segments of the commodity chain fared during the early twentieth century. With the beginning of nearly 14 years of Prohibition in 1920, the profession of bartending was decimated. While it is often suggested that Prohibition actually promoted cocktail innovation because it was necessary to mask the abysmal quality of moonshine,[40] little evidence substantiates this contention. Customers of the day apparently favored straight liquor; it was not an era of cocktail innovation. In fact, innovation moved abroad. "The new drinks that did appear during this era were mostly fashioned in Europe, where at least a few American bartenders fled to pursue their careers," observes cocktail expert Gary Regan.[41] The global market for spirits themselves was largely unaffected, however, due to the fact that so much production occurred outside of the United States.

It is thus notable that post-Prohibition, a considerable wave of cocktail innovation occurs in the United States despite the bartending profession having been largely wiped out. The entire tiki genre, including the now-classic Mai Tais and Zombies, evolved in this era, while the base spirits and hardware remained largely the same. Even today, the three-piece "martini" shaker in the average bar is likely a dead ringer for E.J. Hauck's 1884 combination shaker,[42] and most so-called Hawthorne strainers today are difficult to distinguish from Charles Lindley's 1889 patented "Julep-strainer."[43] To the extent innovation is occurring further up the commodity chain, such as new formulations of lost bitters,[44] or barrel aged gin, for example, these products are responding to demand from cocktail enthusiasts, rather than the other way around.[45]

The absence of protection for cocktails is no historical accident; even more so than food, cocktails are inherently hostile to modern principles of intellectual property. It has been argued that in the culinary context, plating may constitute a form of fixation wherein the dish itself is the work.[46] While there is no reason that some presentations of food could not constitute works of visual art, courts may be disinclined to accept what could present a roundabout way of securing recipe rights, which federal courts have so far refused to allow.[47] As a district court judge recently noted in the improbably captioned *Tomaydo-Tomahhdo, LLC v. Vozary*, "Certainly, plaintiffs cannot be suggesting that somehow the copyright [in a recipe book] prevents defendants from serving chicken salad sandwiches."[48] Other scholars have noted that trade dress claims may also provide protection for certain distinctive presentations of food.[49]

But to the extent that any narrow form of copyright protection or trade dress might be afforded to food preparation, this would be an impossibility in the case of most cocktails. The options for presenting liquids are far more limited than presenting solids. Moreover, the presentations of many conventional cocktails are actually prescribed by semi-formal standard. The International Bartenders Association specifies precise proportions, glassware, and garnish for dozens of classic and common cocktails.[50] A bartender who departs too far from these prescriptions might be thought to not know the craft.

Even setting aside the standards, the number of discrete permutations that are actually palatable are finite. Cocktail confusion is already a problem. Numerous cocktails do business under the same name, or are but one ingredient away from another cocktail. A Bronx, for example, is also a Minnehaha; add bitters and it becomes an Income Tax and also perhaps a Maurice; remove the orange juice and it becomes a Perfect Martini. Similarly, a Ford cocktail also travels under the name Caprice and several others, all of which are essentially variations on the classic martini.[51] Gary Regan's 2003 opus, *The Joy of Mixology*, devotes 30 pages to an extended taxonomy of cocktails that in numerous entries differ only by a single ingredient, or merely the garnish.[52] Were these cocktails the result of "infringement," or independent creation? In most cases, we'll never know.

From the copyright perspective, doctrines like merger and *scènes à faire* thus constrain the extent to which any particular articulation of a mixological idea can acquire protection. From the patent perspective, the obviousness of potential combinations arguably rules out the vast number of potential cocktails. As the Supreme Court reminded an over-zealous Federal Circuit in *KSR International v. Teleflex*, a "patent for a combination which only unites old elements with no change in their respective functions . . . obviously withdraws what is already known into the field of its monopoly and diminishes the resources available to skillful men."[53] A base spirit paired with a fortified wine, bitter, or juice describes a large majority of cocktails. What protection for a cocktail recipe could be granted that would not merely "unite old elements" functioning in their usual manner? While a few certain practices and processes in cocktail preparation might be amenable to patenting, these are the exceptions to a broadly applicable rule.

Explaining Cocktail Innovation

It would seem remarkable that, despite having wiped out our domestic industry a century ago, and having no IP protection to incentivize creativity, there is nevertheless a considerable amount of innovation in the mixological arts. Why is this? Several reasons help explain how innovation thrives in this particular negative space.

As noted, many of the innovations associated with cocktails today were born out of necessity. As discussed before, today's bitters hearken back to the nostrums and elixirs formulated by seventeenth-century apothecaries. These products traded for a half-century before they first obtained patent protection, because physicians, or the nearest equivalent, needed to treat patients, and alcohol provided the most stable vehicle for their ministrations. While it is true that many apothecaries relied on trade secrecy, numerous physicians also disclosed their secrets in treatises.

The need to dilute bitter medicinal alcohols in something more palatable led to the ancient practice of dissolving them in wine, such that we can recognize the primogenitors of modern cocktails by the early eighteenth century. In the same fashion, the necessity of warding off malaria helped construct the modern gin and tonic, as English sailors and colonials took to dissolving quinine in their gin. And the fortuitous union of both gin and rum with lime is similarly associated with the need to ward off scurvy. These innovations were not the result of the carrot of incentive, but the stick of necessity.

Of course, cocktails today are a thoroughly recreational undertaking, and one needs to look further to understand more contemporary cocktail innovation. Various choices regarding business models help to explain the phenomenon.

As Raustiala and Sprigman point out in *The Knockoff Economy*, a cocktail is not a product, but a service; "even more than cuisine, [they] are a performance as much as a product." There's a reason your barman is far likelier than your chef to have a handlebar mustache; his job is both food preparer and entertainer. The difficulty in selling non-scarce ideas leads vendors to focus on selling that which is naturally scarce: access, labor, and skill. Anyone who has ever paid for a round of drinks knows that it is considerably cheaper to buy the stuff and serve oneself. The premium, of course, pays for a comfortable or convenient venue, where one hopefully receives skilled service.[54] As Raustiala and Sprigman observe, "you are not really buying a drink, you are renting a bar stool."

This strategy, referred to by technology pundit and TechDirt editor Mike Masnick as "sell the scarcity," focuses on monetizing inherently scarce resources instead of attempting to control non-excludable intangibles.[55] Yet this alone does not necessarily explain why cocktails are so freely disclosed. After all, one may opt against affirmatively seeking protection, but that doesn't explain affirmatively disclosing what might in some cases be maintained as a trade secret. It is one thing to decline protection, but another to affirmatively publicize one's creation. Why then are cocktail innovations not only unprotected, but publicized?

One reason why recipes abound is that recipes sell the product. It should come as no surprise that to the extent legal tussles have occurred over cocktails, they generally involve not individual bartenders but distillers and distributors, who are concerned not with authorship, but sales. Although the existence of the Bacardi Cocktail may cause heartburn for Bacardi's trademark counsel, Bacardi's marketing department likely regards it as a blessing since the recipe drives demand for the liquor.

More recent trends in spirits marketing focus less on the use of a particular name for a given cocktail, and marketers instead devote attention to producing a variety of cocktails that serve as a vehicle for the product. This intellectual exercise is undertaken at a loss, in order to promote the spirit. The practice is as old as the recipe on the back of the soup can, but distillers have adapted for the Internet age, with numerous spirits' Twitter handles churning out an endless supply of recipes.

Many spirits brands today also employ "brand ambassadors." Although the marketing industry now often casually uses this term to refer to any prominent endorser and even one's own customers,[56] a major subset of brand ambassadors in the spirits industry are practicing mixologists who have gained renown, perhaps by winning competitions. These individuals are engaged to popularize the relevant spirit through events and promotions, and in particular finding ways to showcase their product—including by inventing recipes. In a sense, these brand ambassadors represent a form of market disruption, insofar as the brands are giving away cocktail innovation in order to promote their product.[57]

We see this kind of disruption elsewhere: It is not uncommon for disruptive innovators in the technology sector to provide a complementary product in the course of offering their own. Whether it involves open-source distributors providing free software to sustain a business model involving support and customization, or Internet portals providing free productivity software to gain viewers, most producers resent their product being commoditized by the competition. The free distribution of cocktail recipes is no different. As one industry player complained, "brand ambassadors are ruining it . . . In no other creative field do you find people who are so easily able to insert themselves into the scene." Notably, this is not a complaint about piracy; it is about competition. More people "inserting themselves into the scene" is what the orthodox theory of IP suggests we should see in a *high* IP environment, yet this complaint suggests that a low IP environment is encouraging creativity all too well, at least from the perspective of some market participants.

In addition to promoting the product, recipes may also promote the inventor. Since Sydenham disclosed his formulae in his *Treatise on Gout* in the seventeenth century, experts have disclosed mixological secrets to the public in order to advance their professional interests. Possessing the idea, of course, is not the same as being capable in the execution, and it is on this difference that an expert can trade. A mixologist is not unlike an academic scholar, in the sense that she gives her intellectual product away largely for free, in the hopes that the reputational gain it produces will provide better employment opportunities.

For this reason, we would expect to see the development of strong attribution norms, similar to the strong attribution norms associated with high-end cuisine.[58] In the case of spirits writing, we often see similar attention to attribution. Here, it is common for cocktails both new and old to be credited either to their creators, or in some cases, to their re-discoverers.[59] This is not to say that attribution to other inventors is common in drinking establishments; such an acknowledgment on a menu is rare; just as it is similarly uncommon with cuisine. (After all, if you're paying a premium, you don't expect to be served someone else's recipes.) But because credit is provided in the context of writing, reporting, and reviews—where consumers are likelier to make decisions about whether to patronize an establishment—innovative activity is nevertheless rewarded.

Conclusion

One response to this discussion might be a counterfactual one: that mixological innovation is actually undersupplied by the market, and that the cocktail craft would be doing even better if cocktails were in fact protectable. But for the failure to provide adequate and effective protection behind the bar, this argument goes, we would have accomplished the mixological moonshot by now. This hypothesis can be raised in many of the areas of IP negative space. But it would be wrong to give it much weight; one can equally contend the reverse: that there would be the same amount of innovation in areas where IP exists today, were that protection only repealed.

In sum, what conventional IP theory explains poorly, the incentives of the marketplace seem to explain rather well. Cocktails are an area where we see innovation in the absence of protection in large part because there are external motivators to innovate. Along with other areas of IP negative space, this should be cause for reflection. Any area of regulation should be able to survive a cost-benefit analysis, and intellectual property is no exception to the rule. Having seen that simple necessity, business incentives, and personal self-interest, rather than exclusive rights, are driving one industry to creative activity, we can't ignore that these forces may drive creativity in other comparable sectors as well.

NOTES

The arguments presented here are Matthew Schruers' alone, and should not be attributed to his employer, academic institution, or bartender. Some of the ideas discussed here were previously presented in a blog post, "So, An IP Lawyer Walks Into a Bar," Disruptive Competition Project (Sept. 6, 2013), http://www.project-disco.org

1 Ian Fleming, *Casino Royale* (London: Penguin, 2003), 36.

2 See generally Kal Raustiala and Christopher Sprigman, "The Piracy Paradox: Innovation and Intellectual Property in Fashion Design," *Virginia Law Review* 92 (2006): 1764.

3 Ibid., 1691.

4 Mark A. Lemley, "Property, Intellectual Property, and Free Riding," *Texas Law Review* 83 (2005): 1031.

5 Christopher J. Buccafusco, "On the Legal Consequences of Sauces: Should Thomas Keller's Recipes Be Per Se Copyrightable?" *Cardozo Arts & Entertainment Law Journal* 24 (2007), 1124–1125. See also U.S. Copyright Office, "Recipes, FL-122" (2010), http://copyright.gov.

6 See International Bartenders Association, *IBA Sixty Years On* (2011), 53. While some IBA publications specify Gosling's Black Seal, IBA's *website* conspicuously does not, at the time of publishing. It is entirely possible that Gosling's naked public licensing and the probable widespread unauthorized use of the cocktail's name could result in the Dark 'N Stormy mark being ruled generic.

7 *See* Jonathan Miles, "The Right Stuff (By Law)," *New York Times* (July 2, 2009), http://www.nytimes.com; see also Chantal Martineau, "The Era of Copyrighted Cocktails?," *The Atlantic* (Aug. 31, 2010), http://www.theatlantic.com/health; see

also "Dark 'n Stormy," *Wikipedia*, http://en.wikipedia.org/wiki. In fact, Gosling's specifically abandoned an application for "a prepared alcoholic cocktail consisting of rum and ginger beer" in 1986 (Gosling's trademark counsel apparently caring little for garnish), before securing various USPTO-issued registrations, including for "pre-mixed alcoholic beverage, namely rum and ginger beer" beginning in 1991—specimens of which are canned, and none of which specify a precise recipe. See http://tmsearch.uspto.gov/.

8   More importantly from Gosling's point of view, its rights in the registration extend to the use of name regardless of the recipe. Accordingly, ill-informed bartenders serving other beverages under the name "Dark 'N Stormy" need to be policed, notwithstanding that there's no rum in the equation.

9   See *Ex Parte S.C. Herbst Importing Co.*, U.S. Patent Office Official Gazette 124 (Washington, DC: U.S. Government, 1906), 2178. See also *Heublein v. Adams*, 125 F. 782 (D. Mass 1903); *In re Boston Wine & Spirits Co.*, 39 App. D.C. 421 (1912).

10   "Justice Examines His Club Bartender: Takes Opportunity of Having Him on Stand to Find Out What Goes Into His Drinks," *New York Times* (Apr. 28, 1936), 44. Although not authoritative from a trademark perspective, it is interesting to observe that the contemporary International Bartender's Association standard specifies Bacardi for this recipe. See, e.g., IBA, *Sixty Years*, 42.

11   "Cocktail Must Live Up to Name: Court Decides Drink Should Contain Product Implied by Label," *New York Times* (Apr. 29, 1936), 23 (reported at *Compania Ron Bacardi S.A. v. Wivel Restaurant*, 250 A.D. 837 (N.Y. Sup. Ct. App. Div. 1937).

12   *Bacardi & Co. Ltd. v. Bacardi Mfg. Jewelers Co.*, 174 U.S. Patent Quarterly 284 (N.D. Ill. 1972) (noting actions).

13   Gene Quinn, "Red Bull Wins Trademark Lawsuit," *IPWatchdog* (May 2, 2008), http://www.ipwatchdog.com.

14   U.S. Patent & Trademark Office, "Can Recipes Be Patented?" http://www.uspto.gov.

15   *Uniform Trade Secrets Act with 1985 Amendments* (Chicago: National Conference of Commissioners on Uniform State Laws, 1985), Section 1(4)(ii).

16   *Kewanee Oil Co. v. Bicron Corp.*, 416 U.S. 470, 476 (1974).

17   *Uniform Trade Secrets Act with 1985 Amendments*, Section 1, *commentary*.

18   Foley Publishing Corp., Bartender Magazine, http://www.bartender.com, http://www.cocktailright.com/example.html. (The author's request for comment from this publication went unanswered.)

19   Wondrich, *Imbibe*, 175 (citing 1803 New Hampshire newspaper); David Wondrich, *Punch: The Delights (and Dangers) of the Flowing Bowl* (New York: Penguin Group, 2010), 22 (citing 1798 London newspaper).

20   David Wondrich, *Imbibe!* (New York: Penguin Group, 2007), 170–176. Wondrich points out that the Roman emperor Claudius is recorded as having been advised by his physician to consume various fruit and plant substances dissolved in sweet wine. Ibid., 169.

21   Richard Barnett, "Bitter medicine: gout and the birth of the cocktail," *The Lancet* 379 (London: 2012): 1385.

22 Ibid. (quoting from "A Treatise on Gout," reprinted in John Swan, trans., *The Whole Works of Dr. Thomas Sydenham* (London: 1742), 418).

23 Ibid., 435–437.

24 George B. Griffenhagen and James H. Young, *Old English Patent Medicines in America* (Washington, DC: Smithsonian Institution, 1959), 156–161.

25 Ibid.

26 Office of the Commissioner of Patents (UK), *Patents for Inventions. Abridgements of Specifications relating to Medicine, Surgery, and Dentistry, 1620–1866* (London: 1872), 2.

27 George B. Griffenhagen and Mary Bogard, *History of Drug Containers and Their Labels* (Madison, WI: American Institute of the History of Pharmacy, 1999), 72.

28 The recipe, which consists of Seville orange rind, gentian, and cochineal infused into brandy, lacks the 22 ingredients which Stoughton professed his product contained. Other recipes add various other ingredients, many of which are toxic. For example, Walter Kilner, *A Compendium of Modern Pharmacy and Druggists' Formulary* (Springfield, IL, 1887), 495.

29 Griffenhagen and Young, *Patent Medicines*, 157–161, 166–167.

30 Wondrich, *Imbibe*, 172–177.

31 Brad Thomas Parsons, *Bitters: A Spirited History of a Classic Cure-All* (Berkeley, CA: Random House, 2011), 19.

32 *Siegert v. Abbott*, 72 Hun. 243 (Sup. Ct. N.Y. 1893); *Siegert v. Gandolfi*, 149 F. 100, 104 (2d Cir. 1907).

33 Kal Raustiala, "The Imperial Cocktail," *Slate.com* (Aug. 28, 2013), http://www.slate.com.

34 Jeremy Hugh Baron, "Sailors' scurvy before and after James Lind—A Reassessment," *Nutritional Reviews* 67 (2009): 316. See Swan, *The Whole Works of Sydenham*, 436.

35 Office of the Commissioner of Patents (UK), *Chronological Index of Patents Applied for and Patents Granted for the Year 1867* (London: 1868), 239.

36 Janet Zimmerman, "Any Other Name," *eGullet Forums* (Nov. 23, 2009), http://forums.egullet.org.

37 Baron, *Sailors' scurvy*, 326.

38 See also Justin Hughes, "Champagne, Feta, and Bourbon: The Spirited Debate About Geographical Indications," *Hastings Law Journal* 58 (2006): 301.

39 E.g., *Siegert v. Findlater*, [1878] 7 Ch. D. 801; *Siegert v. Abbott*, 61 Md. 276 (1884); *Siegert v. Abbott*, 72 Hun. 243 (Sup. Ct. N.Y. 1893); *A. Bauer & Co. v. Siegert*, 120 F. 81 (7th Cir. 1903); *Siegert v. Gandolfi*, 149 F. 100, 104 (2d Cir. 1907).

40 E.g., Ted Haigh, *Vintage Spirits and Forgotten Cocktails* (New York: Quarry Books, 2009), 75.

41 Gary Regan, *The Joy of Mixology* (New York: Random House, 2003), 29–30.

42 U.S. Patent No. 300,867 (issued June 24, 1884).

43 U.S. Patent No. 404,204 (issued May 28, 1889).

44 Angostura recently introduced its only new product, orange bitters, in 180 years. Parsons, *Bitters*, 26.

45 M. Carrie Allan, "Gin goes dark: At what point does aging render it unrecognizable?" *Washington Post* (Jan. 14, 2014), http://wapo.st.

46 Buccafusco, *Sauces*, 1131.

47 E.g., *Publications Int'l Ltd. v. Meredith Corp.*, 88 F.3d 473, 480 (7th Cir. 1996).

48 *Tomaydo-Tomahhdo, LLC v. Vozary*, 2015 U.S. Dist. LEXIS 10532 (N.D. Ohio 2015) *at* https://scholar.google.com.

49 J. Austin Broussard, "An Intellectual Property Food Fight: Why Copyright Law Should Embrace Culinary Innovation," *Vanderbilt Journal of Entertainment & Technology Law* 10 (2008): 693–694.

50 See generally IBA, *Sixty Years*.

51 Ted Haigh, *Vintage Spirits*, 137, 166–167.

52 Regan, *Joy of Mixology*, 166–195.

53 *KSR International v. Teleflex Inc.*, 550 U.S. 398, 127 S. Ct. 1727, 1739 (2007) (quoting *Great Atlantic & Pacific Tea Co. v. Supermarket Equipment Corp.*, 340 U.S. 147, 152 (1950)).

54 Kal Raustiala and Christopher Sprigman, *The Knockoff Economy: How Imitation Sparks Innovation* (New York: Oxford University Press, 2012), 91–92.

55 Mike Masnick, "More Artists Recognizing the New Business Model: Sell the Scarcity," *TechDirt* (May 20, 2009), https://www.techdirt.com.

56 Todd Wasserman, "How to Turn Fans into Brand Ambassadors," *Mashable* (July 13, 2011), http://mashable.com.

57 Robert Simonson, "Bartending, a Dead End No Longer," *New York Times* (Aug. 11, 2010), D3; Jeff Gordinier, "The Sorcerer of Shaken and Stirred," *New York Times* (Mar. 16, 2011), D5.

58 Buccafusco, *Sauces*, 1153–1154.

59 "30 of the Best Cocktails Invented Since 2000," *Difford's Guide for Discerning Drinkers* (July 17, 2013), http://www.diffordsguide.com. See also Parsons, *Bitters*, 146 (noting rediscovery of Prohibition-era Seelbach Cocktail); Regan, *Joy of Mixology*, 45–47.

3

Derogatory to Professional Character?

The Evolution of Physician Anti-Patenting Norms

KATHERINE J. STRANDBURG

Physicians have a long history of opposing medical patenting. When the American Medical Association was formed in 1847,[1] one of its first acts was to adopt a Code of Ethics stating that it was "derogatory to professional character" for physicians to hold patents "for any surgical instrument or medicine."[2] Opposition to patents on drugs and medical devices subsided in the early twentieth century and the ethical strictures against drug and device patents were removed. Indeed, physicians now are co-inventors on a sizeable fraction of important medical device patents.[3] While the ethical bans on physician patenting of drugs and devices are a thing of the past, the norm against patenting medical procedures has remained surprisingly robust. As I have described in more detail elsewhere, in the 1990s, a physician movement against medical procedure patents led to the enactment of a statutory provision exempting healthcare workers from infringement remedies for such patents.[4] More recently, medical associations weighed in against the patentability of diagnostic methods in *Lab. Corp. of Am. Holdings v. Metabolite Labs., Inc.*[5] and *Mayo Collaborative Servs. v. Prometheus Labs., Inc.*[6]

Why is it acceptable for physicians to patent drugs and devices, but not medical procedures? This chapter hypothesizes that the evolution of physician ethical norms about patenting in the United States can be best understood through the lens of user innovation. Studies have shown that "user innovators," whose motivation for invention comes primarily from their use of a technology, often form reputation-based communities in which the norm is to share one's inventions and patenting is frowned upon.[7] There are a number of plausible reasons for this choice. First, user innovators benefit from a sharing norm because they can use the inventions shared by other community members. Second, by sharing their inventions with the community, user innovators obtain feedback and suggestions for improvement. Third, sharing a valued innovation with a user community boosts a user innovator's reputation within the community and sometimes even among the broader public. Depending upon the particular community, a reputational boost may lead to non-pecuniary or monetary rewards (or both). Patents may be both costly and dangerous to the viability of a user innovator community with a reputation-based sharing norm. They may introduce transaction costs and deadweight loss without an offsetting increase in innovation or tempt community members to defect from the sharing regime in favor of an exclusivity-based monetary reward.

During the mid-nineteenth century, physicians were the primary innovators of drugs, devices, and procedures for use in treating their patients. Like other groups of user innovators, they formed a reputation-based community with a norm of sharing their innovations. The norm and its enforcement are illustrated by the famous dispute over the patenting of ether anesthesia. During the twentieth century, pharmaceutical companies and medical device manufacturers became major contributors to drug and device innovation. The anti-patenting norm was not enforceable against these companies, who wanted to sell, rather than use, their inventions and were not interested in the physician community's reputational rewards. The demise of the ethical ban on drug and device patents was a natural response to these developments. The robustness of the ethical norm against patenting medical and diagnostic procedures is also understandable from a user innovation perspective. Medical procedure innovation remains primarily the province of physician user innovators who can both benefit from and enforce a sharing norm.

Physician Innovators, Patents, and Ether Anesthesia

During the nineteenth century, so-called regular physicians sought to distinguish themselves from purveyors of secret and potentially harmful "nostrums" and "patent medicines."[8] At that time, so-called ethical medications were prescribed and formulated by physicians according to pharmacopeia.[9] So-called patent medicines were sold directly to consumers. Their formulations were usually secret (and, in fact, rather rarely patented) and of questionable efficacy or even dangerous.[10] The medical profession's rejection of patenting was bound up with its attempts to differentiate itself by its scientific approach from the "quack" purveyors of such suspect nostrums.[11] Much of the debate about the ethics of patenting played out against the backdrop of a notorious and influential controversy over the patenting of ether anesthesia,[12] which solidified the anti-patenting ethical norm and left its mark on patent doctrine through the case of *Morton v. New York Eye Infirmary*.[13]

Before ether anesthesia was developed, surgery was a horrifying experience, performed on conscious patients fortified sometimes with narcotics such as opium, but often only with courage.[14] Ether was well known to physicians and was prescribed orally to treat various maladies. Ether and nitrous oxide also were popular as what we would today call "party drugs." Indeed, ether has been called the "marijuana of the 1830s," though its use was both legal and socially acceptable at the time.[15] When inhaled at "frolics," ether produced euphoria and, sometimes, stupefaction. Physicians believed that inhaling enough ether to produce stupefaction was very dangerous, which apparently deterred exploration of its potential for alleviating pain. Once ether anesthesia was tested and publicized in late 1846, however, it was adopted very rapidly. During the Mexican-American and Civil Wars, it was used in countless battlefield operations.

The discovery of ether anesthesia produced a bitter and long-running controversy over patenting and scientific credit. In November 1846, a patent[16] was issued jointly to dentist, sometime medical student, and reputed con man[17] William T. G. Morton and Harvard lecturer Dr. Charles T. Jackson. Jackson was a highly distinguished polymath, trained in chemistry and geology, as well as in medicine. Morton had studied with Jackson, even rooming in Jackson's house, at some point prior to the ether anesthesia discovery. Later, various others, including Morton's former mentor, dentist Horace Wells, sought credit for the discovery. Many now believe that Georgia physician Crawford Long was the first to use ether for anesthesia, in 1842, though he did not publish his observations until 1849.[18] The story is fascinating, though it was ultimately tragic for its eccentric major characters.[19] Because our interest is in the patent, we focus on Morton and Jackson.

Morton first successfully used ether anesthesia for a tooth extraction on September 30, 1846.[20] The credit dispute between Morton and Jackson revolved around Jackson's role in that first use. Though there are various versions of events,[21] all agree that Morton and Jackson discussed the possibility of ether anesthesia shortly before Morton's first use and that Jackson supplied the ether. Morton, however, claimed that he had had the idea of ether anesthesia before their conversation, while Jackson claimed to have instigated and directed Morton's attempt.

Whatever the real story may have been, after the initial success Morton began immediately to look for ways to make money from the discovery. He advertised painless tooth extraction services, invited press attention, and consulted a patent attorney.[22] He also attempted to keep the composition of the anesthetizing inhalant secret, at least in the beginning.

Morton attracted the attention of Dr. Henry J. Bigelow, then a young surgeon at Massachusetts General Hospital (MGH).[23] After observing several tooth extractions, Bigelow persuaded MGH to allow Morton to attempt ether anesthesia during a surgery at the hospital in mid-October 1846.[24] The success of that attempt sparked interest in adopting ether anesthesia as a standard practice at MGH. As a prerequisite, MGH demanded to know the composition of Morton's anesthetic agent, so that its safety could be evaluated. Morton resisted disclosing his formulation, while moving quickly to apply for a patent.[25]

Jackson, whose primary interest was in scientific credit, was uncomfortable with patenting, reflecting the medical profession's general disapproval of patents. He proposed initially that Morton pay him a consulting fee and patent the invention independently.[26] Morton's attorney advised him that Jackson should be included as a co-inventor on any patent and urged Jackson to join the patent application to ensure that he received scientific credit. Jackson, who had been involved in an earlier credit dispute with Samuel Morse over the telegraph patent,[27] apparently was convinced. Morton and Jackson filed a joint patent application on October 27, 1846. Jackson immediately assigned his rights to Morton in exchange for a sum of $500 to be paid over time at a rate of 10% of licensing revenue.[28] Shortly thereafter, Morton disclosed the composition of his anesthetic agent to the MGH surgeons and more operations ensued.[29] The patent, entitled "Improvement in Surgical Operations" and claiming the use of ether for anesthesia during surgery, issued in record time on November 12, 1846.[30]

After the patent was granted, Morton stepped up his commercialization efforts, viewing the patent as his ticket to great wealth.[31] He circulated a term sheet for five-year licenses to dentists, advertised licenses to surgeons for a royalty of 25% of surgical fees, and hired a number of agents to market the licenses. Somewhat ironically, those agents apparently sometimes credited Jackson with the discovery, since his reputation reassured potential licensees about the procedure's safety.[32]

Bigelow delivered a paper describing his observations of Morton's cases to the American Academy of Arts and Science and the Boston Society of Medical Improvement in early November 1846. The paper was published in the *Boston Medical and Surgical Journal* on November 18,[33] "whereby the news of the discovery was promulgated to the world."[34] Bigelow's article also attempted a preemptive defense of the patent, acknowledging that "discoveries in medical science" have generally been rewarded "indirectly by fame, honor, [and] position," but arguing that special circumstances excused patenting in the ether anesthesia case. Bigelow contended that because ether anesthesia was "capable of abuse, and can readily be applied to nefarious ends," and was "not yet thoroughly understood," its use "should be restricted to responsible persons," which the patentee was empowered to do. He also excused Morton by suggesting that the medical norm against patenting was not shared by practitioners of "the mechanical art of dentistry." Finally, Bigelow argued that the patent would not hamper medical treatment because the patentees' intentions were "extremely liberal with regard to the medical profession generally" and "so soon as necessary arrangements can be made for publicity of the process, great facilities will be offered to those who are disposed to avail themselves of [it]."

While readers of Bigelow's article immediately recognized the potential importance of ether anesthesia, his defense of the patent was less persuasive. Well-known dentist Josiah Flagg's impassioned response to Bigelow[35] noted that ether was a well-known part of the *materia medica* available to all physicians. Flagg scoffed at Bigelow's arguments that special circumstances excused the patent, doubting that a profit-seeking patent holder would best protect society from anesthesia's potential dangers. Rather, Flagg argued: "Who are the most responsible persons to be trusted with this agent? . . . [I]n three words, regular physicians, surgeons and dentists." Flagg advocated resistance to the patent: "I shall not obtain and use it as a *secret medicine*—I shall not purchase and use it as a *patent medicine*. If it is simply sulphuric ether, and it will produce the desired effect, I shall use it, and so will others who wish to do so."

Bigelow replied that the discoverers of an "inestimable boon" to humanity such as ether anesthesia deserve a "substantial return in some shape or other," and argued that the invention might have "slept for twenty years longer, had not Drs. Morton and Jackson demonstrated it to the public." "Suffering humanity," Bigelow suggested, could be assisted equally well by Morton and those licensed under his "reasonable terms" as by those who would disregard the patent.[36]

Flagg's position eventually prevailed. As a practical matter, the patent was widely ignored by physicians and Morton's investments in licensing it bore little fruit. The AMA's ethical prohibition on patenting was adopted soon after the ether anesthesia patent issued. In 1848, the AMA's Committee on Surgery presented an extensive report,[37] collecting the medical community's experience with anesthesia using ether and its close cousin, chloroform, and assessing its safety and efficacy. The report did not take sides in the priority dispute or mention patents explicitly, but "regret[ed] that the early history of the discovery is encumbered with angry disputes amongst rival claimants for the honour, and that attempts were made by those most intimately interested in the claim, to render their private interests paramount to those higher considerations which should animate the disinterested love of truth."

Bigelow continued to engage the issues of patenting and credit along with the science. Just before the 1848 AMA meeting, he published a two-part article in which he ruminated at length about the nature of invention.[38] He acknowledged that nearly simultaneous discovery is commonplace because medical invention is based on shared community knowledge. He concluded, nonetheless, that Morton should be credited as the "real discoverer" of ether anesthesia because he "verifie[d] the suggestion, from whatever source it emanated," "made and modified the experiments at his own discretion," and "assumed the responsibility of danger" in experimenting with it.

An 1856 AMA Committee Report took a decidedly different view of the relative importance of individual and community contributions to improvements in medicine:[39]

> [E]very real improvement in medicine, every contribution to its curative resources which time and scrutiny have sanctioned—all have been results of patient and prolonged investigation, conducted by a succession of cooperative laborers. . . . Never have there been, properly speaking, *discoveries* nor *revelations*, but always *inductions*—not the production and property of an individual, however fortunate or sagacious, but the legitimate fruits of the common efforts and devotion of a venerable and progressive calling.

According to the committee, ether anesthesia could be nothing but an "arrant piece of quackery" until the medical community tested, verified, and improved it:

> Not until it had been stripped of its secrecy, and Letheon [Morton's name for his anesthetic agent] had become sulphuric ether, under the demands of the profession; not until the principles of medical science had been applied to the administration of its vapor by inhalation, by the profession; not until the conditions of safety for this administration had been investigated and approximately determined by the profession, did anaesthetic etherization become a boon to humanity, or anything else than a seductive and dangerous nostrum. We submit, then, that whatsoever debt of gratitude the world has incurred in this behalf was due to the medical profession, and not to Dr. Morton, nor to either of his competitors.[40]

Consistent with its community theory of invention, the report strongly criticized medical patenting, concluding that "it is very plain that no good has come, or can come to [the progress of the healing art and the true character of the profession] from the patronage of the Patent-office."[41] Patents give "indirect discouragement [to] legitimate medicine" by attributing medical progress to "fortuitous events in the practice of lucky doctors, or inspirations vouchsafed to favored ones; lucky hits of some bold experimenter, or rightful rewards of the vaunted devotion and experience of adroit specialists," rather than to the efforts of the community as a whole.

The patent debate ran in parallel with controversy over scientific credit for ether anesthesia, which had begun almost before the ink on the patent application was dry. On November 13, 1846, Jackson wrote to a Parisian colleague describing "his" discovery of ether anesthesia and asking the colleague to transmit a report of the discovery to the French Academy of Sciences.[42] Jackson's letter, and his colleague's later-published report to the Academy, omitted Morton's role in the discovery entirely. The credit dispute, to some degree unresolved to this day, continued unabated for decades. Morton even took his case for credit to Congress, lobbying for official credit and compensation for the discovery's military use and drawing responsive petitions from supporters of other claimants. Congress considered the issue off and on for 25 years, but never came to any resolution.[43]

At first, many physicians, especially in Boston and New York, supported Morton's claim to credit and his petitions for compensation from Congress. They also were sympathetic to the financial plight that resulted from Morton's investments in lobbying Congress. A December 1858 letter to the editor of the *New York Times* described efforts to assist Morton financially after "years of unsuccessful application to Congress for justice."[44] A long list of members of the medical community, topped by MGH, donated to a fund created as a "National Testimonial" to Morton.[45]

All that changed when, his licensing and lobbying efforts having failed, Morton sued the New York Eye Infirmary for patent infringement, turning the tide of medical community opinion against him. Many of his supporters had relied on his representations that the patent would not be enforced.[46] Dr. Willard Parker, one of the primary movers in the "national testimonial" effort, testified at the infringement trial that the profession's efforts on Morton's behalf were premised "on the idea that he had abandoned his patent, otherwise not a thing would have been done."[47] The court invalidated the ether anesthesia patent in 1862.[48] At its June 1864 meeting, the AMA passed a resolution opposing Morton's petition for congressional compensation because of "his unworthy conduct, also because of his unwarrantable assumption of a patentable right to anesthesia; and, further, because private beneficence in Boston,

New York, Philadelphia, and other places, has already sufficiently rewarded him for any claims which he may justly urge."[49]

The opinion in the case is known for its now-classic statement of the unpatentability of natural phenomena:

> A discovery may be brilliant and useful, and not patentable. No matter through what long, solitary vigils, or by what importunate efforts, the secret may have been wrung from the bosom of Nature, or to what useful purpose it may be applied. Something more is necessary. . . . Neither the natural functions of an animal upon which or through which it may be designed to operate, nor any of the useful purposes to which it may be applied, can form any essential parts of the combination, however they may illustrate and establish its usefulness.[50]

Morton's attempts to monetize his patent failed long before the court got involved, however, when he violated the medical profession's sharing norm. Because his attempts to collect royalties from other members of the medical community were viewed as illegitimate, Morton never was able to collect substantial royalties for its use, though prestigious members of the community initially supported his claim to scientific credit. By suing his fellow physicians for infringement, he lost the medical community's support entirely. Morton thus failed in his attempt to have it both ways, by accumulating both reputational credit and patent royalties. Eventually, both Congress and the medical community adopted a "live by the sword, die by the sword" attitude: by relying on the patent, Morton was seen to have opted out of the reputational reward system. When the patent was invalidated, he was left without recourse.

The nineteenth-century medical profession's objections to the ether anesthesia patent reflected a view of medical innovation remarkably aligned with the user innovator community paradigm. Every claimant to the ether anesthesia discovery was a medical or dental practitioner, who developed anesthesia through and for use in his practice. As illustrated by the MGH surgeons' refusal to adopt Morton's procedure until he disclosed his chemical formulation, the community's norms enforced disclosure and punished secrecy. Physicians were expected to publish their innovations in exchange for reputational credit, which was greatly valued, as the long-standing credit controversy illustrates. The medical community was responsible for honing and testing the innovations its members shared. The 1848 AMA Committee on Surgery Report illustrates this user innovator community function, pooling physicians' experiences with the safety, efficacy, range of applicability, and so forth, of ether and chloroform anesthesia. The 1856 AMA Committee Report contrasted this community-based approach with the individualistic "old vulgar idea, according to which valuable improvements in the treatment of disease have originated . . . as fortuitous events in the practice of lucky doctors, or inspirations vouchsafed to favored ones; lucky hits of some bold experimenter, or rightful reward of the vaunted devotion and experience of adroit specialists."

The ether anesthesia story nicely illustrates the operation of a user innovator community's sharing norm. But it also raises the question of whether patents are important for disclosure and dissemination. Bigelow suggested that the invention of ether anesthesia might have been delayed another 20 years without Morton because "the human mind . . . runs in the channels of routine," whereas innovation may require "incredulity and rejection of authority," along with "unyielding perseverance."[51] Bigelow clearly was wrong that, without Morton, the *discovery* would have been delayed. There were several near-simultaneous discoveries of ether anesthesia. But, while Morton may not have been the first to employ ether anesthesia, his discovery certainly was the most widely publicized. Bigelow's article by which "the news of the discovery was promulgated to the world" and Jackson's letter to the French Academy were standard applications of the community's sharing norm. On the other hand, Morton's own efforts at publicizing his discovery—inviting a journalist to observe his first tooth extraction, passing out circulars in Boston, and sending agents to persuade dentists and surgeons to adopt (and license) the procedure—were motivated by the potential for patent-based profits.[52] Without Morton's attempts to drum up business it is hard to know how quickly word of the invention would have spread. Indeed, without the publicity, Bigelow might never have visited Morton to make the observations that he reported in his article.

There can certainly be barriers to disseminating a user innovation. It is unclear why Crawford Long, who apparently used ether anesthesia in his dental practice in 1842, did not publish until 1849, after he heard about Morton's patent. Maybe Long did not see himself as a member of the publishing medical innovator community because he was a dentist, because he lacked academic connections, or for some other reason. Perhaps he was not interested in national recognition or was simply too busy with his practice to make time to publish. The experience of Morton's mentor Wells, who also later claimed credit for the discovery of anesthesia (though he focused on nitrous oxide), illustrates another potential pitfall for a reputation-based innovation system. In this instance the reputation-based system backfired, since Wells abandoned his attempts at developing anesthesia after being humiliated by a failed demonstration at MGH in 1845.[53] The issue of dissemination recently has begun to garner more attention from researchers studying user innovation, who have begun to explore the conditions under which user innovators are motivated to make the effort needed to disseminate their inventions.

The ether anesthesia story also resonates with current debates about the balance between innovation and safety in medicine. At the time Morton conducted his experiments, there was widespread belief that inhaling ether was too dangerous for medical use. Morton went ahead despite those concerns, but at what risk to his patients? Bigelow noted that Morton's initial experiments, on himself and on one dental patient, were "insufficient for the most hasty generalization" and said nothing about the "question of danger," given that "two or three previous cases showed, with equal clearness, that insensibility produced death."[54] Morton plunged ahead nonetheless, using the technique on "twenty or more" dental patients before convincing the MGH surgeons to attempt its use. Bigelow generously attributed Morton's actions to "unyielding perseverance."

Others did not view this trait so favorably. A December 12, 1846, report by a committee of dentists opposed to patenting described disturbing results of some of Morton's uses of ether anesthesia and recommended that the safety of ether anesthesia be investigated by the Massachusetts Medical Society before its wide adoption.[55] More damning complaints about Morton's practices eventually surfaced from dentist Nathaniel Keep, who later became the first dean of Harvard's dental school. Keep entered into what was to have been a ten-year partnership with Morton in late November 1846, only to withdraw from it one month later. Keep claimed that many of the operations under Morton's supervision "were unsuccessful and much distress and suffering ensued" and that Morton's approach to administering ether made inadequate provision for oxygen supply. According to Keep, Morton "was not at all well acquainted with the nature, properties, and safe and proper application of the vapor ether, and [was] reckless in its use, expressing the most perfect unconcern with its effects upon the subjects of his practice, provided they were only made insensible."[56]

The balance between the risks and benefits of medical innovation is a perennial subject of policy debate. Deciding whether Morton is best viewed as a daring patent-spurred innovator unconstrained by the conservative norms of the professional community or as a lucky money-grabber who advanced the dissemination of ether anesthesia only at considerable risk to his patients may be as difficult as fixing that balance.

The Decline of the Norm against Patenting Drugs and Devices

Eventually, technological changes and industrialization moved most pharmaceutical innovation into large chemistry-based research companies and the federal government took over the regulation of drug safety and efficacy. During this shift away from physicians as primary drug innovators, the AMA's stand on pharmaceutical patents evolved from complete opposition to complete acceptance. Physicians continue to play an important role in the invention of medical devices, but regulation and technological change have meant that they rarely work alone. Collaboration between physicians and device manufacturing firms is increasingly important and norms have adjusted to permit device patenting.

By the end of the nineteenth century, developments in both science and industry were planting the seeds of change to the medical profession's patenting norms. The rise of a scientifically based chemical industry, along with the forces of industrialization, eventually moved the locus of drug innovation out of the physician's office and into the commercial laboratory, where the emphasis shifted away from formulations based on the *materia medica* to developing new molecules. In addition, government gradually assumed responsibility for vetting drug safety and efficacy. As drug development became dominated by companies seeking monetary profits, rather than reputational credit, the medical community's anti-drug patenting norm became essentially a dead letter: Community norms can only hope to govern community members. The eventual result was a dramatic retreat from the anti-patenting position that the organization had held for more than a hundred years. In 1955, the AMA's ethical principles were revised to permit the patenting of drugs and medical devices, though the principles maintained that the "use of such patents . . . or the receipt of remuneration from them which retards or inhibits research or restricts the benefits derivable therefrom is unethical."[57] In 1957, the principles were substantially simplified and no longer addressed patenting explicitly. The newly permissive rule about patenting was, however, included in a compilation of sections from the 1955 principles deemed "included within the spirit and intent of the language of the 1957 edition."[58] Nowadays, the AMA's Council on Ethical and Judicial Affairs issues ethics opinions, which, together with the pared down principles, make up what is currently called the Code of Medical Ethics.[59] Not only is drug patenting no longer banned, but, consistent with the shift in the ecosystem of pharmaceutical innovation, no current ethics opinion of the AMA even addresses the patenting of drugs by physicians.

While the 1955 amendments to the AMA principles also permitted patenting of medical devices, the device patenting issue did not fade so quickly from the ethical debate. Physicians continue to play an important role in device innovation. In 1957, an ethics opinion based on the newly revised principles approved medical device patenting, but with significant caveats:

It is not unethical for a physician to patent a surgical or diagnostic instrument he has discovered or developed. Our laws governing patents are based on the sound doctrine that one is entitled to protect his discovery. Medicine, recognizing the validity of our patent law system, accepts it, but in the interest of the public welfare and the dignity of the profession insists that once a patent is obtained by a physician for his own protection, the physician may not ethically use his patent right to retard or inhibit research or to restrict the benefits derivable from the patented article. Any physician who obtains a patent and uses it for his own aggrandizement or financial interest, to the detriment of the profession or the public, is acting unethically.[60]

By 1977, however, the AMA Judicial Council had trimmed away the caveats, in an opinion that remains in force today:

> A physician may patent a surgical or diagnostic instrument he or she has discovered or developed. The laws governing patents are based on the sound doctrine that one is entitled to protect one's discovery.[61]

From a user innovation perspective, medical device innovation is complicated because a physician innovator seeking to design a device often needs collaborators with skills in electrical, material, mechanical, or software engineering. During the nineteenth century, physicians generally were able to design instruments and devices independently (and sometimes owned factories to produce them). Nowadays, medical devices often are technologically complex and subject to significant regulatory requirements. Thus, physicians and device industry engineers must often collaborate to invent medical devices. Patents provide a mechanism by which both physician innovators and industry engineers can be rewarded for their inventive contributions.

The Continuing Persistence of the Norm against Patenting Medical Procedures

During the 1980s and '90s, patenting in the United States seemed to be on a path of virtually limitless expansion. Consistent with the AMA's revised view of drug and device patents, optimism about the potential for patents to facilitate medical advances, particularly through the emerging field of biotechnology, was high. The USPTO, which in 1883 had denied a patent because "[t]he methods or modes of treatment of physicians of certain diseases are not patentable,"[62] reversed its rule against medical procedure patents in 1954.[63] While medical procedure patents apparently remained rare (or at least rarely enforced),[64] it would have been reasonable to assume that the medical profession's aversion to patenting had finally been laid completely to rest.

Seeds of resistance to the continued expansion of patenting in medicine began to be sown in the 1980s, however, when some patentees began to attempt to collect royalties for physicians' use of controversial reproductive medicine procedures. In 1984, the AMA adopted an opinion about medical procedures which, though it did not mention patents, reinforced the norm that "[p]hysicians have an obligation to share their knowledge and skills and to report the results of clinical and laboratory research. . . . [while] [t]he intentional withholding of new medical knowledge, skills and techniques from colleagues for reasons of personal gain is detrimental to the medical profession and to society and is to be condemned."[65] Perhaps surprisingly, the eventual catalyst for a major physician-led movement against medical procedure patents was a patent in the relatively mundane arena of lens-replacement surgery for treating cataracts. Physician opposition to medical procedure patents eventually led to the passage, in 1996, of 35 U.S.C. §287(c), which exempts physicians from remedies for infringement of medical procedure claims.

The story leading up to the enactment of §287(c) begins in 1990, when Dr. James McFarland reported that he had successfully performed sutureless cataract surgery, which alleviated the risk that sutures would distort the replacement lens during healing.[66] Following McFarland's announcement, many surgeons, including Dr. Samuel Pallin and Dr. Jack Singer, worked to duplicate and perfect the sutureless technique. Unlike the others, Pallin applied for a patent, which was directed to a particular shape of the incision through which the replacement lens was inserted. Pallin then attempted to collect royalties from other surgeons who he believed to be infringing his patent.

The response of the medical community is strikingly reminiscent of its response to the ether anesthesia patent. Dr. Jack Singer was one recipient of a demand letter from Pallin. Singer was so outraged by Pallin's royalty demand that he, like Josiah Flagg 150 years earlier, not only refused to pay, but took a very public stand on the patenting issue. He argued at an April 1994 ophthalmology meeting that medical procedure patenting, which he called an "insidious virus," threatened to destroy the medical community's sharing norms:

If allowed to proliferate this will effectively block the timeless way of sharing medical and surgical knowledge, and perhaps more importantly will inhibit the interdependent free exchange of information that is the foundation of good medical care. Other victims of medical and surgical method patents include physician autonomy, the doctor-patient relationship, openness in medical research, and free exchange of medical and surgical knowledge.[67]

Pallin's royalty demands and eventual suit against Singer raised the hackles of many other physicians as well. In a March 1994 interview, for example, McFarland argued:

> It's hard for me to conceptualize why anybody would want to bring this whole royalty scheme into ophthalmology and to introduce the legalities involved and to bring lawyers into the picture and file lawsuits against our colleagues. . . . We ought to get back to trying to figure out better ways to fix folks and to share that with our colleagues for the benefit of the patients.[68]

While a lively and sometimes blistering debate about medical procedure patenting ensued, the debate was one-sided, with medical associations urging support of Singer's defense and forming the Medical Procedure Patent Coalition to lobby Congress to make medical and diagnostic procedures unpatentable.

Legislation that would have banned medical procedure patents attracted a bipartisan group of co-sponsors in 1995. Opposition from the biopharmaceutical industry eventually resulted in the 1996 compromise that became 35 U.S.C. §287(c).[69] Though §287(c)'s passage was widely (though not always accurately) celebrated in the medical press as heralding the end of medical procedure patents, the provision is significantly weaker than the medical community's original proposal. Rather than precluding medical procedure patents or providing a defense to infringement liability, §287(c) only eliminates *remedies against medical practitioners and related health care entities*. Because medical practitioners can still be infringers (even though there are no remedies against them), §287(c) leaves the door open to suits against third parties, such as testing laboratories, for contributing to or inducing their infringement.

After §287(c) passed, the medical procedure patent issue receded. In the wake of the *Pallin v. Singer* uproar, physician innovators, who invent most new medical and diagnostic procedures, likely have been unwilling to risk community opprobrium by pushing the limits of the exemption in suits against other physicians. Indeed, §287(c) was not considered in a single published opinion until 2008, when it came up in *Emtel, Inc. v. Lipidlabs, Inc.*,[70] which remains the only opinion interpreting the scope of §287(c).[71] The silence likely results from the fact that the medical community's norm against patenting medical procedures sweeps more broadly than the statutory provision, which has several carve-outs. In 1995, AMA Ethics Opinion 9.095 made clear in no uncertain terms that "the use of patents . . . to limit the availability of medical procedures places significant limitation on the dissemination of medical knowledge, and is therefore unethical."[72]

The persistence of the norm against patenting medical procedures was evident again in recent medical association opposition to the patentability of medical diagnostic procedures. The AMA and other medical associations filed amicus briefs opposing patent eligibility in *Lab. Corp. of Am. Holdings v. Metabolite Labs., Inc.*[73] and *Mayo Collaborative Servs. v. Prometheus Labs., Inc.*[74] Rather than sue physicians for direct infringement, which probably would have been futile in light of §287(c), the plaintiffs in these cases brought secondary liability suits against test laboratories that provided measurements used by physicians in patented medical diagnostic methods. Unlike *Morton* and *Pallin*, *Mayo* and *Lab-Corp* did not involve physicians suing other physicians for infringement. Instead, the plaintiffs were commercial firms and the defendants were medical laboratories.

Does the medical profession's continued opposition to these patents after the passage of §287(c) make sense? The hypothesis of this chapter, based on the historical evolution of the physician anti-patenting norm and the insights from studies of user innovation, is that the medical community will oppose patents on the types of inventions that can be made by community members without significant collaboration with outsiders. The opposition stems not only from resistance to paying royalties, but also from concern about the survival of the sharing norm.

Physician opposition to the patents in *Mayo* and *LabCorp* is consistent with this hypothesis. The diagnostic procedures claimed in *Mayo* and *LabCorp* not only could have been, but were, invented by members of the academic medical community acting in their normal capacity. The claims at issue in these cases were based on statistical studies of correlations between biological indicators and clinically relevant conditions. These studies were conducted by medical academics. In *Lab-Corp*, the inventors were "three university doctors,"[75] who published the results of their study in peer-reviewed journals the same year that their patent issued.[76] Plaintiff Metabolite Laboratories, founded by one of the doctors,[77] operated out of a university laboratory.[78] In *Mayo*, the inventors were a gastroenterologist and a pharmacologist at a university-affiliated hospital in Canada, who published the results of their research shortly after submitting their patent application.[79] Plaintiff Prometheus Laboratories was a later licensee.[80]

In both of these cases, physicians were routinely capable of using the published results to diagnose their patients without relying on the patents. While it is true that the test laboratories contributed to a physician's *practice* of the diagnostic procedures claimed in *Mayo* and *LabCorp*, the laboratory's technicians were not collaborators in *inventing* the procedures, any more than a scalpel manufacturer is a collaborator in the invention of a new surgical procedure. Thus, unlike the development of modern medical devices, the development of diagnostic procedures of the sort involved in *LabCorp* and *Mayo* can take place entirely within the bounds of the medical community and can be rewarded through its system of reputational and sharing norms.

Conclusion

The history recounted here is consistent with earlier user innovation literature in that physicians oppose the patenting of innovations produced and used within the physician community. It suggests, however, that patenting is likely to be deemed acceptable for innovations that require significant collaboration with outsiders, who must be compensated by something other than use and community reputation. Drug innovation, at one time the province of physicians, is now squarely the province of pharmaceutical companies, with physicians taking a subsidiary or collaborative role. While physician user innovation is still a major source of medical instrument and device innovation, over time it has come to require extensive cross-boundary collaboration with engineers and manufacturers. Medical procedure innovation continues to be primarily the province of physicians, who are compensated with the rewards of reputation and use. Physician opposition to patenting of medical and diagnostic procedures is thus a typical user innovator community response.

Of course, this historical story does not prove that medical community norms about patenting are determined by the interplay between user innovation and the need for cross-boundary collaboration. Other factors almost certainly are at play, and there may be important differences between different areas of medical practice. Further empirical work is required to test and potentially refine the user innovator community hypothesis for physician patenting norms. Norms regarding instrument and device patenting also deserve more attention. Though AMA ethical rules formally permit device and instrument patenting, the user innovator perspective might lead one to expect more complexity in the norms on the ground. For example, one might expect a norm against patenting innovations that can be accomplished by tweaks of existing products and do not require regulatory review. Norms about the patenting of new uses of existing drugs also are of interest, since physicians do not need to collaborate with drug manufacturers or obtain FDA approval to prescribe off label.

Moreover, if the hypothesis of this chapter is correct, technological changes, such as the increasing incorporation of information technology into the delivery of medical care illustrated by *Emtel*,[81] and regulatory changes, such as potential tightening of regulations for medical procedures and the increased influence of payers on medical practice, may lead to further changes in physician patenting norms. *Emtel*, for example, involved claims in the field of telemedicine. The defendants had contracted with physicians and remote medical facilities to provide videoconferencing for telemedicine. Telemedicine and other IT-based medical procedures increasingly may require that physicians collaborate with software engineers to invent new procedures. As we have seen with medical device innovation, the need for such boundary-spanning collaborations strains, and may destabilize, community anti-patenting norms.

The hypothesis that user innovator community patenting norms will be tailored to the need for collaboration with outsiders depends on general theoretical arguments and therefore is testable outside of the medical arena as well. Industries such as tax, business methods, and software, in which there has been significant resistance to patenting, are promising areas to study.

NOTES

The author is grateful to Gail and Al Engelberg for their support of her professorship and of the Engelberg Center for Innovation Law and Policy. The generous support of the Filomen D. Agostino and Max E. Greenberg Research Fund is also gratefully acknowledged. This chapter also reflects the truly excellent research assistance of Zachary King, Elizabeth Kimmel, and Chris Han. Note that the author served as counsel for amici medical associations in briefing in the case of *Mayo Collaborative Servs. v. Prometheus Labs.*, 132 S. Ct. 1289 (2012). The analysis described in this chapter is this author's alone and does not purport to represent the views of those clients.

1 *The Founding of the AMA*, http://www.ama-assn.org/ama.
2 American Medical Association, *Code of Medical Ethics* §4 (1847).
3 Aaron K. Chatterji, Kira R. Fabrizio, Will Mitchell, and Kevin A. Schulman, "Physician-Industry Cooperation in the Medical Device Industry, When Physician-Inventors Team Up with Industry, Is It Collaborative Innovation or Conflict of Interest?" *Health Affairs* 27 (2008): 1532, 1535, 1537–1538 (approximately 20% of medical device patents have at least one physician inventor).
4 Katherine J. Strandburg, "Legal But Unacceptable: *Pallin v. Singer* and Physician Patenting Norms," in Rochelle C. Dreyfuss and Jane C. Ginsburg, eds., *Intellectual Property at the Edge: The Contested Contours of IP* (Cambridge: Cambridge University Press, 2014), 321–342.
5 *Lab. Corp. of Am. Holdings v. Metabolite Labs., Inc.* 548 U.S. 124 (2006). See Brief of Amici Curiae AMA et al., *Lab. Corp. of Am. Holdings v. Metabolite Labs., Inc.* (No. 04–607), http://www.ama-assn.org. (Filed on behalf of six medical associations.)
6 *Mayo Collaborative Servs. v. Prometheus Labs., Inc.* 132 S. Ct. 1289 (2012). See Brief of Amici Curiae American College of Medical Genetics et al., *Mayo Collaborative Servs. v. Prometheus Labs., Inc.* (No. 10–1150), http://www.ama-assn.org/resources. (Filed on behalf of eleven medical associations.)
7 See, e.g., Eric von Hippel, *Democratizing Innovation* (Cambridge, MA: MIT Press, 2005), 77–92.
8 Kara W. Swanson, "Food and Drug Law as Intellectual Property Law: Historical Reflections," *Wis. L. Rev.* (2011): 331, 354–355 (explaining the differences between proprietary medicines and "ethical" medicines).
9 See, e.g., Lewis C. Beck, *Adulterations of Various Substances Used in Medicine and the Arts, with the Means for Detecting them: Intended as a Manuel for the Physician, the Apothecary, and the Artisan* (New York: Samuel S. and William Wood, 1846).
10 See, e.g., H.R. Rep. No. 52 (1849): 5–23, 30 (showing 80 instances of patents on medicines between 1796 and 1843, most of which "combine some active known agent, disguised under colors, and heralded with a name, in many instances, as uncouth as it is insignificant or false").

11 See James A. Johnson and Walter J. Jones, *The American Medical Association and Organized Medicine* (New York: Routledge, 1993): 5–6 (explaining that the AMA was founded in part out of a need to create standards "for effective treatment based upon the most up-to-date scientific principles"); Swanson at 331, 353–56 (discussing how "doctors sought to distinguish themselves as experts who prescribed drugs to treat particular patients, relying on their medical knowledge to be specific, rather than offering general cure-alls").

12 The definitive scholarly treatment of Morton's role in the invention of ether anesthesia is Richard J. Wolfe, *Tarnished Idol: William Thomas Green Morton and the Introduction of Surgical Anesthesia* (San Anselmo, CA: Norman, 2001). For general overviews of the controversy, see "How It All Began," *Anesthesia History Ass'n Newsletter* (January 1992), reprinted from 11 *Middle East Journal of Anesthesiology* (June 1991); J. M. Fenster, *Ether Day: The Strange Tale of America's Greatest Medical Discovery and the Haunted Men Who Made It* (New York: Harper Collins, 2002).

13 17 F. Cas. 879 (C.C.S.D.N.Y. 1862).

14 A vivid description is given in Nathan P. Rice, *Trials of a Public Benefactor, as Illustrated in the Discovery of Etherization* (Pudney and Russell, 1858): 40–42.

15 "How It All Began," 93.

16 U.S. Patent No. 4848 (Nov. 12, 1846).

17 *Tarnished Idol*, 8–26.

18 "How It All Began."

19 For an overview, see *Ether Day*; *Tarnished Idol*.

20 See, e.g., Report of the Committee on Surgery, in *Transactions of the American Medical Association* (1848): 159, 178. (Hereinafter, *AMA Trans.*)

21 See, e.g., *Tarnished Idol*, 57–74; "Massachusetts Medical College—Dr. Jackson's Remarks," *Boston Medical and Surgical Journal* (Mar. 31, 1847): 80; "Letter to the Editor," *Boston Medical and Surgical Journal* (May 7, 1847): 297; "Priority of Discovery of the Use of Ether Vapor," *Boston Medical and Surgical Journal* (May 26, 1847): 333; J.B.S. Jackson, "Review of Dr. M. Gay's Statement of Dr. Charles T. Jackson's Claims to the Discovery of the Inhalation of Sulphuric Ether, as a preventive of Pain," *Boston Medical and Surgical Journal* (June 30, 1847): 1; J. Mason Warren, "Inhalation of Ether: One of the Surgeons of the Mass. General Hospital," *Boston Medical and Surgical Journal* (Mar. 24, 1847): 1; John C. Warren, "Inhalation of Ethereal Vapor for the Prevention of Pain in Surgical Operations," *Boston Medical and Surgical Journal* (Dec. 9, 1846): 375.

22 *Tarnished Idol*, 57–119.

23 Bigelow went on to practice surgery at MGH for 40 years and became well known for his contributions to the field. Oliver Wendell Holmes, Reginald H. Fitz, and Arthur T. Cabot, *A Memoir of Henry Jacob Bigelow* (Boston: Little Brown, 1894).

24 J. Mason Warren, "Inhalation of Ether: One of the Surgeons of the Mass. General Hospital," *Boston Medical and Surgical Journal* (Mar. 24, 1847): 1, John C. Warren, "Inhalation of Ethereal Vapor for the Prevention of Pain in Surgical Operations,"

Boston Medical and Surgical Journal (Dec. 9, 1846): 375; George Hayward, "Some Account of the First Use of Sulphuric Ether by Inhalation in Surgical Practice," *Boston Medical and Surgical Journal* (Apr. 21, 1847): 1.

25 *Tarnished Idol*, 77–80.

26 Ibid., 99–101.

27 Ibid.

28 "Review of Dr. M. Gay's Statement of Dr. Charles T. Jackson's Claims to the Discovery of the Inhalation of Sulphuric Ether, as a preventive of Pain," *Boston Medical and Surgical Journal* (June 30, 1847): 1.

29 *Tarnished Idol*, 80.

30 U.S. Patent No. 4848 (Nov. 12, 1846).

31 *Tarnished Idol*, 103–109.

32 Ibid., 107.

33 Henry J. Bigelow, "Insensibility During Surgical Operations Produced by Inhalation," *Boston Medical and Surgical Journal* (Nov. 18, 1846): 1.

34 "Report of the Committee on Surgery," in *AMA Trans.* (1848): 159, 181.

35 J. F. Flagg, "Letter to the Editor," *Boston Medical and Surgical Journal* (Dec. 2, 1846): 356.

36 Henry J. Bigelow, "Letter to the Editor," *Boston Medical and Surgical Journal* (Dec. 9, 1846): 1.

37 "Report of the Committee on Surgery," *AMA Trans.* (1848): 176–224.

38 Henry J. Bigelow, "Etherization—A Compendium of its History, Surgical Use, Dangers, and Discovery," *Boston Medical and Surgical Journal* (April 19 & April 26, 1848).

39 Joshua B. Flint, "Report of the Best Mode of Rendering the Patronage of the National Government Tributary to the Honor and Improvement of the Profession," *AMA Trans.* (1856): 537.

40 Ibid., 542.

41 Ibid., 534–537.

42 *Tarnished Idol*, 120–121.

43 See, e.g., H.R. Rep. No. 114, 30 Cong. 2nd Sess. (Feb. 23, 1849); 30 Cong. 2nd Sess. Cong. Globe 642 (March 1, 1849); 42nd Congress 2nd Session Cong. Globe 310 (Jan. 9, 1872); 42nd Congress 2nd Session Cong. Globe 377 (Jan. 15, 1872).

44 John Watson, "Letter to the Editor, The Invention of Anaesthesia-National Testimonial to Dr. Wm. T. G. Morton," *New York Times* (Dec. 3, 1858): 2.

45 *Appeal to the Public by Members of the Medical Profession* (1859).

46 See Letters to the Editor in *New England. Journal of Medicine* (Sept. 16, 1858), *New England. Journal of Medicine* (Sept. 23, 1858), *New England. Journal of Medicine* (Sept. 30, 1858); "Law Reports," *New York Times* (Jan. 31, 1862).

47 "The Patent for Sulphuric Ether," *New York Times* (Jan. 31, 1862): 6.

48 *Morton v. New York Eye Infirmary*, 17 F. Cas. 879 (C.C.S.D.N.Y. 1862).

49 *AMA Trans.* 15 (1865): 53.

50 17 F. Cas. at 883–84.

51 Bigelow, *Etherization*, 254.

52 *Tarnished Idol*, 72–74, 103–109.

53 Ibid., 50–52.

54 Bigelow, *Etherization*.

55 *Tarnished Idol*, 110–111.

56 Ibid., 118.

57 "Report of Council on Constitution and Bylaws," *Proc. AMA Clinical Meeting* (1955): 111.

58 *Principles of Medical Ethics 1957* §2 (1958), http://www.ama-assn.org.

59 See http://www.ama-assn.org.

60 "Official Opinions of the Judicial Council," *JAMA* 163 (1957): 1156–1157.

61 "Opinions on Professional Rights and Responsibilities," in *Code of Medical Ethics: Current Opinions with Annotations* (1996–1997 ed. 1996): 150.

62 *Ex Parte Brinkerhoff*, 24 Dec. Comm'r 349 (1883), reprinted in *New Decisions*, 27 *Journal of The Patent & Trademark Office Society* (1945): 793, 798.

63 *Ex Parte* Scherer, 103 U.S.P.Q. (BNA) 107 (B.P.A.I July 23, 1954).

64 See, e.g., "AMA Speaks out on Managed Care," *UPI* (June 14, 1994) (AMA general counsel states that "methods patents" are a new phenomenon in medicine).

65 "Opinions on Professional Rights and Responsibilities," in *Code of Medical Ethics: Current Opinions with Annotations* (1996–1997 ed. 1996): 149–150.

66 For a more detailed discussion of these events, see Strandburg, "Legal but Unacceptable."

67 "Doctor Implores Principles of Hippocrates to Standing Ovation," *Ophthalmology Times* (May 1, 1994): 28.

68 "Sutureless Takes Firm Hold on Cataract Surgery: Interview with Mike S. McFarland," 12 *Ocular Surgery News* 12 (March 15, 1994): 21–32.

69 Pub. L. No. 104–208, §616, 110 Stat. 3009–67 (codified as amended at 35 U.S.C. §287(c)).

70 *Emtel, Inc. v. Lipidlabs, Inc.* 583 F. Supp. 2d 811 (S. D. Tex. 2008).

71 The provision also was at issue in *Lamson v. U.S.*, 117 Fed. Cl. 755 (2014), but the only disputed issue was whether the exemption was available to the government.

72 Opinion 9.095, *Code of Medical Ethics of the AMA* (1996, 2008).

73 Brief of Amici Curiae AMA et al., *Lab. Corp. of Am. Holdings v. Metabolite Labs., Inc.* (No. 04–607), http://www.ama-assn.org. (Filed on behalf of six medical associations.)

74 Brief of Amici Curiae American College of Medical Genetics et al., *Mayo Collaborative Servs. v. Prometheus Labs., Inc.* (No. 10–1150), http://www.ama-assn.org. (Filed on behalf of eleven medical associations.)

75 LabCorp at 128 (Breyer, J.) (dissenting from dismissal of certiorari).

76 See, e.g., J. Lindenbaum , D. G. Savage, S. P. Stabler, and R. H. Allen, "Diagnosis of Cobalamin Deficiency: II. Relative Sensitivities of Serum Cobalamin, Methylmalonic Acid, and Total Homocysteine Concentrations," *American Journal of Hematology* 34 (1990): 99; R. H. Allen, S. P. Stabler, D. G. Savage, and J. Lindenbaum,

"Diagnosis of Cobalamin Deficiency I: Usefulness of Serum Methylmalonic Acid and Total Homocysteine Concentrations," 34 *American Journal of Hematology* (1990): 90–98.

77 See *Metabolite Labs., Inc. v. Lab. Corp. of Am. Holdings*, 370 F.3d 1354, 1358 (Fed. Cir. 2004) (patent in suit is U.S. Patent No. 4,940,658); *Riezler v. Allen*, 2010 U.S. Dist. LEXIS 97853 (D. Colo. Sept. 16, 2010) at *4 ("Commercialization of the technology of the '658 Patent was the reason Metabolite was formed.").

78 *Riezler v. Allen*, 2010 U.S. Dist. LEXIS 97853 (D. Colo. Sept. 16, 2010) at *3—*7 (describing Metabolite's relationship to the University of Colorado).

79 Compare, e.g., U.S. Patent No. 6,680,302, Fig. 1, Examples I and II with M. C. Dubinsky, S. Lamothe, H. Y. Yang, S. R. Targan, D. Sinnett, Y. Theoret, and E. G. Seidman, "Pharmacogenomics and Metabolite Measurement for 6-Mercaptopurine Therapy in Inflammatory Bowel Disease," *Gastroenterology* 118 (Apr. 2000): 705, Figs. 2 and 5.

80 For information about Prometheus Laboratories, see http://www.prometheuslabs.com.

81 *Emtel, Inc. v. Lipidlabs, Inc.*, 583 F. Supp. 2d 811 (S. D. Tex. 2008).

PART II

Countercultural Communities

4

Owning the Body

Creative Norms in the Tattoo Industry

AARON PERZANOWSKI

Twenty-one percent of adults in the United States—more than 65 million Americans—have at least one tattoo; for those under age forty, that percentage nearly doubles.[1] Not surprisingly, the tattoo business is booming, generating billions of dollars in annual revenue.[2] Like more familiar creative industries, the tattoo industry capitalizes on market demand for original creative works. Yet the value of those works is readily appropriable through copying. Predictably, copying is both a practical reality and a source of concern within the industry. But unlike their counterparts in most other creative industries, tattooers nearly uniformly reject formal legal mechanisms for resolving disputes over ownership and copying. Although tattoos fall squarely within the protections of the Copyright Act, copyright law plays virtually no part in the day-to-day operation of the tattoo industry. Instead, tattooers rely on a set of informal social norms to regulate their creative production.

A History of Tattoos

The five-thousand-year history of tattooing, from prehistoric societies to the contemporary tattoo industry, and particularly the dramatic shift in American tattooing over the last five decades, is central to understanding the attitudes and norms surrounding copying within the industry today.

In 1991, climbers in the Italian Alps stumbled upon the frozen corpse of Otzi, the Tyrolean Iceman, a 5,300-year-old mummy adorned with fifty-seven simple geometric tattoos.[3] The Iceman was not alone among prehistoric tattoo collectors. Egyptian mummies dating back to 2100 BC were tattooed, as were a Scythian corpse from 500 BC and a thousand-year-old Peruvian specimen, both of which bore elaborate depictions of animals.[4] Ancient Israelites, Persians, Greeks, and Romans all encountered or practiced tattooing.[5] And in Japan, evidence of tattooing dates to the third century BC.[6]

Aside from the Picts, the pre-Roman inhabitants of modern-day Scotland, Europeans showed little interest in tattoos until Captain James Cook returned to Europe after his second circumnavigation with accounts of Tahitian "tattowing":

> Both sexes paint their Bodys, Tattow, as it is called in their Language. This is done by inlaying the Colour of Black under their skins, in such a manner as to be indelible. . . . The instrument for pricking it under the Skin is made of very thin flatt pieces of bone or Shell. . . . One end is cut into sharp teeth, and the other fastened to a handle. The teeth are dipped into black Liquor, and then drove, by quick sharp blows struck upon the handle with a Stick. [7]

Initially, the European tattooed class comprised primarily sailors, soldiers, and adventurers. But by the nineteenth century, wealthy Europeans were eager to join the tattooed aristocracy with the likes of Queen Olga of Greece, the Duke of York, Lady Randolph Churchill, and King Oscar II of Sweden.[8]

In the United States, Martin Hildebrandt opened the first professional tattoo shop in 1846 in New York.[9] And in 1891, New Yorker Samuel O'Reilly invented the tattoo machine, a device that fundamentally reshaped the process of tattooing.[10] The introduction of electric machinery made tattooing cheaper, faster, and less painful. It also helped develop a distinctive American aesthetic characterized by bold black lines, heavy shading, and a limited color palette emphasizing red, blue, and green.

Tattooers in the United States were generally from the same working-class backgrounds as their clients and typically had no prior art training. Rather than create custom artwork for their clients, tattooers of this era worked almost exclusively from collections of pre-drawn images called "flash." Designs included military insignia, ships, hearts, flowers, skulls, daggers, snakes, tigers, Christian icons, and scantily clad women. When a tattooer came across an appealing new design, he copied it—

sometimes directly off of the body of a willing client—and added it to his stock of flash.

The combination of the electric tattoo machine and simple, pre-made flash designs enabled the industry to capitalize on the popularity of tattoos during the Interbellum period. In many ways, the tattoo industry was structured around the needs of soldiers and sailors who frequented tattoo shops in large groups with limited leave time. But in the postwar period, the popularity of tattoos began to wane. Many soldiers returning from World War II realized that their tattoos were not as enthusiastically accepted outside of the military. And unsanitary conditions in some tattoo shops raised serious public health concerns. After reported hepatitis outbreaks, many state and local governments began to heavily regulate tattooing or ban it altogether.

This period was marked by creative stagnation. Tattooers still relied largely on the same collection of flash designs that were prominent at the turn of the century. These simple, badge-like images met the needs of tattooers, who considered themselves craftsmen, with little interest in artistic expression for its own sake. And it met the needs of clients, whose tattoos often communicated group membership or commemorated milestones through established iconography. But creative torpor set the stage for a fundamental shift.

Beginning in the 1960s, tattooers began to reconceptualize their work. Norman Keith Collins, better known as Sailor Jerry, was among the first and most important tattooers to challenge prevailing practices. Influenced by Japanese tattoo traditions, he sought to elevate tattoo artistry in the United States by creating elaborate, stylistically and thematically consistent tattoos that incorporated the entire human body as a canvas, in stark contrast to the prevailing approach of unsystematically scattering small standalone images across the body.[11]

Over the next few decades, the innovations of Sailor Jerry and protégés like Cliff Raven and Don Ed Hardy helped bring about three interlinked shifts in the industry that led to what some have called the tattoo renaissance. First, a new generation of tattooers was drawn to the industry because of its potential for artistic innovation. Experienced and trained fine artists began to see tattooing as a viable and legitimate career path. Second, the creative output of the tattoo industry changed as a result of the influx of artistically inclined tattooers. New techniques and styles that drew on influences ranging from cubism to graffiti began to emerge. Third, the client base of the industry became more affluent, better educated, and developed higher expectations of technical skill and originality.

These three changes gave rise to the most important development in the industry from the perspective of creative norms—custom tattooing. Rather than simply offer their clients a selection of flash from which to choose, tattooers increasingly created unique bespoke designs for individual clients, customized for both their tastes and their bodies.

As a result of these changes, the tattoo industry today is defined by two very different paradigms. The street shop fits comfortably with the common public conception of a "tattoo parlor." A garish neon sign flickers above the entrance. The walls are papered with flash designs. Clients walk in off of the street without appointments, select the image of their choice, and are tattooed by whichever tattooer happens to be free at the moment. Clients are often charged a pre-determined flat rate. Most simple flash designs can be tattooed in well under an hour, sometimes as quickly as a few minutes. Thousands of tattoo shops in the United States fit this basic model.

Less familiar to the public imagination is the high-end custom tattoo shop. Skull & Sword, a respected shop in San Francisco, is one example. Located on the second floor of a nondescript building, the shop features minimal signage. Rather than accept walk-ins, tattooers book appointments several months in advance. Custom tattoo clients are charged an hourly rate for the time spent applying the tattoo. At high-end shops, rates between $150 and $250 per hour are not uncommon. A sizable custom tattoo can take many hours to complete, often requiring multiple appointments over the course of months.

Most tattoo shops, and most tattooers, operate somewhere along a spectrum between these two paradigms, providing a combination of small, simple, pre-designed tattoos, as well as more elaborate custom work. Since tattooers learn on the job through apprenticeship, they commonly start with simple flash designs, developing the skills necessary for more complex custom designs over time. And because they work in both milieus, many tattooers self-consciously play the roles of both creator and copyist, a duality that informs and complicates industry norms surrounding creative production.

Tattoos and Copyright

Before turning to those industry norms, we should consider the treatment of tattoos under copyright law. Copyright requires originality, that a work is independently created and reflects a modicum of creativity—and fixation—that a work is sufficiently permanent to endure for more than a transitory duration.[12]

In the case of a custom tattoo, copyrightability must be addressed with regard to two distinct but related works. Tattooers occasionally ink an image freehand directly on a client's skin. But more often, they create a detailed line drawing of the tattoo design on paper. Once the line drawing is prepared, the tattooer copies it to a stencil, which when transferred to the client's skin serves as a template for tattooing the outline of the design. But line drawings lack the shading, color, and three-dimensionality often found in the final tattoo.

Line drawings fall squarely within the Copyright Act's definition of "pictorial, graphic, and sculptural" works. A pencil or ink drawing on paper satisfies the fixation requirement. So assuming the work is not merely a copy of a preexisting work and reflects some amount of creativity, the line drawing is eligible for copyright protection. This result is neither surprising nor controversial. The same basic analysis would seem to hold for the tattoo as applied to a human subject. To the extent the tattoo is independently created and satisfies the low bar for creativity, it is original. And as your mother has no doubt warned you, tattoos are permanent. Tattoos then, like their pencil and paper counterparts, are subject to copyright protection.

In litigation over Mike Tyson's facial tattoo, copyright treatise author David Nimmer filed an expert witness declaration that challenged this seemingly straightforward result.[13] Victor Whitmill, who tattooed a Maori-inspired design on Tyson's face, sued Warner Brothers after that design was reproduced on the face of comedian Ed Helms in *The Hangover II*. Nimmer, adopting a position inconsistent with his own treatise, argued that Whitmill was not entitled to copyright protection for Tyson's tattoo. Comparing it to a frosty window pane or wet sand as the tide approaches, Nimmer suggested that skin does not qualify as a tangible medium of expression. But those quintessential examples of transitory media are a far cry from the lifelong fixation of a tattoo. More plausibly, Nimmer pointed to the useful article limitation as a separate basis for denying protection. Pictorial, graphic, or sculptural elements incorporated into a utilitarian article are protectable only to the extent they are physically or conceptually separable from the underlying article. Although Tyson's tattoo is easily divorced from his skin as a conceptual matter, Nimmer insisted that "the only legally cognizable result is to apply the strict requirement of physical separability." Otherwise, he claimed the Copyright Act would "set to naught the Thirteenth Amendment's prohibition of badges of slavery."[14]

At the root of Nimmer's startling equation of willing recipients of tattoos with slaves is a concern that copyright protection could grant Whitmill control over Tyson's public displays of the tattoo as well as reproductions of it in photographs or video. Although the court characterized Nimmer's legal arguments as "silly," these potential consequences are indeed alarming.[15] Luckily, copyright law offers courts many tools aside from the blunt instrument of protectability that they could, and almost certainly would, use to avoid this parade of horribles. But there is another reason of far more practical importance why Nimmer's fears were unwarranted: The scenarios he envisioned are fundamentally at odds with the established norms of the tattoo industry.

Tattoos and Norms

Copyright suits between tattooers and their clients, or suits between two tattooers, are virtually non-existent. Not a single reported decision addresses a copyright claim brought by a tattooer against a client or a fellow tattooer. And the only such case ever filed in the United States—brought by tattooer Matthew Reed against his client, NBA athlete Rasheed Wallace, Nike, and Wieden+Kennedy after his tattoo was featured prominently in a Nike ad—was eventually settled.[16]

Nonetheless, simply by bringing suit, Reed operated outside of the accepted norms of the tattoo industry. None of the tattooers I interviewed had registered copyrights in their custom designs.[17] None had been involved in a formal copyright dispute. Most were dismissive of the notion of bringing a suit against a client or another tattooer. As one interview subject colorfully put it, a tattooer who sued another for copying would be "labeled kind of a wiener with thin skin." This attitude reflects the norms governing both the creative process and the tattooer-client relationship.

Both during and after the design process, tattooers consistently demonstrate a respect for client autonomy. Client input helps shape the design of a custom tattoo. And once an image is created on the client's skin, tattooers uniformly acknowledge that control over the image, with some limited exceptions, shifts to the client.

The design process typically begins with a consultation, where the client presents a basic description of their idea for the tattoo. Because of their greater familiarity with design and composition, as well as a clearer understanding of the limitations of the medium, tattooers frequently guide their clients' choices. After settling on subject matter, style, and composition—typically with significant input from the tattooer—the client pays a small cash deposit before the tattooer draws the design. The deposit fee is then deducted from the eventual hourly-rate price of the tattoo. As a result, tattooers do not ultimately charge clients for their time and effort in creating a design.

Because custom tattoos are both commissioned and collaborative, a copyright lawyer would be tempted to consider the tattooer-client relationship through the lenses of works made for hire and joint authorship. Although strands of both of these approaches can be found in the thinking of tattooers, neither maps onto the norms of the tattoo industry particularly well.

Custom tattoos are almost certainly not works made for hire as defined by the Copyright Act.[18] And while some could be considered joint works, clients typically contribute uncopyrightable ideas, not protected expression.[19] The law would treat most custom tattoo designs as works created by the tattooer alone. Perhaps not surprisingly, the formal conclusions of copyright law do not dictate how tattooers conceptualize their ownership interests in their work. As one tattooer explained, "I don't feel necessarily a strong ownership over [my custom designs], because a lot of the time it's not necessarily my original idea. It's stuff that I'm being commissioned for, so I see myself as more of a paid artist to bring visions to life."

Tattooers invariably express a commitment to the clients' autonomy over their bodies and the tattoos that have become an integral part of them. When asked whether she had any right to control the display, reproduction, or other use of a client's tattoo, one tattooer offered the following response, which accurately captures the industry norm:

> It's not mine anymore. You own that, you own your body. I don't own that anymore. I own the image, because I have [the drawing] taped up on my wall and I took a picture of it. That's as far as my ownership goes. [Claiming control over the client's use of the tattoo] is ridiculous. That goes against everything that tattooing is. A tattoo is like an affirmation that it is your body, that you own your own self, because you'll put whatever you want on your own body. For somebody else to say, "Oh no, I own part of that. That's my arm." No, it's not your fucking arm, it's my fucking arm. Screw you.

Copyright law limits the author's right to control a work after a transfer of ownership of a copy of that work. Notably, the Copyright Act provides that the owner of a copy of work is entitled to display that work publicly.[20] Tattooers embrace an even more robust set of exhaustion rights favoring their clients. In addition to public displays of their tattoos, they acknowledge clients' rights to post images of their tattoos to their Facebook profiles, for example, or even reproduce a picture of the tattoo for commercial purposes. Tattooers also recognize that clients are free to create new works that incorporate or even destroy their original designs. New designs frequently use the client's existing tattoos as a starting point for expansion, regardless of who did the original work. And clients with poorly executed tattoos often ask more skilled tattooers for a "coverup"—a new tattoo that entirely conceals the existing one. None of the tattooers with whom I spoke expressed any reservation about these widespread practices.

But under prevailing industry norms, not all client uses are acceptable. Tattooers distinguish between uses of the tattoo as applied to the body, which are universally accepted, and uses of the tattoo design as a work disconnected from the body, which exist at the edge of the client autonomy norm and may prove more likely to spur formal enforcement efforts. For example, tattooer Christopher Escobedo filed suit against the developer of *UFC Undisputed 3*, a video game featuring Escobedo's client, mixed martial arts fighter Carlos Condit.[21] Escobedo alleged that the game infringed his copyright by including a digital representation of the lion tattoo he created on Condit's torso. The developer's use of the lion tattoo arguably transgressed the limits of the client autonomy norm because its use was detached from the client's body. More recently, a similar suit alleged infringement when the video game *NBA 2K16* accurately depicted the tattoos of NBA stars like Lebron James and Kobe Bryant.[22] The merging pattern suggests that when use is made by third parties outside of the tattoo community, where the client is not named as a defendant, and significant economic value is at stake, the general norm disfavoring litigation may be particularly susceptible to erosion.

Those rare cases aside, tattoo industry norms place a premium on establishing and maintaining the relationship between the tattooer and the client. As one interview subject put it, "To get a great tattoo, it's a full surrender into trust and faith in the tattooer." In part, that relationship of trust is facilitated by the tattooer's recognition of client autonomy. But it also relies on shared assurances against copying.

Tattooers uniformly reported an industry norm against the copying of custom designs. Indeed, that norm is so strong that it extends to the tattooer's reuse of her own designs on subsequent clients. As one tattooer told me, "I designed that custom for that person with an understanding. The agreement I basically made with them was that this design was for that person and that person alone." Although this tacit agreement is not acknowledged expressly, tattooers refuse to reapply the same design without explicit permission from the original client.

Likewise, every tattooer interviewed agreed that literal copying of another tattooer's custom design transgresses industry norms. Literal copyists, considered "the lowest of the low" among tattooers, are referred to as "tracers," "biters," and "hacks." Also derided are tattooers who, while they may redraw or refine elements of a design, closely reproduce the basic subject matter, composition, and style of a custom tattoo.

A custom tattoo designed by Guen Douglas subsequently copied by other tattooers provides examples of both literal and close copying.[23] The first photo shows the original design Douglas tattooed on her client; The second photo depicts a literal copy created by another tattooer. As the images demonstrate, every element of the original custom tattoo was appropriated. The subject matter, composition, outline, shading, color choices, text, and even placement on the body were copied. Of course, given the hand-fashioned nature of tattoos, not to mention variations in

At left, an original custom tattoo; in center, a verbatim copy; at right, a close copy.

skin tone and body shape among clients, no two tattoos are ever identical. Although the tattoo depicted in the third photo offers some variations on the original custom design, tattooers would recognize it as a close copy that violates industry norms.

These examples of literal or close copying present uncontroversial violations of industry norms. At the other end of the spectrum, tattooers generally treat purely abstract ideas, defined in terms of subject matter or style, as free for the taking. Between these two extremes, however, tattooers lack any widely accepted definition of impermissible copying. Interview subjects consistently referred to the wide swath of borrowing, situated between literal tracing and drawing upon common themes or ideas, as a grey area. Whether a particular instance of borrowing runs counter to industry norms hinges on the particular facts and circumstances surrounding the design of the tattoos at issue, rendering ex ante determinations difficult. As one tattooer explained, "In that grey area, there isn't a line until someone draws it. But that's always retroactive. The line is identified as being crossed after the fact. You can't identify it."

Within this grey area, tattooers are sensitive to the risk of treading too closely to another custom design. In response, some adopt strategies to reduce the risk of running afoul of the anti-copying norm. Some decon-struct—or in their words "dissect" or "reverse engineer"—the design to isolate the particular elements that appeal to the client and create a new design. Others try to insulate themselves from the potential influence, conscious or subconscious, of other tattoo designs. But most tattooers are not quite so troubled by the prospect of non-literal borrowing. The tattoo industry is steeped in tradition. And while tattooers value innova-tion, they simultaneously demonstrate reverence for traditional tattoo aesthetics. Clients are likewise drawn to the rich iconography of tattoo history.

Because of the constraints of the form, drawing from the common pool of traditional design elements is often inevitable. "[T]attooing and the imagery within the industry, it's so homogenous and everything is so iconic. You can't just stake claim to something like that." In light of those constraints, tattooers recognize that claims of similarity between cus-tom designs must be tempered by the influence of stylistic and subject-matter conventions.

The scènes à faire doctrine in copyright law is premised on a similar insight. Courts have acknowledged that where two works both contain elements common to a given setting or genre, "infringement cannot be based on those elements alone (or principally) but instead on the ele-ments that are not inevitable in the genre in question."[24] Just as "drunks, prostitutes, vermin and derelict cars would appear in any realistic work about the work of policemen in the South Bronx," traditional American tattoos are likely to depict swallows, anchors, and roses with bold out-lines and bright colors.[25]

The skepticism tattooers express about originality is not limited to traditional tattoo imagery. Regardless of subject matter or style, they see copying as integral to their creative enterprise. In part, this attitude reflects the eagerness with which tattooers have mined other cultures, media, and art forms to satisfy client demands. As Ed Hardy, one of the early pioneers of contemporary tattooing, explained, "tattooing is the great art of piracy. Tattoo artists have always taken images from any-thing available that customers might want to have tattooed on them."[26] Many tattooers embrace the role influence and inspiration play in the creative process. Even for tattooers who create new custom designs for each client, true originality is often more myth than reality: "Everything we're doing is copying. Everything I've ever done is copying. Everything I've done is inspired by somebody else. I'm not doing anything new that [other tattooers] haven't done 20 years ago. I don't feel ashamed about it and I don't feel bummed out on that." Others see copying as a form of creative dialog that should not only be accepted but celebrated. One tattooer explained that "[i]f someone takes something I've done and [he is] inspired by it, takes it, reworks it, and makes it even better[,] [t]hat's not going to make me upset. That's going to make me say, dude, I can step it up too."

Not only do tattooers vary in what they consider a copy; they also exhibit a range of responses to copying. Custom tattoos are generally private works. Therefore, they are less susceptible to copying than mass media products. For this reason, many tattooers were skeptical of the rise of tattoo magazines in decades past because they posed an increased risk of copying.[27] But today, images of custom tattoos are more accessible than ever. Tattooers and tattoo shops post photos of their work on their websites; clients share photos of their tattoos on social media; and Tumblr and Pinterest feature thousands of photos of custom tattoos, often without attribution to either the tattooer or the client. This widespread availability of custom tattoo images—combined with an influx of inexperienced tattooers and clients—has resulted in a marked increase in literal and close copying within the tattoo industry.

The majority of tattooers shared at least one anecdote of their custom tattoo designs being copied. In most of these stories, the Internet played a role in enabling both access to the original tattoo and detection of the copy. Technology also plays a role in the enforcement mechanisms employed by tattooers. Face-to-face responses to copying do sometimes occur if two tattooers happen to work in the same city or encounter each other at one of the many tattoo conventions across the country. But because of the national and international scope of the tattoo industry, enforcement efforts are increasingly digital.

When tattooers encounter what they consider copies of their work, they typically adopt one of three basic strategies: inaction, direct communication, or negative gossip. Many tattooers, typically those with more than a decade of experience, told me that, while they recognize that copying is inconsistent with the norms and expectations of the industry, they have no interest in pursuing any recourse against copyists.

One tattooer, after describing a scenario in which a custom sleeve—a tattoo occupying the client's entire arm, from shoulder to wrist—was traced by another tattooer, explained, "[y]ou can't control other people. . . . It's disheartening, but you have to let that stuff go."

Other tattooers communicate directly with copyists. These conversations range from the friendly to the overtly confrontational. Some veteran tattooers see instances of copying as an opportunity to educate their less experienced colleagues. One tattooer said he "might politely or tactfully offer some guidance" to someone who copied his design. Another tattooer suggested that a common response to minor instances of copying is "teasing" or "calling each other out" in a way that acknowledges the borrowing without any direct accusation of wrongdoing. Less affably, another tattooer described sending "[a] strongly worded email" to confront a copyist.

One subject reported a minor physical altercation between two tattooers over allegations of copying, but physical violence in the tattoo industry today is uncommon. Several interview subjects, however, spoke of the very real threat of violence in earlier eras of tattooing:

> [T]here are nicer people who are tattooing now. That in turn makes people less scared to rip somebody off, because they maybe haven't been in the tattoo world long enough to ever have that fear that someone might break their hand or something, which people did when I first started tattooing.

As tattooers with art school degrees replaced bikers and ex-convicts, instances of physical violence, arson, and other extreme consequences of violating community norms disappeared.

Today, rather than grievous bodily harm, the primary consequence tattooers face for copying is negative gossip. Tattooers mention "public shaming," "blacklist[ing]," and "shit talking" as the most common means of responding to copyists. Despite its size and geographic scope, many interview subjects described the tattoo industry as a tight-knit community. As a result, gossip can have serious social and professional consequences: "[S]ocially, you're screwed. In the community, you're screwed. Being part of the community is a really strong, important part of your growth."

One tattooer described her experience being publicly accused of copying in a widely read blog post:

> I cried in my bed for like three weeks and didn't leave. I was devastated. [H]e said, "Boycott her tattooing. She doesn't deserve to tattoo. She's a hack tattooer." I mean, those are strong statements. Then, to go on his blog or whatever and see what [other] people wrote about me. I'm a girl. I'm sensitive. I fucking cried for weeks.

For tattooers, norms are often identity constitutive. Violating industry norms not only runs the risk of community disapproval, it also undermines a tattooer's self-conception. External enforcement efforts may be less important when, as here, community members have internalized norms. While most custom tattooers take seriously both community disapproval and harms to self-conception, the norm against copying does not apply with the same force in street shops. In many ways, the street shop stands as a holdover of the pre-renaissance tattoo world. In terms of training, outlook, and socioeconomics, street shop tattooers often share more in common with midcentury tattooers than with contemporary custom tattooers. Whereas the custom tattoo community emphasizes artistry and originality, the street shop mentality focuses on speed, efficiency, and client turnover.

These two environments inculcate very different sets of values. Tattooers who learn their craft in a custom shop are taught to avoid copying. One tattooer explained that the "one moral thing [he] got out of [his apprenticeship], was that you just don't copy anybody's work." But a tattooer who started out at a street shop was exposed to a different set of values:

> [W]hen I first started tattooing I was at a street shop with real old salty guys. They had absolutely no problem ripping people off, at all, ruthlessly. To the point where I remember one of the guys that was teaching me to tattoo being like, "Well, if they didn't put it on the Internet, they wouldn't want it stolen."

As a result, copying of custom designs is more prevalent in street shops. Tattooers with artistic aspirations are less likely to copy. "Anybody at a certain level isn't going to try to copy. Only the guys at the bottom rung are going to be willing to do that." And tattooers who operate in the street shop environment are less responsive to the threat of negative gossip among custom tattooers. As one tattooer told me, "usually those scratchers don't give a hoot about the morality, or any sort of industry consequences." But for those who aspire to maintain or achieve a sense of belonging and recognition within the broader tattoo community, including many tattooers currently working in street shops, the anti-copying norm exerts significant influence.

The variety of responses to violations of the anti-copying norm reflects the assortment of perceived harms tattooers associate with copying. Some tattooers subscribe to Charles Caleb Colton's aphorism: "Imitation is the sincerest [form] of flattery."[28] They see copies of their custom tattoos as recognition of the power and appeal of their designs. But for most tattooers, copying inflicts some combination of financial and dignitary harm. Many object to copying for the same reason they refuse to reuse their own custom designs: clients have expectations of a unique, personal tattoo. Tattooers describe custom designs as imbued with "very personal sentiment," an "express[ion of] . . . individuality," or even something "sacred." As a result, when a tattooer copies a custom design, it erodes the value of the client's one-of-a-kind tattoo.

Tattooers see themselves as personally injured by copying as well. When their designs are copied, they are denied some measure of "notoriety," "awareness," or "respect" they would have otherwise derived from a successful tattoo. In the words of one tattooer, "I think the initial harm was somebody else getting credit for something that I created. So someone else [was] receiving some sort of personal gain . . . socially."

The financial impact of copying is at the fore for many tattooers. Because they charge hourly rates, the amount of cash in a tattooer's pocket at the end of each day depends on the number of clients booked and the complexity of the tattoos executed. Worries over business lost to copyists, therefore, can be felt acutely. Many tattooers "are concerned about [copying] because they think it's money being taken out of their mouth . . . because there's a guy down the street now that might be tattooing and doing the same kind of style for, say, $20 less." Other tattooers, however, were dismissive of the notion of direct financial harm from copying. First, unless two tattooers operate in the same city, they rarely compete for the same clients. Second, well-established tattooers, whose designs are most likely to be copied, are often booked with a full slate of appointments many months in advance and therefore may not have the capacity to serve the copyist's client.

Despite disagreement over the magnitude of direct financial losses attributable to copying, the consensus among tattooers is that creating original designs entails significant opportunity costs. Tattooers talked about the "struggle," "effort," and "guesswork" involved in designing a custom tattoo. By tracing the results of another tattooer's labor, the copyist is "just lazy." By free riding on the efforts and opportunity costs of their peers, tracers inflict perceived harms on other tattooers:

> If it's something that took me four hours to draw . . . they're cutting out all that drawing time by just tracing an image of it. They're not putting any effort, whereas I spent hard earned time that I wasn't hanging out with my boyfriend or walking the dog because I was up all night working on this tattoo design that someone else copied.

Although opinions differ on the harms copying imposes, the appropriate responses to those harms, and even the precise contours of impermissible copying, tattooers regard literal or close copying of custom tattoo designs as a clear violation of industry norms. In contrast, copying from other works of visual art is a standard and accepted practice within the tattoo industry.

Readymade flash images, in contrast to custom tattoos, are copied freely within the tattoo industry, with the implicit understanding that those who acquire a copy of a flash design are entitled to reproduce it on as many clients as they choose. However, the unstated rules surrounding flash impose some important limits on its use as well.

For most of its history in the United States, flash served as the lifeblood of the tattoo industry. Even after the dramatic rise of custom tattooing in recent decades, flash continues to play a major role in street shops. And more recently, the industry has witnessed a resurgence of traditional flash imagery among the more discerning clientele typically associated with higher end custom shops.

Historically, tattoo shops acquired their collections of flash in a number of ways. Young tattooers and apprentices were expected to draw new designs and contribute them to the shop. Tattooers might also share flash designs with one another or copy them from their clients' bodies.[29] Early on, tattooers like Lew Alberts recognized the potentially lucrative market in flash designs and began selling sheets of tattoo designs.[30] Tattooers still produce flash today. It is marketed and sold on the Internet, through tattoo supply catalogs, and at tattoo conventions across the country.

When Lew Alberts began selling sheets of flash at the turn of the twentieth century, he did not include an end user license agreement. Contemporary designers and retailers of flash are similarly silent on the question of precisely what rights are transferred when a tattooer purchases flash. While this failure to clearly articulate the scope of the license would strike professionals in many creative industries—and certainly their lawyers—as a troubling oversight, tattooers express no hesitation about what the purchase of flash entails. They describe flash as "meant to be replicated." In their understanding, "if you purchase a set [of flash] . . . you now have purchased rights to tattoo these images should someone want them." Purchasing flash entitles the tattooer to copy that design on as many customers as choose it and to make alterations to the original design by adding, subtracting, or substituting elements or by altering the color palette. As one tattooer explained, "[y]ou do whatever you want to do with it. You can tattoo that on anybody however you want to do it." None of these rules are communicated in writing. Instead, they are "sort of handed down and understood" through observation of daily industry practice. But there are limits. Copying flash images to print t-shirts or competing sheets of flash would violate the industry norms surrounding flash: "If you buy [flash] from a guy and when he leaves town you color copy it and give it to everyone in town, he's going to be pissed."

Like flash, tattooers routinely copy works of visual art. Although at first glance this attitude may seem inconsistent with the strong norm against copying non-flash tattoo designs, the distinctions tattooers draw between copying within their industry and outside of it reveal a great deal about their conception of the underlying wrong copying represents. Every tattooer with whom I spoke had used a piece of fine or commercial art as the basis for a tattoo, and most continue to tattoo such images on occasion. Rather than choosing a pre-designed image from the tattoo shop wall, many clients today arrive at the shop with a pre-designed image located through Google. Tattooers frequently steer clients toward a custom design inspired by the reference material, whether to satisfy their own artistic impulse or to ensure a better quality result for the client. But if a client insists on simply copying a reference, most tattooers will relent.

The reluctance to copy works of visual art has little to do with any concern over the rights of the original artist. In many ways, tattooers see any work other than a custom tattoo as a design intended to be replicated, rather than created for a single use. Discussing tattoos of cartoon characters, one tattooer told me, "Disney designs weren't drawn for tattoos. [They are] icons. . . . Where a custom tattoo design, that was drawn for that human being. It's totally different." Another tattooer used the same example to illustrate what he saw as the natural consequence of media saturation, explaining: "[T]his is something that is pounded into our lives from an early age. Mickey Mouse. So how does society . . . expect us not to take these images and make them our own."

Aside from the sense that commercial art images are fair targets of reproduction, many tattooers talked about the "interpretation" or "translation necessary in order to make a painting a tattoo." They stressed that such a translation is "not a reproduction" or "just ripping off an image and photocopying it." In copyright terms, they see their work as transformative:

> [T]he skill of tattooing is refining something into a tattooable image. Tattoos are tattoos. Paintings are paintings. And you have to make one into the other. . . . An oil painting looks good because it's . . . layered and has a certain sheen to it. It will never look like that on skin. But when you reinterpret it . . . it's like developed a new meaning and developed a new power behind it.

It's hard to say whether a tattoo based on a piece of visual art would constitute a fair use under copyright law. But the rationale tattooers provide for this sort of copying is notable for how closely it echoes the Supreme Court's definition of transformation as "altering the first [work] with new expression, meaning, or message."[31]

Tattooers also echo the market harm inquiry under fair use.[32] Because of the specialized technical skill necessary to execute even the simplest design, tattooers understand themselves as operating in completely different markets than painters, photographers, and illustrators. In other words, a tattoo is simply not a market substitute for other forms of visual art. When asked how she justified tattooing images created by visual artists, one tattooer responded, "Because that person is not a tattooer. . . . Van Gogh can't tattoo *Starry Night* on you, but I can."

Others explain why the norm against copying does not extend to visual artists in terms of group identity. Since they see themselves as a countercultural group existing largely outside of the traditional art world, tattooers are especially unlikely to extend their norms to artists operating within the mainstream. As one tattooer told me, "[W]hen it's a painting or an illustration, it's not another tattooer's work. So in that sense, it's not another pirate you may run across one day. It's a square, a regular artist."

Explaining Tattoo Norms

Descriptively, copying within the tattoo industry is governed entirely by internal industry norms. But why have tattooers developed this particular set of norms? And more fundamentally, why did they develop norms rather than rely on existing formal law? No single narrative fully explains these developments. Instead, the best explanation attributes the emergence of tattoo industry norms to the confluence of cultural and economic forces. As a community, tattooers share a deep skepticism of the legal system. And as an informal guild, tattooers share a collective economic interest in both preserving market demand for their services and restraining entry by new competitors.

Remarkably, the contours of formal law appear to play no appreciable role in the development of IP norms in the tattoo industry. Tattooers are not motivated to create, maintain, and enforce norms because of substantive barriers to legal protection. They do not rely on norms as a second-best alternative to a legal system that denies them protection or leads to substantive outcomes that they reject. But practical barriers to effective enforcement could influence reliance on norms. Chief among those barriers is cost. Copyright enforcement is an expensive proposition. But the same is true for most non-institutional copyright owners. And copyright law anticipates the risk of under-enforcement by allowing recovery of statutory awards far in excess of actual damages.[33]

The most important barrier to legal enforcement within the tattoo industry is cultural. Most tattooers expressed skepticism about the law and the judicial system. Misgivings about litigation are not uncommon in society at large, but there are at least two reasons to suspect that tattooers as a group are more skeptical than most. First, tattooers embrace and celebrate their status as outsiders who reject established social conventions. Second, tattooers and their industry have endured regulations that prohibited their trade within neighborhoods, cities, and entire states.

Because of the outsider mentality many tattooers share, they are predisposed to skepticism about the law. They talk about tattooing existing on the periphery of "respectable society" and operating within a framework that does not "conform to normalcy." Not surprisingly, most tattooers are heavily tattooed. Despite the recent popularity of tattoos, the act of covering the majority of one's body with tattoos remains a conscious rejection of prevailing social conventions. As one tattooer described his compatriots, "We're pirates. This is a fringe art form, no matter what they want to say. It's not a regular square job. It's not a normal way to make a living." Their position at the margins is tied to a sense of detachment from established mechanisms of social control, which in turn reinforces a preference for self-governance. One tattooer's response to a hypothetical peer who turned to formal law to resolve a dispute over copying sums up this attitude: "We govern ourselves. So step off your high horse and un-hire your lawyer." To many tattooers, hiring a lawyer or filing a lawsuit to assert intellectual property rights suggests an "inflated ego" or confirms your status as a "prima donna" or simply "a dick."

In addition, the heavy-handed regulation and criminalization of tattooing colors the industry's perception of the legal system. In the 1940s, state and local authorities began to impose minimum age requirements on tattooing and to more carefully monitor sanitary conditions.[34] After the 1959 death of a recently tattooed client from hepatitis, New York City banned tattooing altogether.[35] Criminal bans across the country followed. While some of these early bans may have been a justifiable response to a threat to public health, the tattoo industry long ago demonstrated its ability to ensure client safety. Nonetheless, tattooing remained illegal in New York City until 1997 and was not legalized in South Carolina and Oklahoma until the mid-2000s.[36] Today, tattooers are still subject to local bans and restrictive zoning ordinances that place tattoo shops on par with strip clubs and pawn shops.[37]

Tattooers have challenged various state and local restrictions on constitutional grounds with mixed success. One of the first courts to hear such a challenge described tattooing as "a barbaric survival, often associated with a morbid or abnormal personality" and asserted that "one-third of the admissions to the U.S. Public Health Hospital at Lexington, Kentucky, for drug addiction were tattooed. If the addict was also a sexual deviant, the incidence of tattooing was markedly higher."[38] In 2010, the Ninth Circuit became the first federal appellate court to recognize tattooing as expression protected by the First Amendment when it struck down a ban on tattoo shops in Hermosa Beach.[39] That decision, while marking a notable departure from prior judicial attitudes toward tattooing, still reflected hints of the hostility that marred earlier opinions. In a begrudging concurrence, Judge Noonan insisted that the court was "not bound to recognize any special aesthetic, literary, or political value in the tattooist's toil and trade."[40]

Tattooers also worry that asserting copyright interests in their own creations might attract unwanted attention from copyright holders whose works are routinely copied by tattooers. By resolving their internal disputes through informal means, tattooers lessen legal scrutiny. More generally, tattooers fear that formal law will open the door to increased legal oversight. As one tattooer explained:

> If you want to [pursue legal action], that's fine. But I don't want to hear any pissing and moaning when you have to fill out contracts for every fucking person you tattoo. Stuff like that, there's going to be a ripple effect from it. It's just getting the government more involved—or any legal body more involved—in something that we've had a lot of freedom with and everyone's enjoyed.

Aside from these cultural features of the tattoo industry, economics offer a separate set of explanations. The economics of the tattoo industry differ from those of traditional copyright-reliant industries in important ways. The publishing, music, and film industries make money by creating original works and selling them to as many paying customers as possible. Very little of what happens in the tattoo industry follows this basic framework. Commercial flash artists fit easily within the reproduction-and-sale business model. But the street shops where those designs are transferred to clients do not. Street shops are in the business of serial reproduction of copyrighted works, but like the local copy shop, they make their income by offering reproduction services, not by selling or licensing copies of their original works. The custom tattoo shop is even further removed from prevailing copyright-reliant business models. Because of the emphasis clients place on bespoke tattoos, a custom tattoo derives its value largely from the fact that it will not be reproduced.

The classic Demsetzian analysis predicts that formal or informal property rights emerge when their benefits outweigh their costs, either because the value of exclusivity increases or the cost of enforcement drops.[41] The tattoo industry fits reasonably well within this model. As client demand for custom tattoos increased, so did the harm tattooers felt from appropriation of their designs. And as technology facilitated both the detection of copying and the spread of negative gossip, enforcement costs plummeted. This story tells us why tattooers would be motivated to assert a claim against copyists. But it doesn't explain why tattooers have opted for informal social norms rather than formal law.

Propertization alone doesn't explain tattoo industry norms because they arise out of collective rather than personal interests. Robert Ellickson, in his foundational study of Shasta County ranchers, suggested that informal norms take root when three conditions are satisfied: the relevant community is close knit, the norms govern workaday affairs, and the norms enhance the collective welfare of the community.[42] Each of these three requirements is met in the tattoo industry.

Although it is geographically dispersed, the tattoo industry bears the hallmarks of a close-knit community. Indeed, more than one interview subject used that precise language to describe it. Through a combination of workplace gossip, conversations at tattoo conventions, and technology-mediated discussion, tattooers have created a decentralized network for the exchange of industry information, including accusations of copying. And that exchange of information carries profound social and professional consequences.

The questions governed by tattoo industry norms are workaday issues, ones tattooers confront professionally on a daily basis: how to
collaborate with clients; how to respond to client requests for tattoo designs that originate from flash, prior custom work, or commercial art;
and how to define their relationship with the images they apply to their
clients.

Most importantly, tattoo norms enhance the welfare of the community. From a tattooer's short-term perspective, defection from the norm
against copying is an attractive strategy. By free riding on the efforts of
another custom tattooer, she can avoid the opportunity cost associated
with drawing an original design. And because she is paid only for the
hours spent tattooing, her compensation holds constant. Similar incentives could encourage a tattooer to violate the norm favoring client autonomy by extracting rents from a client whose public display develops
economic value.

But once client expectations are taken into account, those short-
term strategies reveal themselves as collectively harmful. Clients expect
unique tattoos, and they expect considerable freedom to use the images
on their bodies. Tattooers who upset those settled expectations run the
risk of undermining the market. If clients who desire bespoke tattoos
fear that their design will be tattooed on other clients, or perhaps even
worse, that a design they thought was custom-designed was in fact a
copy of a preexisting tattoo, they may well spend their money on some
other symbol of youthful rebellion. Likewise, if clients worry that their
tattooer will assert some control over their use of the tattoo, they will either insist on contractual guarantees against such interference, demand
lower prices to offset this risk, or simply opt out of the tattoo market
altogether. For the tattoo industry, the creation and enforcement of informal norms is a small price to pay for avoiding the erosion of demand
and the increase in transaction costs associated with defectors.

Ellickson's framework also helps explain why street shops are less
likely to follow industry norms. To the extent street shop tattooers are
part of the same community as custom tattooers, they are on its fringes.
And because their clients are, as a rule, less interested in one-of-a-kind
designs, street shop tattooers are insulated from the erosion of market
demand that results from copying. In other words, the norm against
copying is not obviously welfare enhancing for street shop tattooers.

However, given the nebulous distinction between street and custom tattooing and the mobility of individual tattooers along that professional spectrum, it would be easy to overstate the incentives for defection.

Other non-IP norms within the tattoo industry confirm that collective self-interest motivates tattooers. Tattooers generally accept a number of self-imposed restrictions that are best understood as efforts to preserve the reputational and economic interests of the profession as a whole. For example, most tattoo shops refuse to tattoo clients' faces and—until recently—hands because of the social stigma and economic consequences attached to highly visible tattoos.[43] For similar reasons, most tattoo shops turn away customers seeking tattoos associated with gangs or hate groups. In the aggregate, those norms discourage short-term personal economic gains for the sake of the collective maintenance of industry-wide interests.

These same self-protective instincts sometimes translate into exclusionary anti-competitive practices. In some ways, the tattoo industry resembles an informal guild.[44] It maintains trade secrets. It regulates entry into the profession. And it excludes potential competitors in order to limit competition. These efforts offer a supplemental explanation for tattoo industry norms, particularly the norm against copying custom designs.

Tattooing has long been an "old, magical art" characterized by secrecy. It requires a host of arcane technical knowledge traditionally unavailable to the general public. Historically, tattooers built and repaired their own equipment and mixed their own pigments, to say nothing of the technique necessary to execute a passable tattoo without causing a client inordinate pain. Until very recently, this information was shrouded in mystery. As one tattooer described previous generations, "[T]hey were like magicians; they were able to hold onto those secrets of how to tattoo." By guarding this information closely, tattooers were able to carefully limit entry into the trade. For most of the history of tattooing in the United States, most tattooers learned through apprenticeship.

Tattoo equipment and supply distributors, eager to exploit the untapped market of aspiring tattooers, challenged this long-standing secrecy by marketing pre-assembled tattoo machines, ready-made pigments, and instructional materials. Today, the widespread availability of information on the Internet further disrupts the traditional control tattooers exerted over the secrets of their trade. Some tattooers expressed concern about the impact of this free flow of information:

> [P]eople are being too open with stuff . . . [b]ecause there's too many people. . . . [P]eople are too accepting [and] just let people into the industry. . . . There are way too many people in the industry now. It used to be tattooers were fucking rich. . . . [Y]ou did well for what you did, and it's not like that anymore.

One way to understand the norm against copying is as an effort to reconstruct something akin to the entry barriers secrecy once provided. Custom tattooing involves two distinct skill sets. First, it requires technical skill—that is, a working understanding of how to translate a given design onto the client's body. A good tattooer must understand how to operate her machine, the choice between various needle configurations, and the unique characteristics of human skin, among other specialized knowledge. Second, custom tattooing requires the ability to conceive of and execute original designs. In addition to an understanding of composition, color theory, and a variety of artistic styles, custom design requires creativity, imagination, and time.

Old school tattooers limited market entry by controlling access to technical information necessary to develop this first set of skills. Today's tattooers, though they have largely lost control over those once valuable trade secrets, can rely on the second set of skills to regulate their trade. By emphasizing original designs, in part through the anti-copying norm, custom tattooers have shaped the market in a way that reduces competition from street shop tattooers and new market entrants who may have technical skill but lack the talent or inclination to create one-of-a-kind designs for their clients.

Taken together, skepticism about the legal system, the collective interest in satisfying client expectations, and the desire to limit competition within the trade explain why the tattoo industry relies on norms rather than formal intellectual property protection.

Conclusion

Because tattoo industry norms are largely a function of idiosyncratic cultural and market characteristics, we may question what they can teach us about intellectual property more generally. But two features of the tattoo market offer broadly applicable lessons. First, the tattoo industry's client-driven incentive structure reinforces the notion that formal intellectual property protection imposes uniformity costs when it ignores the creative dynamics within particular communities. Second, the tattoo industry's focus on the provision of personal services, rather than the multiplication and sale of copies, might serve as a useful model for other creative industries struggling with the ubiquity of copying.

An ideally calibrated intellectual property system would provide just enough incentive to prompt the creation of new works. Any incentives beyond the bare minimum impose unnecessary costs on the public in the form of higher prices, reduced availability, and restrictions on the use of creative works. Not all creators require the same incentives. Some face higher upfront costs or greater threats of appropriation. And they create against different backdrops of non-legal and even non-pecuniary incentives. But the rights intellectual property law confers are insensitive to fluctuations in the incentives necessary to induce creative production. Intellectual property protections are uniform, and that uniformity comes at a cost.[45]

To the extent norms form part of the backdrop of existing non-legal incentives, they suggest a more modest need for the additional legal incentives of intellectual property. Tattooers create new original designs because clients and their social code demand them. Even if tattooers were denied copyright altogether, these non-legal incentives suggest that their creative output would remain unchanged. Tattooers, like chefs, roller derby enthusiasts, and other creators should remind policymakers that incentives for creative production take many forms. An intellectual property policy structured around the expectations of a handful of publishers and distributors in a handful of legacy industries is one that neglects the prospect of new creative dynamics and markets in favor of inertia.

Embedded in our copyright system are assumptions about the business models of creative industries. The copyright system envisions a world in which rights holders produce copies of their works and distribute them to the public. But technology has made copying cheaper, easier, and faster, threatening the fundamental premise of this business model. Because the tattoo industry relies on a very different strategy to extract value from its original works, it may offer some lessons for other creative industries seeking to wean themselves from over-reliance on control over the reproduction of copies.

Tattooers do not sell products. As they see it, they are in a service profession. They sell an experience, perhaps even an attitude. Clients don't pay for a drawing; they pay for the time the tattooer spends rendering that image on their skin. As one tattooer told me, "The image is just what happens to be left after you spend a moment in time with a particular person. It's an intangible object." A custom tattoo requires the client and tattooer to spend many hours in a physically—and occasionally emotionally—intimate setting. As a result, clients look for interpersonal skill as well as artistic and technical expertise when choosing a tattooer.

This chapter does not advocate that the music, film, and publishing industries jettison their current business models in favor of one patterned on Sailor Jerry. But taking service and experience seriously could help copyright-reliant industries adapt to new market conditions. Some traditional copyright holders have already begun to embrace the shift from distributing mass-produced copies to providing customized, personalized service. Other industries are emphasizing those aspects of their offerings that remain difficult to copy. The gaming industry's focus on online multiplayer games, for example, can be viewed as an effort to entice consumers with services and experiences that are far harder to duplicate than the static contents of a disc. Tattooing, because it has always functioned primarily as a service industry, and one that made the transition from mass production to bespoke craftsmanship decades ago, illuminates one path forward for other creative industries frustrated by the ever-decreasing value of the copy.

NOTES

This chapter is based on "Tattoos & IP Norms," originally published at 98 *Minnesota Law Review* 511 (2013).

1 "One in Five U.S. Adults Now Has a Tattoo," *Harris Interactive* (Feb. 23, 2012), http://www.harrisinteractive.com; "Tattooed Gen Nexters," *Pew Research Center For The People & The Press* (Dec. 9, 2008), http://pewresearch.org.

2 Max Chafkin, "King Ink," *INC.* (Nov. 1, 2007), http://www.inc.com.

3 Maria Anna Pabst et al., "The Tattoos of the Tyrolean Iceman: A Light Microscopical, Ultrastructural and Element Analytical Study," 36 *Journal of Archaeological Science* (2009): 2335.

4 C. P. Jones, "Stigma and Tattoo," in *Written on the Body* (Jane Caplan, ed., 2000), 2; Pabst, "Iceman," 2337; Leopold Dorfer et al., "A Medical Report from the Stone Age?" 354 *Lancet* (1999): 1023.

5 *Leviticus* 28:19 (New Living Translation); Jones, "Stigma," 4–11.

6 Margo DeMello, *Bodies of Inscription: A Cultural History of the Modern Tattoo Community* (2000), 72; Donald Richie and Ian Buruma, *The Japanese Tattoo* (1980), 11.

7 William J. L. Wharton, *Captain Cook's Journal During His First Voyage Round the World Made in H.M. Bark 'Endeavour,' 1768–71: A Literal Transcription Of The Original Mss. With Notes And Introduction* (1893), 93.

8 James Bradley, "Body Commodification? Class and Tattoos in Victorian Britain," in *Written on the Body* (Jane Caplan, ed., 2000), 145–146.

9 DeMello, *Bodies*, 49.

10 See U.S. Patent No. 464,801 (issued Dec. 8, 1891). Charlie Wagner patented improvements on O'Reilly's device in 1904. *See* U.S. Patent No. 768,413 (issued Aug. 23, 1904).

11 Arnold Rubin, "The Tattoo Renaissance," in *Marks of Civilization* (Arnold Rubin, ed., 1988), 236–237.

12 See 17 U.S.C. §102.

13 Declaration of David Nimmer at 18, *Whitmill v. Warner Bros. Entm't, Inc.*, No. 4:11-cv-00752 (E.D. Mo. May 20, 2011).

14 Ibid., 11.

15 See Joe Mullin, "Tyson Tattoo Lawsuit: Studio's Defenses Are 'Silly,' Says Judge," *Paidcontent* (May 25, 2011), http://paidcontent.org.

16 Stipulation of Dismissal with Prejudice, *Reed v. Nike, Inc.*, No. 05-CV-198 BR (D. Or. Oct. 19, 2005).

17 In 2012, I conducted interviews with fourteen tattooers across the United States. Many of those interviews are quoted throughout this chapter.

18 See 17 U.S.C. §101 (defining works made for hire).

19 See *Erickson v. Trinity Theatre, Inc.*, 13 F.3d 1061, 1069–71 (7th Cir. 1994); *Aalmuhammed v. Lee*, 202 F.3d 1227, 1231 (9th Cir. 2000).

20 17 U.S.C. §109(c).

21 Complaint, *Escobedo v. THQ, Inc.*, No. 2:12-cv-02470 (D. Ariz. Nov. 16, 2012).

22 Complaint, *Solid Oak Sketches, LLC v. Visual Concepts, LLC*, No. 1:16-cv-00724 (S.D.N.Y. Feb. 1, 2016).

23 Guen Douglas, "How to Avoid Tattoo Plagiarism," *Tam Blog* (Mar. 15, 2012), http://tattooartistmagazineblog.com.

24 2 William F. Patry, *Patry On Copyright* §4:24 (2013).

25 *Walker v. Time Life Films, Inc.*, 784 F.2d 44, 50 (2d Cir. 1986).

26 Susan Benson, "Inscriptions of the Self: Reflections on Tattooing and Piercing in Contemporary Euro-America," in *Written on the Body* (Jane Caplan, ed., 2000), 243 (quoting Don Ed Hardy).

27 DeMello, *Bodies*, 34–37.

28 C. C. Colton, *Lacon: Or, Many Things In Few Words; Addressed To Those Who Think* (London et al. eds., 1820), 113.

29 DeMello, *Bodies*, 53.

30 Ibid.

31 *Campbell v. Acuff-Rose Music, Inc.*, 510 U.S. 569, 579 (1994).

32 See 17 U.S.C. §107(4) (2012) (identifying the fourth fair use factor as "the effect of the use upon the potential market for or value of the copyrighted work").

33 See 17 U.S.C. §504.

34 Alan Govenar, "The Changing Image of Tattooing in American Culture, 1846–1966," in *Written on the Body* (Jane Caplan, ed., 2000), 228–229.

35 Ibid., 232.

36 Thomas J. Lueck, "On the Tattoo Map, It's the Sticks: New York Plays Catch-Up at First Skin Art Convention," *New York Times* (May 16, 1998), B1; "Governor Set to Ink Bill Legalizing Tattoo Trade in Oklahoma," *First Amendment Center* (May 6, 2006), http://www.firstamendmentcenter.org.

37 See Gary Nelson, "State High Court Hears Mesa Tattoo Zoning Case," *USA Today* (Mar. 28, 2012), http://www.usatoday.com; Adam Townsend, "Tattoo Parlors Slated for Prohibition in Downtown S.C.," *San Clemente Patch* (May 20, 2011), http://sanclemente.patch.com.

38 *Grossman v. Baumgartner*, 254 N.Y.S.2d 335, 338, 338 n.1 (App. Div. 1964), *aff'd*, 17 N.E.2d 345 (1966).

39 *Anderson v. City of Hermosa Beach*, 621 F.3d 1051, 1059 (9th Cir. 2010).

40 Ibid., 1069 (Noonan, J. concurring).

41 Harold Demsetz, "Toward a Theory of Property Rights," 57 *American Economic Review* 347 (1967): 350.

42 Robert C. Ellickson, *Order Without Law: How Neighbors Settle Disputes* (1991), 167.

43 See Rubin, "Tattoo Renaissance," 233.

44 Robert P. Merges, *From Medieval Guilds to Open Source Software: Informal Norms, Appropriability Institutions, and Innovation* (2004), 5–7 (describing apprenticeship and trade secret protection within guilds); Gary Richardson, "Guilds, Laws, and Markets for Manufactured Merchandise in Late-Medieval England," in *Explorations in Economic History* (2004), 411–412 (noting that "'craft guilds' . . . main purpose and activity was narrow regulation of industrial productivity in order to restrain competition").

45 Michael W. Carroll, "One for All: The Problem of Uniformity Cost in Intellectual Property Law," 55 *American University Law Review* 845 (2006): 856.

5

Painting on Walls

Street Art without Copyright?

MARTA ILJADICA

When a street artist and a graffiti writer are looking at a wall, considering whether to put up a work—a stencil in the first case, an elaborate signature in the second—they may not know that if they produce an original work of authorship, copyright will grant them certain exclusive economic rights.[1] They probably don't care. A typical justification for copyright protection is that it incentivizes and rewards creativity, but this creativity takes place largely without reference to the copyright framework. Yet given the vulnerability of graffiti writing and street art to exploitation, copyright might well be useful in enabling creators to control their works in certain situations. So if it is not the possibility of economic reward that might flow from copyright protection that encourages street art and graffiti creativity, what is it instead? This chapter explores the motivations of graffiti writers and street artists to suggest that these works are produced for the sake of creating something beautiful; to symbolize membership of a creative community; for the sheer pleasure of holding a spray can and giving color to the street. These motivations underpin a number of key norms that regulate the creativity of street artists and graffiti writers: the choice of appropriate surfaces on which to paint, the prohibition against copying, and the prohibition against destruction of works. Moreover, creators hold particular views about how their works ought to be used by members of the public—that is, that copying and dissemination take place for non-commercial purposes.

This chapter argues that while the prospect of copyright protection does not motivate street artists and graffiti writers to produce their works, their creativity is nonetheless regulated by norms that act as a substitute for, and move beyond, copyright law. The first part introduces street art, graffiti, and the empirical work on which the chapter is based before considering what that work reveals about the creators' motivations for producing these works. The second and third parts consider the norm against copying and the norms regulating the placement of works, including which surfaces are acceptable for painting on and when another creator's work can legitimately be destroyed. While these sections consider how creators regulate creativity among themselves, the fourth part examines the creators' expectations around copying by members of the general public, including the exploitation of their creativity. It also considers some of the unsuccessful attempts by creators to protect their work via copyright law and concludes that even when copyright law might apply to graffiti writing and street art, protection may be limited. It is thus unsurprising that creators of graffiti and street art forbear copyright protection, especially since revealing their names may invite criminal prosecution.[2] Subcultural norms by contrast offer a context-sensitive, and hence more appropriate, means of promoting and protecting creativity.

Setting the Scene

The empirical research into rules regulating creativity among graffiti writers and street artists discussed here echoes other studies that have challenged the relevance of copyright law to certain cultural practices, including stand-up comedy, haute cuisine, tattooing, fan fiction, and Irish traditional music.[3] This part considers the scope of the empirical research on which this chapter is based as well as the history and cultural significance of street art and graffiti writing. It then identifies the motivations of the creators interviewed in order to explain why subcultural norms rather than copyright law are more appropriate in regulating their creativity.

While certain forms of street art have met with significant, if not unanimous, public acclaim, graffiti writing—writing a name in a particular style ranging from the tag (the writer's signature) to a throw-up (one-color letter outlines or different colors for the outline and fill) and pieces (large-scale works often with complex lines and shading)[4]— attracts rather less praise. This is not because the creators lack technical proficiency; graffiti writing tends to be done freehand, and it requires considerable skill. Both street art and the writing of letters change the color of the street, but unlike the latter, the former is a "crime of style"[5] and carries significant risks including jail time and public opprobrium.[6]

There are two points to be made about discussing street art and graffiti writing together. First, discussing "street art" as a single phenomenon elides the distinction between diverse forms of creativity that include everything from stencils to paste-ups to sculpture,[7] while precluding a detailed exploration of the more elaborate set of norms present within the graffiti subculture and the particular difficulties graffiti writing poses for copyright law. The difference between graffiti writers and street artists is not simply one of substance—that writers write letters and street artists tend not to—but also of how the works are made, how individuals self-identify and what their mind-set is. As one creator observed: "[I]t depends on what style, how you apply what you're doing. If you're using masking tape and scalpels and stencils and you know all sorts of stuff then you're definitely a street artist . . . Graffiti tends to be done just with cans."

More significantly, perhaps, an argument might be made that stronger norms for the regulation of creativity are to be found in the graffiti subculture because graffiti writers are more likely to identify themselves as belonging to a community of writers than are street artists. Writers are motivated not only by personal fulfillment but also by the attainment of fame within the subculture.[8] Nevertheless, discussing graffiti writing and street art together here allows for a broad discussion of the regulation of usually uncommissioned works found in public places, in particular with respect to copying and competition for space. Where graffiti differs from street art generally, the more specific term is used here in order to highlight the similarities and differences between the two types of creativity.

Second, as Jeff Ferrell identified in his seminal study of Denver graffiti writers, it is only ever possible to provide an insight into graffiti as it relates to one particular time and place.[9] The same might be said of street art. There is no attempt to provide a universal narrative of the regulation of subcultural creativity. The interviews that form the basis of this chapter were undertaken with creators identifying as graffiti writers and/or street artists in 2010–2011, largely in London. It is therefore *that* time and *that* place which inform the creators' responses. The picture is further complicated by the fact that the London scene is the product of the transplant of graffiti culture from the United States and so is heavily influenced by it; the documentation of New York graffiti in *Subway Art*[10] proved highly influential. The creators' responses nevertheless serve to illustrate a more general point about how creativity occurs, what creators expect to be done with it, and how this is regulated without copyright law.[11]

Copyright protection may be justified in a variety of ways.[12] One of these justifications is that copyright provides economic incentives to create works. Yet the prospect of copyright protection does not appear to motivate street artists and graffiti writers. Sketching out these creators' stated motivations thus goes some way toward explaining why street artists and graffiti writers make little or no reference to copyright in the process of producing their works. The empirical research suggests that personality concerns situated within a broader concern with the development of culture animate the production of graffiti writing and street art. It matters to the creators of graffiti and street art works that their works are seen, and it matters that their production allows creators to express their personality and be recognized by others. Indeed, there is an overarching concern with recognition—by both other creators and by members of the public. This is not to say that these things matter to all creators—and indeed, for graffiti writers, gaining fame within the subculture is arguably even more important than either—but considering these particular motivations helps explain why creators would risk putting up their works on the street without permission. Risks are taken both to satisfy the need for personal expression as well as to be seen.

In relation to the more obviously personal motivations, one street artist said, simply: "I do it for me." Another street artist expressed similar sentiments: "[i]t's the fewest strokes of a paintbrush or a spray can to express something really important to me." There is an almost visceral link between the expression of personality and accepting the risks inherent in street art and graffiti creation that make it seem far from any economic considerations. It speaks to the emotional aspects of creativity, including quite simply "adrenaline." For some, the feeling of personal satisfaction is largely unrelated to the creative expression itself. It is the *process* of creation that matters. In choosing a character to repeat on city walls, a street artist said: "I could put that emotion into anything, I've just chosen this character arbitrarily really 'cause it's the quickest thing to do."

For some, this personal drive also translates into a desire to have an impact beyond the personal by communicating with the public at large. This was summarized neatly by a street artist who said: "Putting stuff up on the streets is the most immediate way of getting into the public consciousness." The desire to make their voices heard, to make a social statement, dovetails with the excitement of creation: "[I]t is the purest and most direct . . . form of art I know. There is also buzz and excitement. And I feel it is a way to vocalize my dissent at society, government, corporations etc." For another creator, street art presented an opportunity to change the urban environment: "I just painted a huge painting on [the building] so it's not ugly anymore."

This sketch of creators' motivations with respect to recognition of their expression goes some way toward explaining why creators would need to address scarcity of space—because finding space is necessary in order to be seen—and why creators were happy for their works to be disseminated by members of the public, albeit for non-commercial purposes: It makes the creativity visible. Furthermore, it explains why individual expression is respected by disallowing copying: The prohibition safeguards the personal autonomy of the creators. The subsequent three sections of this chapter thus address the norms that substitute, and move beyond, copyright law. Two issues arise: first, to what extent copying is regulated among graffiti writers and street artists, and second, what happens when there is competition for space on a wall. That is, if personal autonomy and the desire to be seen rather than the prospect of copyright protection provide the motivation to create works, and so street artists and graffiti writers do not generally resort to making copyright claims to settle disputes among themselves, how is their creativity regulated without copyright?

Creating without Copyright

If copyright law is largely irrelevant to the incentivization of creativity, it is perhaps surprising that a loose set of informal norms relating to originality and copying—concepts at the heart of copyright law—are nevertheless adhered to by street artists and graffiti writers. This part of the chapter identifies the broad contours of the norm against copying and its limits, as well as the ideas of personal expression and recognition that creators invoke in order to explain its existence.

Prohibiting copying is a means of respecting the individuality of a creator's expression. The norm that forbids it is thus closely allied to the expectation that works will be original, which in turn is premised on the need for respect among creators: "It is important to get on with your contemporaries or at least acknowledge them, even if they might not personally get on." One of the ways of getting on is to respect others, and one way of respecting others is not to copy. This means not reproducing the works of others and passing them off as your own.

In particular, for graffiti writers, respect means not copying another writer's name or style of writing letters. The prohibition against copying—known as "biting" in the subculture—is of particular importance to graffiti writers insofar as writers aim to get their name up in the most visible places possible, in their own style, and to stay up.[13] While this part considers copying among graffiti writers and street artists generally, it is worth noting that originality for graffiti writers is more circumscribed in that it is based on the production of *letters* in different styles, where minute changes of angle might be sufficient to set the work apart as original even where any such difference is invisible to the untrained eye. "It's a pretty well-known thing," one graffiti writer said, "that you can't go around writing someone else's tag."

The norm against copying is also important because it forces creators to develop their creativity in order to set themselves apart on the street: "[I]f you're going to be in it for the long term you've got to get your own style. As I've developed my own styles, I think you consciously try to veer away from what everyone else is doing."

In steering clear of the creativity others are developing, another creator explained copying was acceptable only to the extent that it will not appropriate someone else's personality: "It's using the principles of it and making your own . . . You don't get respect for [copying] because . . . it's [about] individuality."

The norm must, to some extent, reflect the importance of personality concerns. It is the appropriation of another's personality in your own work that delineates the boundary between acceptable and unacceptable copying. But the prohibition against copying was justified also in terms of not appropriating someone else's effort: "When it's a direct rip of someone's [work] then: not acceptable, because you know that someone worked for long hours and worked for a lot of years to build up a certain thing . . . I think it's just morally incorrect." The norm against copying is thus situated within an understanding of how creativity occurs, that is, with creators working alongside each other who see their work in the context of the works of others.

Furthermore, there would appear to be an intuitive acceptance, especially in relation to graffiti writing, that rules circumscribing individual creativity are employed in the context of participation in, and enrichment of, a common graffiti culture. For graffiti writers in particular, and perhaps less so for street artists because they are not similarly constrained regarding the content of their works, the acknowledgment of a common pool of creativity from which to draw is important: Any writer can write letters, what matters is the originality of an individual style. One creator, identifying as a graffiti writer but open to employing street art aspects in their work, observed: "you tend to adopt a memory bank of different styles in your head." A writer's style might take "aesthetic cues" from the work of New York writers chronicled in *Subway Art*, for example, but will be unmistakably the writer's own. There is neither a sense here that copying can be, nor that it should be, at all costs, prevented. Copying, while respecting the core of another's individual expression, is part of the development of creativity generally. In other words, the norm against copying—at least within the graffiti subculture—is important in helping an individual distinguish themselves from others, to express themselves and be recognized but in doing so to consciously help the culture evolve. The norm against copying balances the protection of individual creativity and the preservation of culture.

There appear to be limits placed on the prohibition of copying—that is, circumstances in which copying is accepted as permissible—which include the appropriation of popular culture, the appropriation of mere ideas as well as certain practical concerns. Some level of appropriation, from popular culture for example, is expected to occur when creators draw upon the material available to everyone in order to create their own works. Indeed, creators recognized that some copying was inevitable. As one street artist explained: "The thing is, I think in anything there's always a level of plagiarism isn't there? Even if you don't set out to do that, everything has been done before, nothing is new. . . . I think the whole idea of originality is completely rubbish."

This understanding would also seem to implicitly recognize the idea/expression dichotomy[14] that is familiar to copyright lawyers:

> I'll do stuff that [I'm] not necessarily copying from other people but I'm aware that other people have done before but I always set out to do it the best. . . . [T]here are times when you will do something, and I'm not talking about something incredibly specific . . . I want to do that myself, I want to do my own kind of personal representation of that. Artists have done it for thousands of years. At the end of the day, how many paintings of bowls of fruit are there out there really?

While particular ideas might be reproduced by different creators, it is what sets the work apart—its execution—that is important. A further limitation on enforcing the copying norm is a practical one: Copying may be accepted by street artists because of a recognition that their creativity is transient and may, at some point, be beyond their control. In extreme cases, it may be necessary to simply change their work: "If someone kept copying [the character] I might just have to do something else."

The preceding discussion makes clear that the norm in question is highly sensitive to context. This is especially the case with graffiti writers, where the protection of a name and style is important to gaining, and maintaining, status within the subculture. In short, there is an awareness that creativity draws from the broader culture but, more importantly, that creativity occurs within a community of creators. As such, the norm against copying is not solely directed at the protection of an individual creator's works. It is not the prospect of copyright protection but rather the subcultural norm against copying that is supporting creativity.

Finding Space on the Wall

Unlike other artistic endeavors that might require only a canvas or a sketchbook, graffiti writers and street artists must consider not just the substance of their work—whether it copies someone else, for example—but also its placement. In some instances, desirable wall space will be scarce. This part of the chapter addresses three issues, the first relating to placement and the second and third to the management of scarcity: first, choosing an appropriate surface; second, how street artists and graffiti writers compete for space; and third, the acceptability of destroying another creator's work when space is scarce.

Both street artists and graffiti writers temper their desire for visibility by adhering to a norm relating to the acceptability of certain surfaces. The choice of where to place a work depends on a number of factors, including whether the space is deemed to be "individual" property such as a house or a car, or, public or commercial property such as a shop-front shutter.[15] A street artist, echoing aspects of graffiti writers' views on the choice of surface, said: "Private houses, cars, historic buildings . . . I do not believe in damaging another individual's property. For me, corporate and civic spaces, industrial spaces, abandoned shops etc. are where I prefer to paint."

It seems likely, too, that the choice of abandoned places provides an element of safety and freedom to paint: the sense that a creator is less likely to be interrupted or, indeed, to have their work removed by property owners or local authorities. Another street artist, considering the acceptability of surfaces with respect to their aesthetics more generally, rather than the type of property, said:

Some places people clearly don't want painted. You know if someone's got something out the front of their home and they clearly care about it and they maintain it, or if someone's got a look going I don't want to mess with their look, you know. It's disrespectful. I think if somebody clearly doesn't care about a wall or if someone clearly wants graffiti on a wall . . . I think then it kind of implies consent. Really, just go ahead. I try to make a good job of it, try to use the whole surface.

There was no clear consensus on this point among creators, but a further motivation relating to the choice of surface is worth considering here: the impact of street art on public space and the effect it has on the public. One street artist described the potentially positive aesthetic impact of choosing a surface as follows: "I'm always doing it because I want to brighten up people's lives and make them smile, make them think."

The choice is made specifically with the public in mind. Regulating placement then is arguably a means of respecting by leaving alone certain types of property while at the same time designating enough surfaces as appropriate in order to potentially transform the experience of public space. This opens up the possibility of using street art to, as Alison Young puts it, "contest social arrangements and indicate new attitudes to shared public spaces."[16]

Having chosen an appropriate surface, the next decision a creator needs to make relates to any work that already occupies that surface. Before considering the circumstances in which a creator may decide to cover someone else's work and replace it with their own, the next section provides context by considering the competition for space between street artists and graffiti writers.

The regulation of the appropriateness of a surface creates scarcity insofar as certain surfaces—on places of worship, houses—are effectively not available to creators to paint on. In addition to these are surfaces that are physically difficult or impossible for most creators to access in order to paint on. Scarcity is also the product of competition between creators for the remaining public spaces leading to contests over territory. As the following discussion shows, finding and keeping a spot where a work will remain visible is likely to be difficult.

Although it is important not to overstate the competition for space among and between graffiti writers and street artists, it is worth highlighting that, in the experience of some of the creators interviewed, graffiti writers were more successful in making space for their works. That is, they were more likely, though this was certainly not routine, to go over the works of street artists than vice versa. One street artist described the position as follows: "There is this old school, new school thing that sometimes you get from traditional graffiti writers . . . [Writers] can sometimes all look down on the new school of street artists, but it's only a minority thing in my experience."

Moreover, street artists are much less likely to retaliate either among themselves or with respect to graffiti writers, as one creator explained: "[I]t doesn't happen really in the street art world. Street art gets dogged, capped, crossed out but it never leads to tit for tat between the street artist and graffiti writer, that I know of anyway." Another creator made a similar point: "[I]t gets quite territorial and so it's like you've got over my tags and my throw-ups with your paste-ups, it's like, why don't I just put my tag and throw-ups back over your paste up? . . . [But] street artists won't hardly ever retaliate against graffiti writers."

This perhaps points to a different, more territorial, approach to space by graffiti writers as opposed to street artists. Competition between creators, combined with day-to-day vulnerability to destruction by local authorities and property owners, also means creators may need to keep going back to a surface to keep their work visible. "I don't get off on that kind of competitiveness, I'm not really into that game," one street artist said, while acknowledging the importance of going back when works have been erased: "You've got to be very tenacious to actually keep your work there."

Notwithstanding the above points regarding scarcity of space, competition between creators also has positive aspects. A street artist described competition for space as a potential driver for creativity in terms of the space that is available for those wanting to get up:

> Climbing up fire escapes, hanging off bridges . . . It's a very competitive field but I think it's a very healthy competition . . . It's a very vibrant thing and I think it keeps the whole scene in check . . . [T]here's this territorial thing going on and I don't like the idea of street art getting too smug and cushy. I like that there's this constant battling for space.

There seems to be an implicit acknowledgment that producing art in public space is a process requiring constant engagement not only in relation to the acceptability of surface choice but also in regard to the actions of other creators. Competition for space might thus make individual works vulnerable but nevertheless contribute to the development of street art culture as a whole.

Popular types of spots tend to be those that are "in full view of the public."[17] Thus certain places are more desirable than others. For example, a wall hidden away may be less desirable than one that is on a busy street and is thus prominent. Though, of course, it may well be easier to paint in the former compared to the latter. The choice of place is of particular relevance to graffiti writers since visibility is key to attaining respect within the subculture, and writers are highly adept at choosing spots.[18] A creator, having chosen the right surface, may well be facing a wall that is already covered with other creators' works, making some form of regulation, however loose, helpful where a creator must decide whether or not to go over an existing work. Perhaps the most relevant norm arising as a response to the scarcity of space thus relates to the acceptability of going over another creator's work and replacing it with one's own.

The regulation of scarcity has a number of aspects, three of which are highlighted here: first, that going over another's work is undesirable and should be avoided if possible; second, that the acceptability of destruction will depend on the quality of the work in question including the effort that has gone into it and whether it is in good condition; and, third, that destruction may be unacceptable regardless of the quality of the work because of the creator's status or, related to this point, because the work is memorializing a particular creator.

Creators expressed the view that if there is blank space available on a wall with a work or works already there, the blank space ought to be taken up first. As one creator explained, there are "spaces where it is expected that works will not last" but clearly, if there is space on the wall then "it would be out of order to paint over someone else's work just for the hell of it." Similarly, another creator said that the work is "on the street" and while "it's natural" to expect that it might not last, "you wouldn't purposely go out to ruin someone's work."

In considering the appropriateness of going over another creator's work, the *quality* of the work matters. Taking quality into account means considering two things: whether the work that will potentially be destroyed is already significantly damaged and whether the new work is superior in style. This was relevant to street artists and graffiti writers but especially to the latter in terms of whether the work is stylistically impressive in some way. Certainly, copyright law is not interested in the relative merits of different works in quite the same way, except perhaps in the narrow field of the moral right of integrity when considering destruction of works of "recognized stature."[19]

A graffiti writer summarized the prohibition against going over works of a superior aesthetic quality as a rule, stating simply: "don't go over [something] better than you." As another creator put it: "I don't tend to [go over other's work]. I don't see any need, there's enough, the world is big enough that you don't need to go over someone else's work especially if it's a piece of importance."

Relating to the quality of the work, the interesting question here is what exactly it means for the work of a fellow creator to be better. The traditional graffiti writing approach was described by one creator as follows: "It is old school rules. Throw up over tag, piece over throw up, never the other way around. If someone puts a throw up or tag over a piece they are seriously disrespecting the artist and the piece." The quality of the work replacing the original creator's work is important to street artists too:

> [I]t was a new fresh clean space in London and everyone just kind of went crazy on it but it was fine, they didn't go over the actual artwork, just the background . . . It's weird how you sometimes get this respect. It's nice how some people think, "I want to work on that wall but I'm not going to go over that, I'll just find my own little space. . . ." If someone comes along and does something over my work I don't care if they start doing it as I'm finishing as long as what they're doing is better or at least on a par.

Similarly, another creator said: "I really respect the bigger pieces that people do, the multi-colored stencils, multi-layered and quirky."

An assessment of quality also relates to the condition the work is in. When a work has been significantly damaged already, it may be appropriate to simply go over the work by putting a new work in its place. Similar concerns were expressed by street artists, though in slightly different terms when considering whether to go over graffiti writing. Relating to the damage a work might have suffered already, a street artist explained:

> The only reason I would go over someone else's work is if there was a need to so, for example, you had a piece that had been so heavily tagged that it was completely unrecognizable, the artist had made no effort to keep it there or change it or whatever and then you just think, well, hang on, anything is better than that and it's time for the piece to evolve and it's time for the area to evolve.

Making the same point, another street artist said going over would be fine: "If their work is looking shoddy, out of condition, out of context . . . and it doesn't seem that it would be missed . . ." To complicate matters, however, even where a work is damaged and destruction appears to be acceptable, a creator will need to consider whether the *status* of the creator indicates that the work should be left alone regardless.

The relevance of status is especially important within the graffiti subculture because graffiti writers operate within a hierarchy where, in any particular city's scene, a writer will know who is up and who is not—that is, who is famous within the subculture.[20] A work may be "better" by virtue of a creator's renown. Thus it is not necessarily the aesthetic quality of the work that matters, though that may have contributed to the creator's fame. As one creator explained: "The rules of the game are really important. You gotta respect writers who display superior skills or who have been in the game a long time."

What this means is that a creator will need to have a good understanding of who the other active creators are and, crucially, how prolific they are. A key source of knowledge is that gained through an awareness of the works in a creator's city: Prolific creators will, quite simply, be visible over a long period of time. A creator will need to, as one street artist put it, "take a walk, have a look and see what's going on, learn about different artists." Of course, there is no official arbiter of a creator's standing vis-à-vis other creators, making conceptions of status, at least to an extent, fluid.

The recognition of status does not, however, only apply to creators currently producing works. A specific prohibition that was noted by graffiti writers, and also some street artists, is that memorial works—either produced by a creator who subsequently died or created in such a person's honor—must be left alone. As one street artist explained: "[I] don't like going over people's work but it's a matter of how much work has gone into it and, you know, the significance of it, whether that person's alive or dead. [. . .] Memorial pieces tend to be untouchable."

It is also worth noting here that, unlike the norm against copying, the regulation of scarcity moves beyond the substitution of copyright rules. It provides an additional, context-sensitive norm addressing the specific problem of scarcity by considering the nature of street art and graffiti writing practice, including taking account of competition between creators. The notion of respect among creators underpins the resulting norm against destruction and might be seen as the fundamental basis on which scarcity is addressed.

This concern with respect also suggests that the norm against going over potentially helps to preserve works that are significant to the community of creators, in particular as exemplified by the respect afforded to memorial works. It suggests that creators are willing to give up space because they do not appear to see themselves as atomized creators but rather as creators alongside others. At the same time, the norm against destruction appears to act as a shield for the individual labor expended in creating a work.

Copying and Copyright

The preceding section considered competition between graffiti writers and street artists as well as different aspects of the norm against destruction of works. Of course, street art is not only visible to other creators; how the other people on the street interact with the works of graffiti writers and street artists also matters. This part traces creators' expectations about the acceptable copying of their works by members of the public before turning to consider recent cases in order to determine whether, outside of their own creative communities, creators are likely to succeed in making copyright claims.

The interviews with graffiti writers and street artists indicated that there was a keen awareness of how their works should be used. This either was articulated without reference to copyright or was considered quite separately from the potential application of copyright law. Several points are relevant in examining creators' views on exploitation of their works by others: first, placement of their works in public makes copying inevitable and, to an extent, welcome; second, sharing street art and graffiti is potentially beneficial for the development of street art culture; and third, commercial copying of works is unacceptable both because of the lack of remuneration provided to creators and because it debases graffiti and street art creativity.

The fact of public placement of works on the street effectively meant, according to a number of creators, that reproduction of these works is to be expected. Indeed, some creators were bold in their acceptance of copying, specifically where it took the form of photographs. One creator commented that their work should not be protected from such copying, "nor should anyone else's."[21] The expectation that copying would occur is grounded in an understanding that the physical situation of a work must change how that work can be used. As a graffiti writer asked: "If you do it in a public place how can you then comment when it's in the public?" In particular, creators articulated an awareness that when their work was in public it was no longer only their interests as creators that mattered. Giving up rights, up to a point, to works in public space appears to stem from the motivation to be seen by others, suggesting a sort of implied license to copy.

Reproduction is accepted as a precursor to sharing street art and graffiti. Members of the general public making copies, in particular making works available for others to see on the Internet, "keeps the scene alive." Such reproduction increases creators' visibility and becomes a part of how the culture develops; it is not antagonistic to the creator's interests as members of the creative community being celebrated. For example, taking photographs of graffiti writing contributes to the documentation of graffiti writing culture, and in turn, may inspire its further creation in the manner of *Subway Art* and other books that inspired the first generation of UK writers. Indeed, a prevailing view of non-commercial use was that it is flattering: "I'm flattered if people take the time to photograph the work [for] their own personal documentation, that's wonderful. What really frustrates me is when people take photos to sort of make a commercial gain from it."

The important thing to note is that sharing graffiti writing and street art is not simply justified on the basis of benefit to an individual creator. As one street artist put it: "I am part of the public. I am painting for us, really inasmuch as I can gauge what other people are feeling, what the area means to them." There appears to be a disjuncture between what copyright can do—provide a remedy to an *individual* creator—and the creator's expectation that this recognition of individual creativity is *part* of the development of street art culture that is experienced by creators and members of the public alike.

However, creators did not state that there was no limit to what they would be happy to see done with their work, despite comments such as "[you] give up all rights to have a say." Rather, once the work is in public, it matters how that work is consumed. Creators' expectations regarding copying gleaned from the interviews might be summarized thus: Sharing with others is acceptable while copying for commercial gain—for example, placing works on canvas or on clothing or using works in advertising without permission, and without compensating the creator—is usually unacceptable. Two explanations, among others, were given for this: that such copying ought to be compensated, but that even when compensated it may be unacceptable because it negatively exploits the cultures of graffiti writing or street art.

One street artist was clear that the use of graffiti and street art ought not to exploit it negatively: "I think it's further encroaching on our individual freedom, onto our social freedom. That's why I strongly object to commercial graffiti." And it is not only the appropriation of the images but also of the process and style of street art that the creator objected to. Considering a bank using stencils in its advertisements, the same street artist said: "This is so offensive, that in the guise of offering you a service they're actually trying to make money, trying to draw you in and use the cachet of a folk art . . . [They] are trying to hijack that social forum for their gain. I think that's really wrong." There is an underlying plea here for the recognition of the social value of works aside from their potential economic value: "There are emotional and social motives and these are pure, really pure motives. That is beautiful."

This is not to say that graffiti writers and street artists in general eschew commercial opportunities. Some creators will, apart from producing works on the street, also participate in solo or group exhibitions, undertake commissioned work, or sell their works.[22] Whether creators are opposed to the commercialization of their work appears to depend on whether they are in control of the nature and range of uses of the work. As one creator said: "[S]treet artists have come in and kind of branched out in different ways, making furniture and making clothes. . . . I don't think it's selling out."

Where reproductions exploit the creator's works without recompense of the moral or economic variety, far less tolerance was expressed. Discussing the experience of a fellow street artist, a creator expressed distaste at a well-known clothing store that "blatantly ripped off" other artists' works.[23] A small number of creators also mentioned that their work had been copied by big clothing stores. At least one creator felt resigned to this happening: "[The company] has copied an idea of mine and made a t-shirt they sell in their shops, also places sell photographs of my street work printed on canvas. There's nothing that can be done about that."

It was, for a number of creators, problematic that their works were being reproduced without compensating them: "[W]hen you do street art you are allowing people to publish your work, but if they earn money you can control it." The street artist above does not consider copyright specifically as a means of control here but rather raises the expectation of being rewarded in some way. This came up for other creators too. For example: "If someone's making money out of my art I wouldn't mind seeing some of that money, but when someone takes a photograph, it's their photograph . . . [I]t can be stealing or it can be a new artwork in itself depending on how well that photograph's been taken."

Interestingly, for another street artist, changes made to a photograph of their work would not necessarily matter. Asked about this, a street artist said: "I don't know, I can't imagine it happening but it'd be interesting if it did . . . I'd have to see it before I made any judgment." This again points to the importance of sustaining the culture as a whole—for example, by sharing the work.

It is worth noting that the creators' expectations regarding copying by the public described here echo the prohibition in copyright law against reproduction without a copyright owner's permission.[24] The expectations also broadly track existing copyright exceptions in the United States and UK: fair use/fair dealing and the public place exceptions. First, the expectation that copying will be non-commercial seems to suggest something of the fair use[25] approach to copying. Second, the acceptance that publicly visible works will be reproduced is akin to the architectural works exception in U.S. law,[26] albeit covering pictorial works, and section 62 CDPA in the UK, which provides an exception to infringement for copying buildings and three-dimensional artistic works on public display. Yet the creators' more expansive approach to copying works on public display is, at the same time, potentially narrower than section 62 because it disallows commercial reproductions.[27]

Alongside the expectations creators have about how the public can interact morally with their works, they may well be aware that their creations are potentially protected by copyright; the question remains whether these rights can be enforced. As the remainder of the discussion shows, creators are not likely to have their expectations regarding appropriate public copying met by making copyright infringement claims.

Some creators, assuming they are able to meet the costs of litigation, have been pushed to seek redress under copyright law in an effort to prevent the exploitation of their works for commercial ends and without remuneration. Yet two recent examples of U.S. litigation relating to economic and moral rights highlight the shortcomings of copyright law in protecting graffiti writing and street art. Specifically, copyright law cannot protect the process of making these works nor the process of creation as part of a community, especially in the case of graffiti writing, by recognizing and protecting particular letter styles.

In relation to economic rights, for example, *Reece v. Ecko*[28] concerned, among other things, the ultimately successful motion to dismiss the author's copyright infringement claim regarding reproduction of graffiti writing—specifically, the stylized word "Dip"—in the defendant's video game.[29] In granting the motion, the court first identified the potentially protectable parts of the plaintiff's graffiti work, namely the name "Dip," letter style, color schemes, geometric shapes, and backgrounds.[30] As the discussion above suggests, for graffiti writers, the reproduction of a name, even in a different style, and/or the reproduction of certain elements of style including the style of letters and associated shapes, would contravene the norm against copying within the subculture. In *Reece v. Ecko* such subcultural sensitivities were considered somewhat obliquely.

The court noted that the expression of the word "Dip" was copyright protected and that for "graffiti art, the form of the lettering at issue is arguably central to the artistic expression of particular words"[31] and that the "personalized, artistic variations of lettering" were relevant to determining whether an infringement had occurred.[32] Nevertheless, the court found that Reece would not have been able to demonstrate copyright infringement: The two works were similar but the "ordinary observer" would not find that their "aesthetic appeal" was the same.[33] This, the empirical research suggests, is in marked contrast to graffiti writers who, in determining whether copying has occurred, are highly attuned to apparently minor stylistic differences. It remains to be seen what the outcome of a recent complaint by two graffiti writers over the appropriation of the stylized forms of "Revok" and "Steel" for clothing will be.[34] Even so, perhaps this is the start of a greater assertiveness by graffiti writers and street artists in resisting the exploitation of their works, as demonstrated in the recent complaint by Rime against Moschino and Jeremy Scott for reproducing his work on a dress worn by singer Katy Perry.[35]

With respect to moral rights, courts may also be willing to at least entertain such claims. In *Cohen v. G & M Realty*,[36] the District Court for the Eastern District of New York, while initially granting a restraining order, declined to grant a preliminary injunction to the plaintiffs to prevent the destruction of works of visual art at a site known as 5Pointz alleged by the plaintiffs to be works of "recognized stature" under VARA. In *Cohen*, the position was more fraught because the site itself was being demolished and redeveloped; the best chance to save the works lay in engaging with formal copyright law and making a moral rights claim. Yet the works were whitewashed before the judgment denying an injunction was handed down and the whole building was demolished some time afterward.[37] The merits of the claim for destruction of works of "recognized stature" are yet to be fully litigated,[38] but the reasoning in the judgment suggests that subcultural creativity in the form of graffiti writing and street art will prove difficult to protect. The stature of street art is difficult to demonstrate unless subcultural fame is taken seriously as a mark of esteem and street art is accepted to have (potentially) broader cultural significance that makes it worth protecting even when this conflicts with real property rights. Both the lack of recognition of the reproduction of style in *Reece v. Ecko* and the lack of recognition of the respect afforded to the works in *Cohen v. G & M Realty* present a marked contrast to the informal norms for regulating creativity among graffiti writers and street artists that are highly sensitive to the creative processes in a way that copyright law is not and, perhaps, cannot be.

Conclusion

Recent controversies over street art and graffiti creativity suggest that such creativity will continue to beguile members of the public and commercial enterprises alike. Copyright claims may increase and creators may come to find success. And yet, for graffiti writers and street artists, and indeed many of the other creators featured in this edited collection, intellectual property will only ever be a minor part of the normative framework within which they operate. Certainly, the outline of the norms regulating street art and graffiti writing presented here raises questions about the justifications for copyright and its efficacy in promoting and protecting creativity. Copyright law cannot, for example, protect the process of creating street art and graffiti; it cannot protect pleasure, nor can it promote the community-led development of subcultures. Copyright does not incentivize this form of creativity, nor does it present the most effective means for regulating it, at least as considered from within the relevant community itself.

Instead, this chapter suggests that graffiti writers and street artists adopt copyright-like norms—relating to copying by other creators as well as members of the public—which differ from copyright in that they are attentive to not only the subject matter of the works but also the process of creating them. Indeed, the discussion here suggests that creators' norms are not only directed at regulating works but are constitutive of communities of creators. Especially in the graffiti subculture, the norms demonstrate a communitarian approach to creativity in which the rules addressing individual behavior are finely balanced so as to protect individual creativity only to the extent that this enables graffiti culture as a whole to flourish by, for example, reducing the chances of works being destroyed and encouraging letter style innovations.

It seems unlikely that a more sensitive copyright system would be capable of incentivizing the production of more street art and graffiti writing. Even without such a system, street art and graffiti writing will likely continue to flourish. This continued flourishing, combined with the currently limited copyright enforcement where graffiti writing and street art are concerned, however, ought not to be used as an excuse to exploit the creativity of the street without regard to the moral or economic rights of its creators. Rather, it is another reason for wanting to reform copyright in a manner that is sensitive to the creative processes of the creators it seeks to protect and the culture(s) it hopes to promote.

NOTES

This chapter reflects a part of the empirical and other research (undertaken during doctoral studies at King's College London, 2008–2012) forming a detailed study of copyright and graffiti writing norms published as: Marta Iljadica, *Copyright Beyond Law: Regulating Creativity in the Graffiti Subculture* (Oxford: Hart Publishing, 2016).

1 In the United States, as a pictorial work under U.S.C. §102(a)(5); in the UK as an original artistic work under s. 1(1)(a) Copyright Designs and Patents Act 1988 ("CDPA"). Authors have certain exclusive rights including to reproduce their works: U.S.C. 17 §106(1); s. 16(1)(a) CDPA.

2 E.g., in the UK, under s. 1 Criminal Damage Act 1971.

3 Dotan Oliar and Christopher Sprigman, "There's No Free Laugh (Anymore): The Emergence of Intellectual Property Norms and the Transformation of Stand-Up Comedy," *Virginia Law Review 94*, no. 8 (2009): 1787–1867. Emanuelle Fauchart and Eric von Hippel, "Norms-Based Intellectual Property Systems: The Case of French Chefs," *Organization Science* 19, no. 2 (March 2008): 187–201; Aaron Perzanowski, "Tattoos & IP Norms," *Minnesota Law Review* 98, no. 2 (2013): 511–591. Rebecca Tushnet, "Payment in Credit: Copyright Law and Subcultural Creativity," *Law & Contemporary Problems* 70 (2007): 135–174; Luke McDonagh, *Does the Law of Copyright in the UK and Ireland Conflict with the Creative Practices of Irish Traditional Musicians? A Study of the Impact of Law on a Traditional Music Network*, PhD thesis (School of Law, Queen Mary, University of London, 2011). For an overview of creativity that flourishes despite copyright forbearance see: Elizabeth L. Rosenblatt, "A Theory of IP's Negative Space," *Columbia Journal of Law and the Arts* 34, no. 3 (2011): 317–365, 330–334.

4 For definitions of types of graffiti see, e.g., glossary in Henry Chalfant and James Prigoff, *Spraycan Art* (London: Thames & Hudson, 1987), 12. See also Craig Castleman, *Getting Up: Subway Graffiti in New York* (Cambridge, MA and London: MIT Press, 1982), 26–31.

5 Jeff Ferrell, *Crimes of Style: Urban Graffiti and the Politics of Criminality* (Boston: Northeastern University Press, 1996).

6 On the different treatment of graffiti writing and street art, see Alison Young, "Criminal Images: The Affective Judgment of Graffiti and Street Art," *Crime, Media, Culture* 8, no. 3 (2012): 297–314, 298–299.

7 For descriptions of the different "genres" of street art, see Alison Young, *Street Art, Public City: Law, Crime and the Urban Imagination* (Abingdon and New York: Routledge, 2014), 10–14.

8 On the hierarchy, fame, and recognition, see Mark Halsey and Alison Young, "The Meanings of Graffiti and Municipal Administration," *Australian and New Zealand Journal of Criminology* 35, no. 2 (2002): 165–186, 172–173. Also, see generally Nancy Macdonald, *The Graffiti Subculture: Youth, Masculinity and Identity in London and New York* (Hampshire and New York: Palgrave Macmillan, 2001).

9 Ferrell, *Crimes of Style*, 27–28.

10 Martha Cooper, and Henry Chalfant, *Subway Art* (London: Thames & Hudson, 1984). Referred to by a number of people during the fieldwork as the "bible of graffiti."

11 That intellectual property law might not be a good fit has been discussed in other contexts. See, e.g., Jessica Silbey, *The Eureka Myth: Creators, Innovators and Everyday Intellectual Property* (Stanford: Stanford Law Books, 2015); Kirsty Robertson,

"No One Would Murder for a Pattern: Crafting IP in Online Knitting Communities," in *Putting Intellectual Property in Its Place: Rights Discourses, Creative Labor, and the Everyday*, ed. Laura J. Murray et al. (Oxford and New York: Oxford University Press, 2014).

12 For an overview of the justifications for intellectual property, see William Fisher, "Theories of Intellectual Property," in *New Essays in the Legal and Political Theory of Property*, ed. Stephen R. Munzer (Cambridge: Cambridge University Press, 2001).

13 Jeff Ferrell and Robert D. Weide, "Spot Theory," *City* 14, no. 1–2 (2010): 48–62, 55.

14 For an overview of the UK/EU position, see Lionel Bently and Brad Sherman, *Intellectual Property Law*, 4th ed. (Oxford: Oxford University Press, 2014), 212–217.

15 The complexities of this norm in particular are beyond the scope of this chapter and are discussed elsewhere: Iljadica, *Copyright Beyond Law*.

16 Young, *Street Art, Public City*, 29. For another empirical account of street art in the city, including an exploration of street art creativity as a ritual, see Rafael Schacter, *Ornament and Order: Graffiti, Street Art and Parergon* (Farnham and Burlington, VT: Ashgate, 2014).

17 Ibid., 51.

18 For an account of how to choose and the norms relating to this choice, see Ferrell and Weide, "Spot Theory." Though train writing is outside the scope of this chapter, it is important to note that trains are an especially desirable surface for graffiti writers. For empirical accounts of the regulation of graffiti writing including train writing, see, e.g., Andrea Mubi Brighenti, "At the Wall: Graffiti Writers, Urban Territoriality, and the Public Domain," *Space and Culture* 13, no. 3 (April 15, 2010): 315–332.

19 Under the Visual Artists Rights Act ("VARA"), U.S.C. §106A.

20 On these dynamics, including on "off-limits" spots: ibid., 55.

21 Another creator assumed their work could not be legally protected: "The law doesn't protect the work, I don't know if [it] should." There may be a legal basis for this, at least in the UK where courts could potentially refuse to enforce copyright on public policy grounds (s. 171(3) CDPA) where a work was placed on property without permission.

22 For example, by selling prints, see Luke Dickens, "Pictures on Walls? Producing, Pricing and Collecting the Street Art Screen Print," *City* 14, no. 1–2 (2010): 63–81. This commercial engagement, however, is unlikely to be attractive to graffiti writers concerned first and primarily with writing their name and attaining fame within the graffiti subculture.

23 It is worth noting, however, that imbalances of bargaining power means that even licensing works would not necessarily prove lucrative. On the position of UK creators of visual art see Martin Kretschmer et al., *Copyright Contracts and Earnings of Visual Creators: A Survey of 5,800 British Designers, Fine Artists, Illustrators and Photographers* (CIPPM, Bournemouth University, 2011).

24 U.S.C. §501(a); U.S.C. §106 grants authors the exclusive right to reproduce their works. Similarly, in the UK, it is an infringement to copy: s. 17(1) CDPA.

25 Echoing, in particular, U.S.C. §107(1) by taking into account whether it is a "commercial" use.

26 U.S.C. §120(a): "ordinarily visible from a public place."

27 Since it appears that this would also allow for commercial copying. See New Zealand case decided on a very similar provision: *Radford v. Hallenstein Bros Limited*, HC Auckland CIV 2006–404–4881 [2007] NZHC 1654.

28 *Daniel Reece v. Marc Ecko Unltd et al.* 10 Civ. 02901 (JSR)(DF)(SDNY) 2011 US Dist Lexis 102199 201.

29 The motion to dismiss also included a moral right of attribution claim: *Reece v. Ecko*, 41–44.

30 Ibid., 24.

31 Ibid., 28.

32 Ibid.

33 Ibid., 36.

34 Complaint, *Williams et al. v. Roberto Cavalli SpA et al.* CV 14–06659-AB, February 12, 2015, Central District Court of California.

35 Complaint, *Tierney v. Moschino* CV 2:15-cv-05900, August 5, 2015, Central District Court of California, Western Division.

36 No. 13-CV-5612 (FB)(JMA) Eastern District of New York, November 20, 2013.

37 Cara Buckley and Marc Santora, "Night Falls, and 5Pointz, a Graffiti Mecca, Is Whited Out in Queens," *New York Times*, November 19, 2013, www.nytimes.com; Amand Holpuch, "New York's graffiti mecca 5Pointz torn down," *The Guardian*, August 22, 2014, www.theguardian.com.

38 Complaint, *Castillo et al. v. G&M Realty LP et al.* Case No. 15-CV-03230 (FB) (RLM) Eastern District of New York, June 3, 2015.

6

Subcultural Change and Dynamic Norms

Revisiting Roller Derby's Master Roster

DAVID FAGUNDES

I will never forget attending my first roller derby bout in November 2007. I was hooked at first sight by the sport's distinctive blend of counter-cultural style with serious athletic competition. The next year, listening to Chris Sprigman and Dotan Oliar present their work on comedians' norm-based regulation of their standup routines,[1] it occurred to me that roller derby offered not only an unparalleled entertainment spectacle, but also a natural experiment in the extralegal regulation of intangible property. A major feature that sets derby apart from other sports is skaters' use of pseudonyms in lieu of "government names" to identify competitors. Did derby girls care whether their names were unique? If so, how did they keep track of and enforce the uniqueness of their pseudonyms in a sport that was then transitioning from an obscure sub-culture to an international phenomenon?

In a 2012 article, "Talk Derby to Me: Intellectual Property Norms Governing Roller Derby Pseudonyms,"[2] I answered these and other questions about the roller derby community's use of social norms rather than law to regulate the distinctiveness of their skate names. While its subject matter was situated in the punk-inspired world of derby, the article's substantive inspiration was the tradition of legal literature about order in the absence of law that dates back to Ellickson's seminal work on the topic.[3] "Talk Derby to Me" sought to explain skaters' preference for non-legal rules over state-created law, and to explore how those rules operated in terms of their creation and enforcement. All of the conclu-sions rested on descriptive claims about how the derby world worked, including its highly close-knit character and the importance of main-taining unique skate names.

My research for that article concluded early in 2011, and while I was able to update it throughout that year,[4] it has now been about four years since I completed that snapshot of roller derby's name-regulation norms and practices. In this chapter, I revisit those norms and practices, and illustrate how they have—and have not—changed in the intervening time. This investigation enables a descriptive account of roller derby name norms that is dynamic rather than static, and allows insight into several under-explored issues: How norm-based regulation changes over time, what exogenous and endogenous forces lead to that change, and how this dynamic story further illuminates our understanding of how social ordering rooted in law contrasts with that rooted in norms. The first part of this chapter quickly introduces readers to the world of roller derby and summarizes my claims in "Talk Derby to Me." Next is an exploration of how roller derby's name-regulation norms have changed in the intervening four years in terms of subcultural preferences about name uniqueness, use of legal regulation, and preferred forms of norm governance. Finally, the discussion reflects on how these changes in norms, preferences, and practices interact, and what lessons they bear for the study of extralegal regulation and informal order generally.

Talk Derby to Me Then

This section provides two types of background. First, it provides a quick sketch of contemporary roller derby's unique subculture and style. Second, it reprises my substantive claims about the norms that prevailed in that community regarding performance pseudonyms and the means used to maintain the distinctiveness of those names.

Understanding how roller derby's name norms work requires an understanding of the derby world itself. Before outlining the substantive claims of "Talk Derby to Me," I will briefly describe the strange and wonderful world of contemporary roller derby.[5] While the origins of the sport may be traced to the 1800s, present-day roller derby has its roots in the robust alternative subculture of Austin, Texas, where a group of rowdy women gathered in the early 2000s to re-imagine derby as a blend between an all-girl, full-contact sport and a chaotic rock-and-roll show.[6] Roller derby provides its participants with much more than just an athletic extracurricular. In the countercultural niche within which it flourishes, derby provides a sense of community and identity to its participants.[7] Competitors forge close bonds thanks to both the rigors of training and shared aesthetic tastes.[8] The appeal of derby led to the sport's explosive growth from a handful of leagues in Austin, Los Angeles, and New York in 2003 to its current global status.[9] Derby leagues now span the globe, from Australia[10] to Argentina[11] and from Scotland[12] to South Africa.[13]

Derby skaters are not your usual athletes. The sport's countercultural roots give it a decidedly punk-rock aesthetic, so skaters tend to feature more tattoos and piercings than competitors in other sports, and the atmosphere at a bout has far more edge than a trip to the old ballpark.[14] What may set derby skaters apart from other athletes more than any other feature, though, is that they compete using fanciful and/ or fierce pseudonyms in lieu of their legal names. Spectators thus root for such varied competitors as Juana Beatin, Ivanna S. Pankin, Tara Armov, Helen Wheels, Penny Dreadful, or—my personal favorite—the Arrested Development-inspired Raven Seaward.[15] These pseudonyms— known in subcultural parlance as "skate names" or "derby names"—not only differentiate skaters in the eyes of their fans, but also provide a sense of identity within the derby community.[16] The continued vitality of derby names is, however, very much in question as the sport grows more popular and less limited to the alternative subculture from which it emerged.[17]

The regulation of derby names supplied the subject matter of "Talk Derby to Me." The need for regulation of derby pseudonyms grew out of skaters' desire that those pseudonyms remain unique. At least during the first decade of contemporary roller derby, skaters took very seriously the notion of name uniqueness, and typically reacted with rancor at the mere suggestion that someone would compete under a very similar or identical name.[18] This concern for name uniqueness derived from three separate considerations. First, derby names distinguish skaters, so that duplicative names would lead to confusion both among fans and within the derby world.[19] Second, and probably more important, skate names are a repository for the identities that skaters work so hard to create.[20] Third, while names are theoretically infinite, they are in practical terms increasingly scarce,[21] so that skaters attach high value to finding a truly distinctive moniker. These three considerations led to the descriptive conclusion that undergirded much of the analysis in "Talk Derby to Me": that the uniqueness of their pseudonyms is highly important to derby competitors.[22]

This descriptive claim about the importance of unique pseudonyms to roller derby competitors led to a pair of claims about how that uniqueness is maintained. The first is that skaters rarely, if ever, used state-created law as a means of managing and enforcing the exclusivity of their monikers. This may, at first, seem puzzling to those formally trained in law. A derby name is a kind of brand,[23] after all, and trademark law provides the primary legal route to protect marks associated with commercial goods and services.[24] In "Talk Derby to Me," though, I showed that while some skaters had indeed trademarked their skate names, this practice was very rare and limited to the dozen or so skaters who had sought to start a business related to derby or otherwise commercialize their reputations as top competitors.[25] In contrast to the legal centralist account that animated most literature on IP norms, the case of roller derby suggested that people may prefer norms over IP law even when the latter was substantively available.[26] Of course, one might argue that trademark law is unavailable to derby skaters, few of whom are wealthy, not because it is substantively inapplicable to nicknames, but rather because the time and expense of formally securing a trademark renders the option practically unavailable. While this conjecture is plausible, all of my research revealed that derby skaters' preference for norms arose independently of, rather than as a second-best response to, the absence of, legal options.[27]

So if skaters did not use trademark law to protect the distinctiveness of their pseudonyms, what did they use? The answer was the International Rollergirls' Master Roster, an elaborate skater-created and -managed registration system that, as of 2011, provided a reasonably effective means to maintain name uniqueness.[28] The Master Roster sought both to establish priority among skate names and to make this information public, so that if a new derby competitor ("fresh meat" in subcultural parlance) desired to adopt a nickname, she would be able to tell quickly from the Master Roster (which was and remains publicly available online[29]) whether that name had already been taken and was therefore off-limits.[30] The Master Roster also featured the "Derby Name Checker," a program written by Minnesota Rollergirl Soylent Mean, that would allow aspirants to quickly determine not only whether their exact proposed name was in use, but how many preexisting names were similar to it, and even how similar those names were to theirs.[31] While the Master Roster formalized the registration of roller derby names, the adjudication and enforcement of name priority was left to informal means such as shaming sanctions.[32] While far from perfect,[33] the Master Roster provided a flawed but basically effective means for managing the uniqueness of skaters' pseudonyms even as the derby world continued to grow explosively.[34]

Talk Derby to Me Now

The previous section highlighted three claims I made in "Talk Derby to Me": first, that the uniqueness of performance pseudonyms is highly important to roller derby skaters; second, that skaters eschew formal law, including the seemingly plausible option of trademark, as a means of ascertaining name uniqueness; and third, that the Master Roster provides skaters with a basically functional and generally accepted source of name regulation. I now revisit each of these propositions four years after completing my original research.

First, consider the proposition that formal law proves irrelevant to skaters' attempts to assure the uniqueness of their pseudonyms. When I finished writing "Talk Derby to Me," there were only about a dozen roller derby nicknames formally registered as trademarks with the Patent & Trademark Office (PTO).[35] My most recent search of the PTO's database revealed that this number has about tripled in the intervening four years, with thirty-nine roller derby names featured on the principal register.[36] At first glance, this several-fold increase may seem an indication that trademark has recently become an increasingly favored form of name protection for skaters.

Such a conclusion needs to be tempered by the background of roller derby's enormous expansion during that time. The sport has, by all accounts, undergone enormous growth since 2011, especially in terms of the number of participants both in the United States and abroad.[37] To provide just one indication of this ongoing expansion, the membership of the dominant roller derby trade association, the Women's Flat Track Derby Association (WFTDA), grew by more than 10 percent in December 2014 alone.[38] The increase in trademarked derby names could simply reflect the increase in the number of participants in the sport. Nor did my recent research reveal a cultural shift in how skaters regard the role of formal law in protecting their names. On the contrary, skaters still tend to find trademarks a waste of time, at least as a way of maintaining name protection within the derby world. New York Gotham Girl and Team USA star Sexy Slaydie considered the trademark option, but decided against it because her stature within the derby world would likely deter anyone from copying her skate name.[39] And less well known skaters who have contemplated trademarking their names have typically dismissed the idea as too time-consuming and expensive, as well as unnecessary in light of the derby community's informal norms against name copying.[40]

So if the relative increase in derby-name trademarks since 2011 is meaningful, it is probably not because the derby world has become more reliant on formal law in lieu of social norms. Rather, it is more likely a product of an increase in skaters' translating their notoriety and reputation on the track into derby-related businesses. As I noted in my earlier work: While skaters found trademark both cost-prohibitive and ineffective as a means for assuring name uniqueness within the derby community,[41] what linked the few skaters who registered their pseudonyms even then was that they were creating commercial entities linked to their names.[42] What they sought from trademark law was, like any other owner of a valuable brand, protection from infringement from the world at large.[43] Most of the new spate of registrations fit this model. For example, Bonnie D. Stroir, an elite skater for the San Diego Derby Dolls, has translated her derby expertise into a successful trade in coaching, seminars, and videos.[44] It is thus not surprising that in 2013, Bonnie applied for and received trademark registration for her skate name, under which she sells her derby-related services.[45] Finally, it is worth noting one skater's interesting—though outlier—opinion that in light of the recent decline in the importance of maintaining unique derby names, the minority of skaters who truly do care about having sole exclusive rights to their monikers should have to demonstrate that preference by going through the time and expense of securing a formal legal trademark.[46]

A major premise of "Talk Derby to Me" was that skaters consider the uniqueness of their names important, and the evidence from 2008–2011 certainly bore this out. While community norms theoretically allowed derby folks to share names, so long as the senior user of the name permitted it,[47] the Master Roster revealed as late as 2011 only a handful of instances in which this actually took place, though that number had grown to just under twenty by later that year.[48] The very premise of the Master Roster was that registrants should get property-like exclusive rights over their names,[49] reflecting the general consensus at that time in favor of uniqueness and against duplication.

More recent evidence, though, indicates that this norm has changed dramatically. Now, skaters tend to express opinions ranging from decreased concern to indifference or even scorn for the idea that they should insist on unique names. Sausage Roller of Manchester (UK) Roller Derby indicated that he is fully aware of and copacetic with at least two other skaters, one with an identical name (Sausage Roller of Bay Area Derby Girls) and one with a phonetically indistinguishable one (Sausage RollHer of Otway (Australia) Derby Girls.[50] Sexy Slaydie echoed this reaction from a different perspective, observing that if another skater took her name, she would find it laughable rather than offensive.[51] Each of these two expressions of indifference toward name duplication could be explained differently. Sausage's name-twins are so geographically far-flung as to eliminate any risk of confusion, while Slaydie enjoys enough international renown that a newbie seeking to take her name would likely be jeered off the track as a rank poser. A noob adopting the name "Sexy Slaydie" would be an absurdity on par with a garage band taking the name "U2." Slaydie also benefits from what some have termed the "unwritten rule" that you "can't take a name of a skater that's well known or famous," which would lead to "a lot of kickback" from the derby community.[52]

Still, these opinions do not square with the consensus I reported five years ago, where insistence on name uniqueness overbore even practical concerns such as likelihood of confusion.[53] Sausage and Slaydie's observations appear to reflect a more general trend, one noted by Frisky Sour, who observed that people care less about derby names than they used to five years ago. Comments on derby-related Internet sites confirm the increasing sense that name uniqueness is no longer a highly prized value in the derby community. Kim Penetrable expressed a typical opinion that is the polar opposite of the mine-alone approach that was typical some years ago: "[I]n my opinion, don't stress[] if someone else is using your name or similar, say hello, make a friend and keep skating!!"[54] The volunteers who run the new registration site Roller Derby Roster, discussed in more detail below, report that not a single skater has complained about their policy of registering duplicate derby names.[55]

The shift from a strong sense that names should be exclusively associated with individual skaters to the current norm that sharing names is acceptable represents a major change in the preferences that underlie the norms of the derby world. What explains this? Part of it may simply be a concession to the practical challenges of securing the exclusivity of derby names as derby continues its sprawling global growth.[56] The past four years have seen thousands, and possibly tens of thousands, of new participants join the sport, with an increasing percentage of this growth coming from outside the United States. The explosion of new skaters, combined with the related collapse of the Master Roster, as detailed below, left newbies unable to conclusively determine whether their preferred names are already in use.[57] Large-scale coordination is impossible without an effective coordination device. The rapid expansion of derby has also exacerbated the problem—complained about by fresh meat skaters even five years ago[58]—that nearly all the good derby names are taken.[59] Sexy Slaydie recently lamented that she hadn't heard of a great and truly original derby name in years.[60] In light of this, name exclusivity begins to seem like a selfish move by derby veterans at the expense of newbies, unless perhaps it promotes some other important value. And in the increasingly far-flung world of contemporary derby, it is hard to identify what that value would be. Most skaters agree that not copying the name of a local competitor is an important courtesy and means of avoiding name confusion, but with the exception of the few skaters who compete internationally, the confusion-based harm that a Tokyo-based Anita Kill would inflict on her Boston-based namesake is negligible.[61] The move away from insistence on name exclusivity may thus be not only a product of necessity, but also of this changing cost-benefit calculus as well.[62]

And, while derby names remain a distinctive and fun element of the sport for most observers and many participants, there is also a growing chorus of criticism about them. Some skaters have pointed out that the old approach whereby derby people would be entitled to an exclusive name was inconsistent with derby's community ethos. Roller derby is supposed to be a share-alike world, not one that is characterized by self-aggrandizement,[63] and the kinds of disputes that will necessarily arise in a world where skaters feel wronged by others using similar names threatens this sense of unity. Some skaters regard those who make an issue of the exclusivity of their names as creating unnecessarily selfish conflict that undermines derby's sense of amity. "It's definitely not sportswomanlike to get all bent out of shape," observed tennesseefrisky, "Derby is supposed to be unifying!"[64]

The decreasing concern about name uniqueness may also be due to the growing sense that derby is a serious sport that should be defined by the excellence of its athletes, not the countercultural vibe that set the sport apart in its early days.[65] In contrast to the former sense that names were central to one's identity within the sport, some skaters have dismissed them as mere "vanity plates,"[66] admonishing those who have "their panties in a bunch" over name disputes to "put on [their] big girl skates and . . . uh . . . skate."[67] "There's a lot more to this sport and having an impact," commented DCB, "than what you're called."[68] Related to and reflecting the decline in concern for derby name uniqueness is the increasing trend of skaters competing under their own names.[69] While this remains a minority practice,[70] it has been adopted by a majority of competitors in one league[71] and on some all-star teams,[72] and a number of skaters have cited it as part of the explanation for declining anxiety about the exclusivity of derby names.[73]

The move away from concern for unique derby names does not mean that skaters have grown entirely indifferent to who is skating under their name. Some skaters continue to insist on name exclusivity. New York Gotham Girl Fisti Cuffs, for example, declined a request by an Australian skater to compete under her same name.[74] And Rose City Roller Leet Seeking Missile has expressed her will that no one else will have her name[75]—even though she has retired from skating. Still other skaters remark that while they think tolerating name duplication is the right thing to do in an age of scarce monikers and numerous skaters, they would be somewhat disappointed to find their derby name used by another competitor.[76]

The foregoing two descriptive points raise a puzzle: If skaters cared deeply about name exclusivity, but declined to use formal law to enforce their names, how did they do it? The answer, at least some years ago, was a formal but extra-legal system by which administrators vetted the uniqueness of proposed names and posted approved ones to a publicly available registry, the Master Roster. I described the Master Roster in detail in "Talk Derby to Me," extolling its virtues as a form of spontaneous order but acknowledging the extent to which it was already beginning to crack under the strain of more submitted names than its handful of volunteer administrators could handle. Even when the Master Roster was first initiated, nearly a decade ago, skaters were complaining about long delays between submitting a name and its registration and appearance on the Roster.[77] Elsewhere, I have reflected on the challenges faced by a system that depended on a handful of people to register thousands of new names a month—as well as clear a years-long backlog of names that had already been submitted but were never processed.[78] In early 2012, there appeared to be some hope that the Master Roster could right itself. A new administrator, Elaina B., brought energy and diligence to the challenge, and through months of extracurricular effort had reduced the name backlog substantially.[79]

Nearly four years on, though, the Master Roster has finally ground to a halt. Those in the derby community with long enough memories speak of "olden times" when the Roster "worked just fine."[80] The current consensus is that derby has long since entered a post–Master Roster era, leading to a vacuum where there was once a sense of order.[81] Elaina B. confirms that by late 2012, even her valiant efforts at clearing the backlog of submitted names and managing the onslaught of new proposed names outstripped what little time she could spare with competing derby and family duties.[82] She threw in the towel in late 2012,[83] and the fact that no one volunteered to replace her likely illustrates the shared sense that the derby-name-registration system as it was then conceived could simply no longer function effectively.

The reason for the collapse of the Master Roster is no mystery. The structure of the Roster required the administrator, and perhaps a few helpers, to individually vet each name, process it, and post it online.[84] While some leagues had designated "name wranglers" whose job it was to clear names and submit them in groups, their work was invariably imperfect, so that the Roster administrator would still typically check whether a submitted name was identical to a preexisting one (in which case it would be rejected outright) or similar (in which case it would be returned to the proposing skater to seek clearance from the preexisting registrant). The degree of similarity would determine different outcomes—a highly similar name would likely be rejected, while for a less similar name, the administrator might ask the proposing skater to seek clearance from the senior user. Making these kinds of judgment calls meant that registering names on the Roster moved at a snail's pace. And, in addition to registration, administrators also had to negotiate complaints from dissatisfied skaters, answer questions from league name wranglers, and handle all other kinds of time-consuming minutiae. So when the number of submitted names continued to skyrocket throughout 2012, it slowly became clear that the system as currently conceived had become unsustainable.[85]

The collapse of the Master Roster did not, however, lead to a free-for-all in terms of duplicate name usage. The registration system did not constitute, but rather reflected, roller derby's name norms. The core derby principle—don't be a douche bag[86]—admonished skaters to treat each other with dignity, including not copying names, or at least asking permission to do so.[87] And competitors with international reputations report even today that the respect and notoriety they have earned on the track effectively prevents name duplication regardless of any formalized claim to their derby pseudonym.[88] What did change in the wake of the Master Roster's demise was any reliable notion that one's name was truly unique, since newly registered names stopped appearing in 2012 (and some report that their names never appeared despite earlier submissions). The result of this was an uptick in simultaneous name usage, though much more likely as the result of good-faith accidents in light of the global and numerical expansion of the derby population rather than intentional copying.[89]

Another reason that respect for derby names has persisted following the demise of the Master Roster is that other sites have risen up in its place to enable name registration, albeit with different administrative and conceptual approaches. Roller Derby Roster (RDR) is the closest lineal successor to the Master Roster.[90] The site is run by administrators who manage incoming name submissions and, once cleared, add them to a solely advisory database that includes all the names registered on the Master Roster,[91] as well as the ability to search the roster for preexisting names.[92] RDR requires registering skaters to first create an account, after which they can submit a name and modify it through their online profile. A skater who quits derby can, for example, indicate on her profile that her name has been "retired," and that status will be reflected on the name-registration database.[93] And in terms of name exclusivity, the site advises:

> We strongly suggest that you check all of your league names and skater names against the current version of the master roster before submitting them. Duplicate and similar league and skater names are allowed, but really, what is the fun in that? Most of us didn't get to choose the name our parents gave us, so here is your chance to go wild. Pick something that fits YOU, your unique personality and skating persona.[94]

RDR thus seeks to strike some balance between the need to tolerate duplicate names and the desire not to abandon the notion of originality entirely. Their official rules reflect the new norm that overlapping names are formally permitted, but appeal to skaters' sense of adventure to push in the direction of encouraging name uniqueness.[95]

Another relatively new site,[96] Derby Roll Call (DRC),[97] eschews the Master Roster and its administrative approach entirely. DRC is the brainchild of Manchester Roller Derby skater Sausage Roller, a computer programmer by trade who developed the site when he attempted to come up with a coding solution to the derby-names coordination problem. DRC allows skaters to register their names by filling out a simple online form with only their derby name and email address (league is requested as optional information). Once a skater has submitted these two pieces of information, their name will appear on DRC's list without any intervention by an administrator. DRC touts its automated approach as a way to allow its registry to "cope with the amazing growth our sport is seeing."[98] The lack of approval as a precondition for registration also necessarily means that the site tolerates duplicate names, but DRC embraces this openly: "Given how many people are finding out about derby every single day, it's inevitable two people will come up with the same name at the same time. Who are we to decide who got there first? The site's approach is to accept this duplication and try to inform everyone about the situation."

DRC thus serves a mainly informational function: It maximizes the ease with which skaters can register names in the hope that this will create awareness of preexisting identical and similar names.[99] The site also aspires to facilitate dialogue between skaters with similar names by sending emails to existing registrants when a new skater registers a name similar or identical to theirs,[100] further facilitating the ability of skaters to resolve name disputes among themselves. The site's approach has proven very popular. Since DRC was launched in early 2014, nearly 20,000 skaters have registered their names on the site.[101]

These two sites represent very different strategies to derby name registration in the post–Master Roster era. RDR uses the same basic structure as the Master Roster, but with some tweaks, most notably a greater degree of automation and streamlining of submitted data.[102] DRC represents a more radical departure from the Master Roster model, doing away with the notion of name approval entirely, and instead seeking only to provide information to and facilitate resolution between skaters regarding their names. It also bears noting that there are a handful of other specialized registration sites that (unlike RDR and DRC) are available only to a subset of the derby community. The Junior Roller Derby Association (for skaters under age eighteen) operates its own registry for which "the only rule is that the name be G—PG"[103]—i.e., that it not have sexual, violent, or other adult content. The list is not, however, meant to create enforceable, exclusive name rights for registrants. On the contrary, its administrators remind users that "this listing is *PURELY* for entertainment purposes! Please do not ask someone to change THEIR name at any time because it's 'too close to your name.'"[104] Roller Derby Australia also operates a registry that is limited to skaters from that country. It still uses the Master Roster model, where skaters (or leagues) submit names via email to one central administrator for approval.[105] Unsurprisingly, the Australian registry has experienced similar backlogs to the Master Roster, and has apparently received the same kind of impatient emails from skaters frustrated that their names have not been registered more promptly.[106] In contrast to other sites, the Australian registry does not openly take a position on the registration of duplicate names.

Cultural Change and Social Norms

In the past four years, attitudes toward skate names in the roller derby world have undergone a significant change. What skaters tended to want in the early days of derby's countercultural resurgence was name uniqueness. As a result, the informal regulatory system that emerged to manage derby names used exclusion-oriented property strategies. The Master Roster provided a basis for claiming a derby name exclusively, so long as a skater successfully showed that she was the first to register it. This is a race approach to first possession, similar to law's means of securing property rights in wild animals and works of authorship, and the winner of that race could expect that no similar names would be registered without her permission.[107] The most significant shift in the derby rosters that have arisen in the wake of the Master Roster's desuetude is not that they use technology to streamline the name submission process, but that the new rosters reject the idea of name uniqueness. RDR tolerates the idea of duplicate names, but acknowledges that they are acceptable. DRC, though, embraces the idea of name duplication as a necessity in the increasingly large and global new roller derby world.

This regulatory change raises a question: Why have a registry at all if name uniqueness is a thing of the past? What is the point of letting the community know you are using a name if this will not prevent others from using the same name? The answer is coordination. Traditionally, property owners register their interests, such as in chains of title memorialized in public records. This public memorialization brings the twin advantages of securing the priority of an owner's interest and facilitating coordination with other interested parties: If you discover while searching title that a parcel of land is saddled with a mortgage, that enables you to avoid acquiring an encumbered property, or to enter into a negotiation with the mortgagee to resolve the cloud on title. The new derby name registries may not declare a name to belong exclusively to a skater, but they do still serve this valuable coordination function. If a newbie skater thinks up a name, the fact that it has been registered already does not mean that she cannot use the name, but it would certainly affect how she approaches its use. It may mean that the moniker no longer appeals to her, if she has a strong desire to find a truly unique name. But if the skater does continue to want the name, the registration may allow her to determine whether—despite the increasing tolerance for duplicate names—she considers the other skater's name too similar, or their location too proximate to permit name duplication as a matter of courtesy.[108] Finally, discovering a preexisting name on a registry is useful because, as with physical property, it enables dialogue between skaters about how and whether to share the name. DRC, for example, features information about a skater's league when it returns names similar to a proposed one, thus making it easier to locate and contact skaters who already use a proposed pseudonym. And DRC's in-process function that seeks to notify skaters when a name similar to theirs has been registered would do even more to facilitate the kind of dialogue that furthers the coordination function of the new roller derby name registries.

Two trends emerge from this analysis: The norms governing roller derby names have moved from exclusion to sharing;[109] and the systems used to regulate those names have moved from seeking to secure unique names to facilitating coordination between skaters with interest in the same name. Both norms about name exclusivity and the systems used to regulate names have changed. This points toward an interesting and difficult question regarding the causal relationship between these two trends. Did the collapse of the Master Roster force the derby community to become more tolerant of name sharing? Or did other trends—globalization and explosive growth—lead to the collapse of name-exclusivity expectations, so that the new registries simply reflected this preexisting trend? This kind of chicken-and-egg question may not be possible to answer, so it is important to be cautious about any conjectures. One skater did suggest that she thought the notion of unique derby names could have survived had the Master Roster not collapsed, suggesting that the inability to secure exclusive name rights led skaters to abandon their old expectations. Frisky Sour observed that the difficulty of registering a name on the Master Roster—which typically required complying with league prerequisites and having your name approved by your league's name wrangler—made skaters value their names more when they were finally approved under the old regime. But most skaters emphasize independent explanations for the new norm of name openness, chiefly the impossibility of finding unique derby names for thousands of new skaters per year, but also the move from derby as a subculture where everyone knows each other into a global sport and widely shared passion. There is little evidence, though, that the Master Roster's demise occurred simply because no one cared about derby name exclusivity anymore. On the contrary, the evidence indicates that concern for names persists, but that this concern has changed in its character and intensity.

The evidence is too thin to assay any strong conclusions, but one possibility is that the above chicken-and-egg phrasing of the problem (did the collapse of the Master Roster lead to increased indifference to derby names, or vice versa?) miscasts the inquiry. Another explanation, and likely the most plausible one, is that they were not causally related to each other, but instead were different products of the same external phenomenon. The numerical growth of skaters and the international reach of the sport made it impossible for the Master Roster—at least, as it was traditionally constructed with no automation and one or only a few administrators—to function. These two trends also eroded skaters' concern for unique derby names because it was increasingly difficult to find any such names, and the possibility of offending or being confused with skaters elsewhere in the world also diminished. Both the strong preference for exclusive derby names and the major system used to preserve it were epiphenomenal of each other. The recent changes along both of these metrics were, in all likelihood, caused by the geographical and absolute growth of roller derby itself.

At first glance, this updated account of the extralegal regulation of roller derby names may look like a story about the failure of such regulation: The Master Roster worked well enough to a point, but when demands grew too great, it collapsed. This was not because it was impossible to register all submitted derby names. Rather, it was because the time investment required to process those names overwhelmed the time and resources available even to committed volunteers for whom the Master Roster was a labor of love.[110] This failure must be attributed to the norm-based character of roller derby's name regulation system. The defining characteristic of social norms is, of course, that they operate independently of the state. Were the Master Roster a state-supported bureaucracy, it would likely have persisted despite roller derby's expansion. For instance, the various state-funded Departments of Motor Vehicles continue to do their dreary work, despite that they are labors of love for no one. Indeed, this may still have been true had roller derby been a for-profit sport with a professional association that embraced name registration as a function on which it was willing to expend capital.[111]

Upon closer examination, though, the localized failure of the Master Roster is more accurately seen as part of the overall success of norm-based regulation of roller derby names generally. The Master Roster's demise took place at a time when community expectations about exclusive derby names were already diminishing. Its collapse would look very different if it had happened in an environment when skaters still felt very strongly about unique names, so that the absence of a registry created chaos and an inability to secure name exclusivity. Instead, though, the Master Roster's demise was thus part of an overall change in name ownership norms. By the time it had ceased to function in late 2012, its relevance was much more limited than it was even a couple of years previously.

The decline of the Master Roster may be recast as a success story for derby norms for another reason. Though the existence of a registry is very useful, it is not absolutely necessary to maintain roller derby name norms. Even absent a central registry, skaters can and do still research nicknames they imagine for themselves. Often when they find from word of mouth or another league's website that a preexisting skater has the same name, they will reach out to contact that skater to ask whether she would tolerate use of a similar name. Roller derby's community ethic leads to a degree of self-policing in name usage—even absent a registry—that is governed by norms of courtesy rather than exclusivity. Some degree of name exclusivity persists in the post–Master Roster era for a related reason: Top skaters have earned enough fame and credibility that they have something like brand recognition. International stars like Sexy Slaydie or Fisti Cuffs, or old-school derbyists who have successful derby businesses like Ivanna S. Pankin or Bonnie Thunders, don't need to worry too much about new skaters taking their names, since that would seem like an outrageous and inauthentic ripoff that no one would take seriously.[112] These skaters' brands are so strong that they need fear neither confusion nor dilution.

But perhaps the most compelling reason that the decline of the Master Roster is a story of the success, not the failure, of norm-based regulation of derby names is that it facilitated the rise of registries that better reflect the emergent tolerance for name duplication in the roller derby community. The Master Roster, as we have seen, was premised on a property-like notion of exclusion: Once your name was registered there, it was understood that you had an informal, subcultural entitlement to use that name to the exclusion of another. The registries—RDR and especially DRC—that arose following the collapse of the Master Roster reflected a very different ownership strategy that made name-sharing presumptive, and these registries were constructed in order to facilitate this coordination approach rather than the exclusion approach that prevailed before. So while the decline of the Master Roster was not a conscious response to the decreasing interest in name uniqueness, it still fortuitously dovetailed with this change in the derby community's attitude toward their pseudonyms.[113] The demise of the Master Roster may thus be regarded as a positive development, retiring a registry that no longer reflected prevailing norms, and paving the way for the emergence of systems that were based on and better reflected those new norms.

Regulation via social norms, as the story of the Master Roster's decline illustrates, is likely more susceptible to change than is regulation via formal law. The replacement of the Master Roster by newer registries happened organically. It did not require the approval of legislatures or the intervention of judges. So is this malleability a feature or a bug of regulation by social norms? The answer likely depends heavily on context. The story recounted here is an optimistic one of creative desuetude, where the decline of the Master Roster created the space within which alternative systems arose that more accurately reflected the derby community's new attitude toward skate names. Here, the malleability of norms-based regulation worked well in concert with changing subcultural preferences, and the insistence of WFTDA not to effect centralized control of the Master Roster appears wisely prescient. But it bears reflecting that this was not the only possible outcome. The Master Roster ceased to function at the same time that the derby community's insistence on name exclusivity weakened, but it did not cease functioning *because* of this norm change. Had the Master Roster broken down while skaters still had a stronger desire for name uniqueness, its unavailability would have been a problem rather than a blessing.

Conclusion

The great studies of norms—Ellickson, Bernstein, Ostrom—tend to take long, detailed looks at particular systems of informal order. This approach generates deep analysis and important insights about how such systems function. But these pictures tend to be static. They are snapshots, albeit highly detailed and useful ones, that exist outside a temporal context. This chapter, by contrast, has sought to introduce the element of time into the study of social norms by examining how the extralegal regulation of roller derby names has changed since I completed my research for "Talk Derby to Me" in 2011. Those changes have been substantial. While state-created law (trademark) remains marginal, the Master Roster is no more, having collapsed under the weight of too many submitted names for one volunteer administrator to handle. Even more significantly, the desire for name exclusivity on which the Roster was based has also eroded, replaced by a new tolerance for name sharing. This norm shift has ushered in a new generation of derby name registries that seek to facilitate coordination rather than exclusion.

Examining norm systems—or at least this one—across time showcases the greater pliability of such systems as compared to state-created legal regimes. That norms-based regulation has this quality is not terribly surprising; it is a familiar point that the apparatus of the state—whether the sclerotic legislative process or the deeply conservative common law approach to adjudication—slow the passage of new legislation and the establishment of new rules of law. Norm-based systems, unhindered by the state's administrative ballast, can respond more quickly to changes in social norms. This claim is solely descriptive. While the story of derby name regulation is an object lesson in which the flexibility of extralegal regulation worked well in combination with developing social norms, this may not always be the case. It remains necessary to state the implications of this case study conservatively: One factor that recommends, or disfavors, social norms is the appeal of relatively rapid over glacial systemic change.

NOTES

Thanks to Kristen Brown, Peter Gerhart, Blake Hudson, and Jessica Roberts as well as participants at the 2014 Creativity Without Law conference at Case

Western Reserve Law School and the 2015 Annual Meeting of the Association of Law, Property & Society for thoughtful suggestions about this project. And as always, thanks to the derby folks, without whom this project would not have been possible—Elaina B., Frisky Sour, Ivanna S. Pankin, Sausage Roller, and Sexy Slaydie, among many others.

1 This was the IP Scholars' Conference (IPSC) at Stanford University in August 2008, where Sprigman and Oliar presented "There's No Free Laugh Anymore: The Emergence of Intellectual Property Norms and the Evolution of Stand-Up Comedy," 94 *Virginia Law Review* 1787 (2008).

2 90 *Texas Law Review* 1093 (2012).

3 This work, of course, is Robert Ellickson, *Order Without Law: How Neighbors Settle Disputes* (1991).

4 I chose to include the conclusion, "The Twilight of Derby Names," in "Talk Derby to Me," 1149–52, shortly before the article went to press, following conversations with skaters who were increasingly skeptical about the practice of skating under pseudonyms.

5 I summarize the history and context of roller derby in "Talk Derby," see ibid., 1099–1115, and mostly cite that article in this chapter's descriptive account of derby. But for those justifiably fascinated by the sport, two outstanding books that provide a deeper examination of its roots and culture are Jennifer "Kasey Bomber" Barbee and Alex "Axles of Evil" Cohen, *Down & Derby: The Insider's Guide to Roller Derby* (2010) and Catherine Mabe, *Roller Derby: The History and All-Girl Revival of the Greatest Sport on Wheels* (2007).

6 Fagundes, "Talk Derby," 1100.

7 Ibid., 1101.

8 See Barbee and Cohen, *Down & Derby*, 72–73 (discussing community as a source of derby's appeal).

9 Fagundes, "Talk Derby," 1100–1101 (discussing the global expansion of roller derby).

10 E.g., the Sydney Roller Derby League, http://www.sydneyrollerderby.com/.

11 E.g., Buenos Aires Roller Derby, http://buenosairesrollerderby.com/.

12 E.g., Glasgow Roller Derby, http://www.glasgowrollerderby.com/.

13 E.g., C-Max (Johannesburg) Roller Derby, http://cmaxrollerderby.com/.

14 Back when I was going to LA Derby Dolls bouts regularly, for example, the Dolls were supported by gothically styled "fearleaders" in lieu of cheerleaders and their bouts featured NSFW—but highly entertaining—narration by Evil E.

15 Get it? If not, see "5 Tips on How to Create Your Roller Derby Name," *Caroline on Crack* (July 13, 2010), http://carolineoncrack.com (quoting Raven explaining her name).

16 Fagundes, "Talk Derby," 1102–08 (discussing the relevance and importance of derby names within the derby community).

17 See ibid., 1151 (reflecting on the then-nascent phenomenon of skaters rejecting pseudonyms and competing under their government names).

18 Ibid., 1108–09 and nn.76–79 (quoting Cheap Trixie as saying, "When you bite on someone's style you look like a douche and so uncool").

19 Ibid., 1110–11 (explaining that this concern is especially salient as derby competitions become national and international).

20 Ibid., 1111–12 (noting that overlapping name usage inflicts dignitary harm on preexisting users' identities within the derby world).

21 This is because the growth of derby has expanded faster than available pop culture references has grown, so that skaters often find themselves thinking of five or six names before they come up with one that has not been used before. Ibid., 1112–13.

22 Ibid., 1113.

23 Ibid., 1111 (discussing skate names as bases for subcultural skater identity); see also the interview with Sexy Slaydie (observing that skaters choose names to build identities around them).

24 See generally 15 U.S.C. §§1051, 1053, 1114 (establishing protection for marks used in connection with goods and services used in commerce); e.g., *Hirsch v. S.C. Johnson & Son, Inc.*, 280 N.W.2d 129, 130 (Ill. 1979) (upholding the registration of the "Crazylegs" nickname for former football star Elroy Hirsch).

25 Ibid., 1129–30.

26 Ibid., 1131–32 (discussing the legal-centralist implications of much of the IP norms literature); e.g., see chapter 1, "Norms-Based Intellectual Property Systems," by Emmanuelle Fauchart and Eric von Hippel (arguing that "conditions [are] favorable to norm-based IP systems" when "any extant law-based . . . IP protection [is] inadequate or unsatisfactory").

27 Fagundes, "Talk Derby," 1132–33 and n.202 (citing evidence from founding members of early roller derby leagues that norm-based derby name regulation arose independently of consideration of legal alternatives).

28 See ibid., 1114–29 (discussing the operation of the Master Roster generally).

29 As I explain below, though, the Master Roster has ceased to include new names, so that its utility is limited to the informational function of reflecting names that were registered as of late 2012. http://www.twoevils.org/rollergirls/.

30 Fagundes, "Talk Derby," 1118 and n.128 (citing as the first rule of the Master Roster the "uniqueness requirement [that] only one skater can skate under a given name").

31 Ibid., 1119 (describing and explaining the operation of the Name Checker).

32 Ibid., 1121–31 (discussing adjudication and enforcement).

33 One constant complaint lodged by skaters was the lapse of time after they submitted their name and before it was approved and posted by the site's administrators. This gap was due to the understandable challenges undertaken by the administrators of clearing thousands of submitted names per month, which in addition to day jobs and league responsibilities, could be an overwhelming task. See Dave Fagundes, "The Varieties of Motivation and the Problem of Supply: A Reply to Professor Ellickson," 90 *Texas Law Review*. See also 311, 313–14 (2012). As I discuss below in more detail, it was the understandable inability of the site's administra-

tors to manage the ever-increasing influx of names that led to the Master Roster's desuetude.

34 Fagundes, "Talk Derby," 1117 ("[W]hile there are (and have been for some time) movements afoot to supplant [the Master Roster] with a newer, better version, it remains for now the dominant, unique means by which roller derby girls can register their skate names[.]").

35 See ibid., 1129–30 (discussing rare instances of derby girls registering their skate names as trademarks). The PTO website is publicly available at http://www.uspto.gov/.

36 I performed this search on April 12, 2015, using the Trademark Electronic Search System (TESS) on www.pto.gov. I searched the "goods and services" field of all live and dead trademarks for the phrase "roller derby," which returned 188 results. I then sorted through each entry to identify the marks that were claimed by individual skaters as opposed to leagues, derby-related businesses, or other entities.

37 Interview with Sausage Roller (commenting on the roller derby explosion, including internationally, over the last several years).

38 WFTDA added 29 leagues in December 2014, raising its total league membership from 273 to 302. "Roller Derby Rankings, Tournaments, and Growth," *Derby Central* (Jan. 13, 2015), http://www.derbycentral.net.

39 She explained that because of her international profile, everyone is aware that the name Sexy Slaydie belongs to her, and other skaters would consider it a painfully unoriginal breach of subcultural norms even to try to use it.

40 Interview with Brett Rogers (explaining that he decided not to trademark his daughter's junior derby name for these reasons). These are more or less exactly the same reasons that skaters reported for their indifference to registering their skate names when I researched "Talk Derby to Me." See Fagundes, "Talk Derby," 1132–33.

41 One skater reported that her teammate had "received a cease and desist letter from a skater with the same name." Comment of Breaking Back Sunday, in "Duplicate roller derby names," *littleanecdote.com* (Jan. 23, 2014), http://littleanecdote.com. But this remains an isolated and unconfirmed reference, and Breaking confirmed the anomalousness of this purported resort to formal law: "To me, that was just so extreme and against the spirit of the derby world." Ibid. Other skaters concurred. See comment of Frisky Sour, ibid. ("YIKES.").

42 Fagundes, "Talk Derby," 1129–30 (noting, for example, that O.G. skaters Trish the Dish and Ivanna S. Pankin both trademarked their names as part of their starting Sin City Skates, a business that vends derby-related goods).

43 For this reason, leagues and some teams tend to trademark their names as well. Ibid., 1130 and n.192.

44 See Bonnie D. Stroir Official Site. http://www.bonniedstroir.com/.

45 PTO word mark BONNIE D. STROIR, serial no. 85717219, approved for final registration Apr. 23, 2013.

46 See comment of VicGoria, in "Duplicate roller derby names," *littleanecdote.com* (Jan. 23, 2014), http://littleanecdote.com ("My two cents is: If you care enough about your derby name then you can trademark it like some skaters have").

47 See Fagundes, "Talk Derby," 1118 and n.128.

48 Ibid. 1121, n.147. From today's vantage, this relatively rapid growth in name-sharing likely represents one of the first instances of the eroding concern for name uniqueness.

49 For example, the Master Roster's accompanying rules stated that duplicate names were allowed only with the permission of the prior skater who had registered the name. Ibid. 1118, n.128.

50 Interview with Sausage Roller.

51 Interview with Sexy Slaydie.

52 Email exchange with Frisky Sour, June 9, 2015 (on file with author).

53 Fagundes, "Talk Derby," 1110–13 (discussing this point and citing examples).

54 Comment of Kim Penetrable, in "Duplicate roller derby names," *littleanecdote. com* (Jan. 23, 2014), http://littleanecdote.com; see also comment of Jessica Rabid, ibid. (noting that she learned another skater is using her name, but "I don't really mind"); SINnamon Challenge, ibid. ("Should someone else take SINnamon Challenge, chances are I'd hardly notice.").

55 Email from Roller Derby Roster Support, June 16, 2015 (on file with author).

56 Interview with Sausage Roller (explaining the decline in concern over name exclusivity as a function of the growth of derby from a few hundred skaters to nearly a hundred thousand); email from Roller Derby Roster Support, June 16, 2015 (on file with author) ("[S]katers understand the sport is growing and eventually duplication becomes a side effect of that growth.").

57 See comment of DCB, ibid. (noting that "in the time since the 'demise' of the fully functional twoevils [Master Roster] . . . duplicates have become more present (mostly by accident)").

58 See Fagundes, "Talk Derby," 1112 n.92 (discussing The Boogiewoman's regret that she ended up skating under her fifth- or sixth-choice name).

59 See comment of Kim Penetrable, in "Duplicate roller derby names," *littleanecdote. com* (Jan. 23, 2014), http://littleanecdote.com ("Considering the growth of roller derby, it's not possible that there are enough unique names out there that aren't at least close to someone else's already used name.").

60 Interview with Sexy Slaydie.

61 See, e.g., comment of SINnamon Challenge, in "Duplicate roller derby names," *littleanecdote.com* (Jan. 23, 2014), http://littleanecdote.com (explaining that because she skates in Japan, she would be indifferent to uses of her name elsewhere in the world). This, too, represents a different sense than the one I observed in the derby community several years ago. Then, skaters insisted on the exclusivity of their names regardless of concerns about likelihood of confusion. See Fagundes, "Talk Derby," 1106–08 (discussing non-confusion-based reasons for insistence on name exclusivity).

62 Frisky Sour observed that "I would be mildly bummed if someone used Frisky Sour, but that's not a compelling argument against duplicate names." Posting of Frisky Sour, in "Duplicate roller derby names," *littleanecdote.com* (Jan. 23, 2014), http://littleanecdote.com. Her comment epitomizes the new perspective on derby names, prioritizing the community need for good derby names above her personal preference for exclusivity.

63 Skaters who are self-interested at the expense of the group are said to violate derby's core principle: "don't be a douchebag." See Fagundes, "Varieties of Motivation," 317 n.33.

64 Comment of tennesseefrisky, in "Duplicate roller derby names," *littleanecdote.com* (Jan. 23, 2014), http://littleanecdote.com; see also posting of Breaking Back Sunday, ibid. (characterizing a skater's sending a cease-and-desist letter as "so extreme and so against the spirit of derby").

65 Comment of Kim Penetrable, in "Duplicate roller derby names," *littleanecdote.com* (Jan. 23, 2014), http://littleanecdote.com (dismissing the importance of exclusive derby names in part due to the effort to "make the game more sport than spectacle if you get my drift, no fishnets, but instead compression tights, often called Grown-Up derby by my team mates"); see also the interview with Sexy Slaydie (agreeing with the proposition that contemporary roller derby is much more professional than it used to be, and that the sport's focus is increasingly on athletic competition rather than aesthetic or alternative flair).

66 Comment of Kim Penetrable, in "Duplicate roller derby names," *littleanecdote.com* (Jan. 23, 2014), http://littleanecdote.com.

67 Comment of VicGoria, ibid.; see also email from Roller Derby Roster Support, June 16, 2015 (on file with author) ("At the end of the day, playing roller derby is about athleticism, teamwork, and having fun. If your heart is set on having the same name as someone 1,000 miles away from you, who are we to tell you that you cannot take on that persona.").

68 Comment of DCB, in "Duplicate roller derby names," *littleanecdote.com* (Jan. 23, 2014), http://littleanecdote.com.

69 I noted this then-nascent trend in "Talk Derby to Me," 1107 n.71 ("It bears noting that a small number of skaters have begun skating under their legal names.").

70 Interview with Sexy Slaydie (noting that most skaters still use and enjoy pseudonyms despite a vocal minority who do not).

71 A majority of skaters for Denver Roller Derby use their own names. DRD also changed its league name from "Denver Roller Dolls" to solidify the legitimacy of the sport in the local community. "Rebranding for Equality: Dolls Set Precedent with 'Denver Roller Derby' League Name," *DenverPost.com* (Feb. 9, 2015), http://yourhub.denverpost.com.

72 E.g., Team Legit, https://www.facebook.com (a flat-track all-star team that used government names as far back as 2008, and took its name in part from this feature).

73 Comment of Roarshock Tess, in "Duplicate roller derby names," *littleanecdote.com* (Jan. 23, 2014), http://littleanecdote.com ("All in all, I really don't mind duplicate

names. Personally, I think we should just make a move to use our real names [don't hate me].").

74 See interview with Sexy Slaydie (recounting this story about Fisti Cuffs). What is less clear, interestingly, is whether the Australian skater actually honored Fisti's admonition and chose a different name.

75 Email from Frisky Sour ("my friend swears that no one else will ever be Leet Speaking Missile EVER").

76 See posting of Frisky Sour, in "Duplicate roller derby names," *littleanecdote.com* (Jan. 23, 2014), http://littleanecdote.com (reflecting that she would be "mildly bummed if someone used Frisky Sour").

77 Fagundes, "Talk Derby," 1149–50 and n.279 (discussing increasing problems with and complaints about the Master Roster even four and five years ago).

78 See generally Fagundes, "Varieties of Motivation."

79 Elaina B. had high hopes at the time she initially signed on to help with the Master Roster around late 2011. Ibid., 313 ("If I say I'm going to do a job, I'm going to do it. Even if it kills me. And I'm going to do it right."). As of early 2012, she had actually reduced the Master Roster backlog significantly. Ibid., 312 n.4.

80 Posting of Frisky Sour, in "Duplicate roller derby names," *littleanecdote.com* (Jan. 23, 2014), http://littleanecdote.com. Frisky actually pegs the days when the Roster "worked just fine" as around 2007, noting that "a few years later" delays were already becoming problematic. Ibid.

81 See comment of Kim Penetrable, ibid. (lamenting that "[i]f [the Master Roster] worked, then the whole unique name thing could probably have worked").

82 Interview with Elaina B.

83 Ibid.

84 The puzzle that I've never been able to solve is why the organizers of the Master Roster insisted that names had to be registered only by a handful of administrators. The stated rationale was always that the administrators had to be consistent with their choices and that too many decision makers would lead to disorganization and confusion. But any such downsides seem minimal in comparison with the upsides of actually getting enough names registered. The Master Roster seemed ideally suited for the kind of community-based crowd-sourcing solution that roller derby has so effectively used elsewhere.

85 Interview with Elaina B.

86 See Fagundes, "Varieties of Motivation," 317 n.33 (discussing roller derby's ubiquitous no-douchebag rule).

87 Fagundes, "Talk Derby," 1118 and n.128.

88 Interview with Sexy Slaydie.

89 See comment of DCB, email from Roller Derby Roster Support, June 16, 2015 (on file with author) (noting that "in the time since the 'demise' of the fully functional twoevils [Master Roster] . . . duplicates have become more present (mostly by accident)").

90 The site acknowledges that it was "adopted from the original Roller Derby Master Roster[.]" http://www.rollerderbyroster.com ("guidelines" tab). RDR's volunteer managers also report that "[t]o help keep the legacy of the original names we imported the list that Two Evils had." See email from Roller Derby Roster Support, June 16, 2015 (on file with author).

91 Nothing about the original Master Roster suggested it was mandatory—in fact, many skaters noted that it simply enabled courtesy—but RDR takes an even lighter approach, stating that the site "has been put together just for fun, and to carry on the spirit and importance of the Roller Derby pseudonym." Ibid.

92 Ibid. ("search" tab).

93 These innovations have the salubrious effect of both cutting down on and streamlining name registrations. The Master Roster simply required that any skater could submit derby names via email, so that administrators themselves had to enter information that skaters input on RDR via their profiles. See Fagundes, "Talk Derby," 1120 (discussing the technical details of how skate names were submitted to the Master Roster, including the role of "name wranglers").

94 http://www.rollerderbyroster.com ("guidelines" tab).

95 The site also suggests, per Slaydie's suggestion, that in the case of very famous skaters, duplication is unacceptable. "The world isn't big enough for two 'Bonnie Thunders,'" RDR admonishes. Ibid. ("guidelines" tab). Bonnie is a star jammer for the New York Gotham Girls. See http://www.gothamgirlsrollerderby.com.

96 Derby Roll Call launched on January 20, 2014. See interview with Sausage Roller, April 14, 2015.

97 Derby Roll Call. http://www.derbyrollcall.com/.

98 Ibid. ("The registration process is automated, allowing it to cope with the amazing growth our sport is seeing.").

99 For this reason, the DRC home page offers a simple name-search functionality that returns all identical and similar nicknames to a given proposed name. For example, the proposed name "Ida Slapter" has ten similar names (including Ida Stroyder and Ida Slapabitch) but no identical matches on the site.

100 See http://derbyrollcall.com ("You may also be emailed if somebody submits an identical or similar name to you. Sausage Roller told me that this feature of the site remains in development. See interview with Sausage Roller.").

101 Ibid. ("Number of registered names: 19,724.").

102 See email from Roller Derby Roster Support, June 16, 2015 (on file with author) ("What is different about our site is that people submit their own names and then they are approved by us with the click of a button. Once approved you can come in and edit your number or league or even change your status. . . . [T]he automation helps us stay on top of things significantly.").

103 Junior Roller Derby Names Listing. http://www.juniorrollerderby.org ("Any names that are deemed inappropriate for an organization such as the JRDA, will be removed without warning.").

104 Ibid.

105 Derby names roster registration. http://www.rollerderbyau.net/ (stressing in bold-face and red type that "we currently only have one volunteer tending to the roster updates").

106 This is clear from the site's twice asking visitors in boldface, underlined text to "please be patient" with the registration process. http://www.rollerderbyau.net. The site also implores users to "Please refrain from sending check-up emails [be-cause] we often have limited time to process emails, enquiries about your roster fill our inbox and delay roster updates."

107 There were several instances of duplicate names registered on the Master Roster, but this was permitted only when the senior skater permitted the junior skater to do so. The notion that prior registration gave skaters the right to share or decline to share their name illustrates the exclusivity approach that animated the Master Roster regime.

108 These factors remain relevant even in the post–Master Roster age. Sausage Roller's tolerance for duplicate names was to a large extent a result of the other skaters' be-ing located on other parts of the globe, and he emphasized that skaters would still consider it taboo to take the same name of someone in their league, or even in the local area.

109 In another respect, the norms have changed to more closely reflect substantive trademark law. I noted in "Talk Derby to Me" that derby norms mapped trade-mark law to the extent that skaters used many of the factors at play in the *Polaroid* test to determine whether two marks were excessively similar. Fagundes, "Talk Derby," 1122 n.149. But this more recent change brings the substantive (norm-based) rights of skaters more in line with what U.S. law promises trademark own-ers: An entitlement that is limited to the scope of its geographical recognition; see *Dawn Donut v. Hart's Food Stores, Inc.*, 267 F.2d 358 (2d Cir. 1959), rather than one that operates independently of practical considerations.

110 David Fagundes, "Labor and/as Love: Roller Derby's Knowledge Commons," in *Governing Knowledge Commons* (Oxford University Press, 2014).

111 Registries for American racehorses' names, for example, functions well because it is controlled and funded by the well-heeled Jockey Club. In Australia, racehorse name registry is a public function bankrolled by the state.

112 Sexy Slaydie remarked that if a newbie skater competed under her moniker, it would be cause for laughter rather than concern.

113 And while no one was vocally critical of the Master Roster and its exclusion approach, neither did anyone fight too hard against its decline. Elaina B. recalls a few people raising their voices to keep the Roster alive after she retired, but no one ultimately followed through to actually do the work. RDR is the closest equivalent, but it explicitly embraces duplicate names, and in that respect repre-sents a sharp departure from the Master Roster's exclusion approach.

PART III

Content Creators

7

Architecture and Morality

Transformative Works, Transforming Fans

REBECCA TUSHNET

As the editors of this volume write in the Introduction, "nearly every community is deeply influenced by the physical and technological architecture in which it is situated." Online fandom communities, which have been a focus of my research, offer excellent illustrations of this principle. Fans have created spaces where noncommercial creativity can thrive, as participants in online communities create new stories, videos, artwork, and other artifacts based on existing works, from the Avengers to Zorro and everything in between.

Creative fandoms are particularly attractive to groups underrepresented in American mass culture: women; lesbian, gay, bisexual, transgender, and queer people; and racial minorities of all sexes and orientations. "Talking back" to dominant culture using its own audiovisual forms can be particularly attractive to disempowered speakers. Rewriting a popular text to show the alternative paths it might have taken readily permits critique of existing structures—by creating possibilities and alternatives, such remixes demonstrate that there is no single, necessary story. Fanworks cover every imaginable topic, from alternate universes in which the characters from the *Avengers* films are ordinary high school students to stories exploring what might have happened after the final scene on *Mad Men*. Not all fanworks are critical, but all of them involve the addition of new thoughts to existing characters and situations, and therefore represent someone's creative expression.

Media fans were among the first to see the liberatory possibilities of the Internet, and much, though not all, of media fandom has moved online. Fans regularly take technologies not made for them and adapt them for fannish purposes, such as the writing platform Wattpad, the image-heavy blogging platform Tumblr, and the visual art site DeviantArt. Vidders, who make new works by combining video clips from TV shows and films with songs in order to use the songs to tell a new story about the visuals, often put their fanvids up on YouTube, where they sit alongside many other types of video. Vidders therefore encounter groups of people with different norms about what kinds of appropriation are acceptable.[1] Fans also create their own sites, such as Fanfiction.net and AnimeMusicVideos.org; however, because fans are people, that doesn't prevent conflicts over norms and boundaries from breaking out.

The diversity of transformative work-creating fandoms is so great, it can't be encompassed in any one chapter, and there will be counter-examples of everything I say here. Thus, I will simply attempt to sketch out some current trends and matters of debate in areas of fandom with which I am familiar, which largely come from Western media fandom. However, scholars of media fandom have identified similarities among Western media fandoms, non-Western fandoms, and other fannish creative endeavors such as cosplay (short for "costume play," creating costumes to emulate existing characters or altered versions of them), including the use of norms to bring new members into fan communities; internal policing of specific types of commercial activity to keep the fandom "noncommercial" on its own terms; and the use of pseudonyms to create identities within fannish communities and protect fans from ridicule from the outside.[2] So, while my perspective is necessarily limited, there are some general features of creative fandoms that can offer larger lessons about "low-IP" spaces.

In search of some larger lessons, this chapter will discuss the role of individual identity in online fandom communities; the role of community itself in shaping the content of creative works, and of helping to form individual identities; the idea of *transformativeness* as a unifying idea justifying fannish creation; and the competing idea of noncommerciality, which has never been pure but is now under new pressures as the formal economy intervenes into fandom in new ways. Fans have complex and often contradictory relations with commercial productions; the most widely shared fan value regarding intellectual property, that of attribution, is flexible in implementation and of substantially less interest to the commercial entities now engaging with fandom than fans' economic potential. As I will discuss, there is in fact significant variation in what fans consider acceptable in the intersection of money and fandom. Like most communities, fandom is divided; and yet communities survive without complete consensus and without eternally fixed norms.

Though a noncommercial ethos is an important part of many fandoms, what *noncommercial* means is up for debate in a world that does not in fact have separate spheres for the market and the private. As with many subcultures, the prospect of monetizing the love and productivity of fandom spurs outsiders (and some insiders) to attempt to separate fans from their dollars. Partially in response, some fans created the Archive of Our Own to host fanworks, run by the nonprofit Organization for Transformative Works (disclosure: I was a co-founder of the OTW). Other specifically fannish spaces are free to use, but ad-supported, such as Fanfiction.net. These spaces prioritize the concerns of fans: sharing, crediting fannish creativity, and offering feedback, but they also have servers to run, and servers cost money.

Copyright law gives copyright owners control over derivative works—works based on or adapted from the copyright owner's initial work, such as the movie version of a book. If fanworks aren't fair use or otherwise protected, fanworks may infringe the derivative works right. Although moral rights don't exist in the United States, except in limited circumstances not relevant here, some authors also assert moral claims to control how their works are interpreted and reinterpreted. But fandom has almost the opposite norm: change in the form of adding new creative expression produces a separate work that the copyright owner should not control, at least when that new work circulates only within fandom.

The expressed preferences of original creators don't matter to a large number of the fans who create fanworks—after all, one reason they create is that the original text left them dissatisfied in some way. The largest general fan fiction site on the Internet, Fanfiction.net, doesn't allow fan fiction where authors object, but that choice is probably more understandable as a function of legal risk aversion than an implementation of internally felt norms, and it would be a mistake to confuse the two.[3] The Archive of Our Own, by contrast, explicitly does not consider whether an author objects to fan fiction, instead taking a blanket position that noncommercial fanworks are fair use. Attribution, however, does remain a constant, with plagiarism off-limits and credit to fan authors vital because credit is the only recognition most fans receive. The Archive of Our Own has very few limits on the fan-related content it will accept, but a fundamental rule is still attribution, whether explicit or implicit. No one needs to footnote "Use the Force, Luke!"

At this point, the legal status of fan fiction is unlikely to be contested in the United States. It's now common for fan fiction to be part of the "test suite" for a theory of copyright; that is, a theory that doesn't allow noncommercial fan fiction is prima facie not a good theory. Moreover, the U.S. Copyright Office has recognized that fan videos may well be fair use, accepting the arguments of fan video makers that using short clips from existing works deserves an exemption from the Digital Millennium Copyright Act's prohibition on circumventing technologies that prevent copying from DVDs and digital downloads and streams. It's true that we don't have a court case opining on the fair use status of online fanworks, but one reason for that absence is that, when fans have secured legal representation in response to rare copyright owner cease and desist letters, the copyright owners have declined to press their claims. I believe this pattern represents a sensible recognition that they're likely to make fair use precedent rather than to win their cases.

Thus, bolstered by fair use claims where necessary, media fandom offers an example of a functioning creative ecosystem embedded in, but not fully absorbed by, late capitalism. Media fandom is low-IP in that there are few interactions with lawyers or courts. But concepts of right and wrong still both structure communities and are subjects of debate within those communities. Ultimately, creative fandom is not about purity in any sense, but rather constitutes itself from the play of individual self-definition and community norms. It's in the hybridity and messiness of fandom structures that we can get a better sense of what creative practices look like.

Identity

Even under a legal regime without much in the way of attribution rights, authors regularly seek and receive credit, with exceptions requiring some explanation—for example, the need for political responsibility that submerges the authorship of politicians' speechwriters and judges' clerks. Fan authors are no different: Identifiability is important, especially since fannish endeavors usually pay off only in reputation, if that. Most profit-seeking creative works are similar in that regard, of course.

Fannish identities are often pseudonymous, but that doesn't mean they don't matter. At the most basic level, a popular pseudonymous author will have a wider platform for her next endeavor.[4] Even for less popular creators, pseudonyms serve important functions. Pseudonymous members of a community can play particular versions of themselves, disclosing personal information while still feeling safe because of the pseudonym's distance from a legal identity. This safety then allows a fan to express herself in ways she might not have elsewhere, including taking some risks in creating new works.

Pseudonymity's shielding functions can therefore be tightly linked to its creative functions. Many fans even choose names related to their fandoms, signaling membership in fannish groups and openness to interactions with other fans. Kirklovesspock may find kirklovesmccoy's opinions misguided, but they share a certain kind of public signal. Pseudonymity is so common in fannish spaces that even people otherwise willing to use their legal names may choose pseudonyms, just to fit in. The pseudonymous norm is enforced against other community members: People who publicly connect a fan's pseudonym with her legal or "wallet" name face social sanctions from other fans.[5] The fannish community thus collaborates in the fan's production of a separate identity, enabling her to play more freely.

Choosing a name is only the beginning of a fan's journey. People find out who they are by making things, including fanworks. *Making* thus involves creative productions but also the production of the creative self, which emerges in the course of doing the work. Jessica Silbey's qualitative interviews with professional creators of various types reveal the importance of *process* in creation: a creative end product is the result, but it's not the thing on which creators focus, which is instead the value they find in doing the work itself.[6] *Work* is a noun in copyright, but a verb in the everyday practice of creativity.

One of the implications of the centrality of process is that valuable acts of creativity occur even when the results are similar to those that have come before, because work furthers the creative development of the *individual.* As explained by theorist Tisha Turk:

The value of an undergraduate student paper seldom lies in its originality. (Anyone who thinks it does has never read eighty papers explaining the significance of the title of *Pride and Prejudice*.) Those papers are valuable not because they make original, innovative scholarly arguments but because they are a mode of learning; what matters is the practice, the process. . . . For the most part, undergraduate papers are not practice for anything in particular; their value is in the habits of mind that they encourage. The practice is the point.

This, for me, is part of why it's valuable to address fannish processes, not just fannish artifacts. Even a celebratory vid—a vid that doesn't transform the story, or re-read it, or whatever—does require work; it requires ripping, clipping, converting, editing, tweaking, lots of different kinds of decision-making, even if those decisions feel completely intuitive and easy in the moment. . . . Looking at process gives us a way of explaining why reproduction, in a fannish sense, is never simply mechanical: The practice is (at least part of) the point.[7]

As the similarity between Silbey's and Turk's accounts indicates, commercially motivated authors and fans are not all that far apart in their needs and concerns. One might say: But professional authors produce work that is, on average, of higher quality than undergraduate papers or fanworks. There's no doubt that low barriers to entry lead to works of low quality, but so what? As the influential science fiction writer Theodore Sturgeon pointed out, 90 percent of science fiction is crud, but 90 percent of *everything* is crud. Even if we only cared about quality, no culture produces a Shakespeare without also producing a great number of prosaic and easily forgotten playwrights. It is from the vast numbers of people experimenting that we get the peaks of human achievement. Even indifferent fanworks should thus be understood as products of the freedom that also produces artistic triumphs.

It is also notable that very few other low-IP creative communities are routinely subject to judgment based on the quality of their *average* creative work. And it's hard to shake the feeling that media fandom associated with women, and particularly with young women, faces an often gendered distaste. A lot of chefs' new creations disappear without notice; a lot of tattoo artists do at best indifferent work; a lot of stand-up comics perform painfully unfunny routines; and so on. But somehow, we don't spend a lot of time worrying that most of those creators aren't very good, and very few accounts of these groups in popular media feel the need to nod at how bad most participants are, whereas a sentence of this sort is common in articles about fan fiction.

Copyright's nondiscrimination principle is on to something here. Creative work deserves recognition as the production of an author, even if it's not "good." The process, and the people who engage in it, deserve our respect. At the very least, fans' deep commitment should lead others to ask why fandom is so important to many people. The OTW collected fans' stories as part of its mission to promote the legitimacy of fanworks, and the following two are typical. Chelsea S. explained how it was the importance of seeing a *rewriting* that enabled her to understand herself:

> [F]anfiction gave me a small segue into some insight about myself. I am bisexual. If I think hard, my first crush on a girl was probably in the first grade. Not that I could ever admit it to myself. Growing up in east Texas, one just didn't do that. Even my own brother coming out of the closet couldn't assist me in what should have been a comparatively small step. It wasn't until I was older and stumbled upon the infamous "slash fiction" that I saw one of my favorite television characters, one with whom I identified deeply, recast as a bisexual man. His character was not significantly altered, he didn't suddenly become something unrecognizable. The stories I read featured him having more or less the same adventures he always had. It was the first step to greater tolerance and greater self acceptance for me.[8]

Balun S. used fandom to help herself and others:

> I was an engineer, or at least I had been, I had lost my job and was dealing with the hopelessness and depression that are part and parcel of long-term unemployment and dwindling savings. . . . I turned yellow and racked up two years' gross wages in debt in just a few days in medical bills. I was beyond low. I was in the dark place were staying alive was no longer a priority and death would have been a release, a kindness. However, we received gift[] cards for dinner and a movie. We saw Disney's *Tangled*. It was fun, but they skipped over some obvious things to get to the happily ever after in a reasonable amount of time.

It bothered me, and there was no way Disney would ever do that part of the story, so I did. . . . I posted to FanFiction.net and people liked what I wrote. For the first time in years I received validation that I was a worthwhile human being! Something a job had never given me. Life was worth living again!

Through my fanfiction, I worked through my emotional pain. Then I found that others shared that pain. People would read and re-read my stories to help them out of depression and suicidal thoughts. We would communicate and I helped lead them through their own dark places. I have had several people tell me that they are alive now and wanting to stay alive because of my stories and our interactions, all because we are able to connect through the shared love of a movie. . . .

I would like to help people, but the only way I know to find some of these people in trouble is through the love that is shared with a movie or other story.[9]

Sometimes, seeing yourself reflected in a work of art can be vital to your own survival. Sometimes, making art can be the same. And because inspiration regularly comes from the world around us, fanworks are one way that people can perform this necessary, sustaining work of living.

Community and Change

As Balun's story indicates, many of the individual benefits of creating fanworks come from the experience of community. Fandom as creative practice is communal because it is inherently iterative. As one commenter wrote, "Fanfic is all about asking 'what if' and the answer is always yes."[10] A classic rule of improv theater is that participants are not allowed to refuse another participant's gesture, though they may reinterpret it, add to it, or otherwise send it in a new direction. Fandom is very much like improv: Many fannish creations exist in a web of other creations, and an individual work may be difficult to understand without knowing about its connection to the larger community and about the debates or tropes to which the individual work is a response or contribution. Should I write this story? Should I draw this picture? In fandom, the answer is always yes. This ethos leads to weird and wonderful results. And it also supports immense experimentation, diversity, and plenitude.

Community is also where architecture becomes important. Communities need places, even virtual places, to be communal. Many times, fan communities make do with platforms not designed for them, adapting sites for their own purposes and existing in the interstices. Karen Hellekson describes fans' use of various sites, some of which can be actively hostile to fanworks, as "making use of" whatever comes to hand. When the answer to "should I make this?" is always yes, then "why not throw some fan fiction up [on the general publishing site Scribd] and see how it does?"[11] is also a plausible conclusion.

Fans will often experiment with different sites and functions to see how they can be adapted. For example, the blogging site Tumblr provided "tags" for posts in order to allow users to search and categorize content with short descriptions of post content. Tags were meant to guide topic-based searches, like Dewey Decimal numbers or Library of Congress categories. But fans now use Tumblr tags for commentary, humor, and indecipherable-to-outsiders argot, sometimes conducting entire discussions in tags. Top-down expectations from the site's creators were overwhelmed by actual practice.

Worries about suppression of fannish content and fears that commercial motives would lead to exploitation or control of fanworks have also led fans to develop their own sites, primarily archives of collected works from numerous authors. This practice is furthest entrenched with fan fiction, though there are also sites for fan video and art. The OTW's Archive of Our Own (popularly known as AO3), with a name deliberately referencing Virginia Woolf's discussion of a female author's need for her own private space in order to write, was specifically designed to support fan communities. Potential users participated in focus groups on the AO3's terms of service, which were written in an attempt to make them understandable to ordinary fans, though there's still no way to make them read the terms of service in the first place.[12] The AO3 has minimal restrictions on content and takes the position that fans have broad fair use rights. One reason for its creation was to make sure that fan creators would have a place to go if commercial motives led to their ouster from other spaces—something that happened when, for example, Fanfiction.net banned sexually explicit fan fiction, apparently because advertisers worried about having their ads placed next to erotica.

Even with fair use considered as settled, there are still other issues in fandom about what kind of content is acceptable. For example, many fan communities historically considered "real person fiction" (RPF)—pretty much what it sounds like—far more ethically dubious than "fictional person fiction," even though RPF poses no copyright problems and very few other legal issues when the stories are, as they almost inevitably are, plainly fictional. Changes in celebrity culture and fan practice, however, have made RPF much more broadly accepted than it once was in Western media fandom, highlighting one difference between norms and laws: norms' greater susceptibility to evolution. By accepting RPF in pari materia with other fanworks, the AO3 consolidated this emerging norm in its sector of fandom. The beliefs of the particular group of fans who participated in discussions about the AO3's terms of service became the rules of one of the first sites many new fans are likely to encounter, teaching about acceptable boundaries by example.

Other recent changes include changing aesthetic conventions in fiction (a wave of third-person present-tense stories, and then a backlash) and fan video (moving to heavier editing to take advantage of new capabilities in editing software), as well as changes in how feedback is solicited and delivered. Fandom's growth and increasing reliance on audiovisual modes have led to changes in platforms and wider dispersion. As the text-heavy blogging site LiveJournal has declined, the image-friendly Tumblr has risen. Tumblr's structure makes it easier for "strangers" to encounter each other—although not always in friendly fashion—because they follow the same topics. LiveJournal allows users to "lock" entries to limited audiences, as Facebook does for those who understand the settings, but Tumblr does not.[13] As a result, Tumblr users more easily encounter other users who don't share common backgrounds or assumptions and who are willing to disagree vigorously. But Tumblr is not a pleasant place to post long texts; fans who write fan fiction often post to AO3 and/or Fanfiction.net and then solicit readers on Tumblr and other sites, from Instagram to LiveJournal. In this way, fans continue to piece together an ever-more-scattered existence, using whatever tools seem to be most useful at the time.

The AO3 has implemented a "kudos" button that functions similarly to a "like" or "thumbs up," but unlike, for example, YouTube or Reddit, it does not offer a "thumbs down" option. This feature cements a fannish norm that the threshold for saying something negative ought to be higher than the threshold for saying something nice. Before the kudos button, email or publicly posted comments were the only way to offer feedback, and still are the only ways to offer criticism. The architectural choice to include it arguably changed the balance between fan creator and fan audience. Some people appreciate the ability to give kudos as a quick acknowledgment and believe it increases the willingness of users to interact with authors, while others fear that it supplants more detailed feedback. Probably both addition and displacement occur, changing the shape of the community in ways whose long-term effects are hard to predict.

Likewise, Mel Stanfill identifies some recent changes in the balance between individual and community: "Posting fiction that has not been beta read and is thus riddled with errors relating to both show canon and to writing is now routine. Leora Hadas has described this attitude in the context of *Doctor Who* fandom as the sense of a 'basic right' to create and post fic, and it points to prioritizing individual desire to create over any sense of obligation to produce something others will find worth reading."[14] Older archives sometimes required works to be "beta read"— checked for grammar, spelling, and even plot and characterization—but AO3 and Fanfiction.net do not. A beta reading requirement does not scale, so large fan sites don't use prescreening measures any more than large non-fan sites do.

Yet fan spaces aren't just subject-specific versions of the broader Internet. For example, a common feature of commons-based production is that norms can distinguish between the appropriate treatment of insiders and outsiders, and fandom is no different. Creating unauthorized new stories based on the work of profit-seeking copyright owners isn't just accepted, it's *constitutive* of creative fandom. However, doing the same thing to a work of fan fiction—creating a fanwork of a fanwork— without the original fan creator's permission is highly controversial. A major debate erupted some years back when one *Stargate Atlantis*[15] fan community ran a challenge asking people to rewrite existing fan stories (with credit to the originals). One argument for treating fanworks differently than the commercial sources was that fan authors only have a story, not cultural acceptance as creators or financial reward. Thus, the argument went, it was more important to grant fan authors moral rights of control over their works than to allow commercial copyright owners to control fanworks. Other fans found this position hypocritical or at least misguided, since a story once told is in the hands and minds of the audience, and reactions—including creative reactions—are inevitable. Similarly, there have been vigorous debates about whether a fan who records herself reading a story out loud (known as podficcing) requires the original author's permission.

The AO3 attempts to moderate these different positions by the practice of reciprocal links: For a podfic, for example, the podfic creator can indicate that it is a "related work" to a written text. If the text is also hosted on the Archive, the writer can decide whether to accept the link, in which case the podfic will be easily available to readers of the written text, or to decline the link. The concept of related works allows creators some control over the visibility of works based on their own fanworks. This design feature of course does not solve the moral problem, but it may well help to shape norms on an ongoing basis.

Medium also matters. A person who, without asking first, draws a picture illustrating another fan's story is likely to be praised and considered to be offering the highest form of flattery because she is contributing her own artistic talents to realize the fan-author's world. Fan art is routinely sold, but "filing off the serial numbers" and "pulling to publish"—removing fan fiction from online distribution and rewriting it so that it can be sold as a separate work—is controversial, perhaps precisely because it seems to be withdrawing a gift that has been reciprocated with gifts of feedback and praise.[16] These differing norms by medium are an example of the kind of context sensitivity, and lack of fully settled rules, that communities routinely produce and that generic legal regimes find hard to replicate.

Likewise, there is a general fannish norm against making a creator's works publicly available without permission, though that norm is not universal and even people who generally adhere to it may also recognize exceptions. However, interpreting that norm creates some interesting questions as time passes and archives change hands or threaten to disappear from the Internet for want of maintenance. If a fan put her works on Geocities, a now-defunct website, and then died, may her friends preserve her works on a new site if they sincerely believe she would have wanted them to remain accessible? The correct answer is not obvious.

Another OTW project, Open Doors, works to preserve at-risk archives, usually by importing them into the AO3. As long as the archivist wants the archive to be preserved as a collection, the OTW has generally taken a creator's original choice to deposit a work in an archive as a continuing desire to keep it online, even if the archive moves domains. However, Open Doors also allows individual creators to remove or "orphan" their works from an imported collection. "Orphaning" is a concept borrowed from copyright's "orphan works" debates: A creator may choose to leave a work available, but to remove all identifying information so that the work is no longer associated with even a pseudonym. The new code was deliberately designed to allow individual opt-out and deletion or orphaning of works, even though older archive software generally didn't allow easy changes once a work had been added to an archive. Orphaning preserves access to the work but means that the creator no longer gets the credit—or the blame—and stays truly anonymous. Coding the AO3 to allow orphaning is a deliberate choice and may have long-term effects on preservation if creators use it to preserve access to their works even when they no longer wish to be known as fans. This is a different kind of balance between audiences' interests in access and authors' interests in economic control than that attempted by formal copyright law; where formal law has resort to detailed legal codes and limited exemptions for libraries to engage in preservation work, the AO3 has only programming code designed to break the attributional link between an author who doesn't want to be known as an author anymore and her works.

All of these norms about preservation and alteration are at least related to IP concepts, but they're far from the only relevant norms. Fans recognize other specific ethical duties to others in fandom. Some content is disturbing to some users, or even "triggering"—it may force them into flashbacks of trauma. Or users may simply want to avoid content they know they don't like. While warnings are not an intellectual property issue, they are very much an information issue. As a result, fans have developed extensive systems of warnings and content tags that allow users to screen out works with content they want to avoid, from sexual assault to violent death to characters behaving "out of character." Volunteers have even coded extensions that can be used on the AO3 and Tumblr so that works containing a user's blacklisted terms won't appear in search results.

At the same time, warnings can be highly controversial, and some creators don't want to use them; they consider warnings to interfere with artistic freedom or to spoil the outcome of a narrative.[17] As a result, the AO3 does require a creator to choose from a menu of major warnings—but one of the choices is "Choose Not to Warn." Under the archive's policies, creators who use Choose Not to Warn have satisfied their warning duties, and users proceed at their own risk. In order to implement the major warnings, the AO3 uses Choose Not to Warn as the default; this choice has consequences of its own as a signal about appropriate behavior (and may be misunderstood by some users). The possibility of adding as many varied "Additional tags" as the creator desires allows creators to customize their signals to audiences considering whether to access their works. The very availability of the additional tags field helps support a custom of active tagging and content disclosure, in a way unavailable in previous archives. Code can't make norms, but it can make some practices easier to implement. The rapid adoption of extensive content tags, often even by authors who choose not to "warn" as a matter of principle, suggests that the ability to tag using the neutral term "additional" is of great value to creators and audiences alike. Although the concept of "trigger warnings" has been debated and often derided in the academic context, this grassroots invention has value outside fandom. Users of book review sites such as Goodreads often adopt similar tagging practices, and some professional authors and publishers—especially those connected to media fandom—have begun using similar "advisories" and tags.[18]

When we talk about architecture shaping behavior in this way, it's worth noting that architecture requires architects, not to mention construction engineers, janitors, and the occasional security guard. The Archive of Our Own relies on huge amounts of volunteer labor to make all these systems work. In order to allow users to navigate more easily, it uses a curated "folksonomy," in which creators are allowed to tag their works in almost any conceivable way, and then "tag wranglers" associate tags with the same meanings. Thus, one creator can use "Harry Potter/ Severus Snape" to designate the relationship explored in her fanwork, and another creator can use "Severus Snape/The Boy Who Lived," and both will turn up in a search for "Severus Snape/Harry Potter." Maintaining this curated folksonomy requires the efforts of 500 tag wranglers, not to mention numerous others on the Support and Abuse teams, as well as the system engineers and coders who help make up the largest female-majority open source project on the Internet. The AO3 thus has a complicated governance system. Mailing list administrators and archive administrators have similar roles within other communities. These volunteers are vital to the survival of the systems that bring fans together. As David Fagundes has written: "shared infrastructure and altruistic motivations lie at the heart of, rather than as a mere sidelight to, the story of IP production. Much IP production would not be possible without infrastructure resources that are best managed as commons."[19]

In other words, community doesn't just happen. It takes work. And not everyone will agree with the choices of would-be community-makers. When the OTW was founded, a number of fans expressed concerns that it would wrongly attempt to speak for all fans or make creative fandoms so visible that copyright owners would backlash and suppress us. The fear of excessive visibility, at least, has faded as other events, such as the popularity of *Fifty Shades of Grey*—an international bestseller that began its creative life as *Twilight* fan fiction—have brought fans into mainstream visibility regardless of anyone's efforts to hide. While the OTW can't speak for all fans, it does contribute to the development of fannish norms. As the next section will detail, one significant part of this contribution comes from the legal concept of "transformativeness," embedded in the OTW's very name.

Transformativeness and Activism

"Transformativeness" as a copyright concept refers to the extent to which a new work or use adds new meaning or message to an original work. The more transformative a use is, the more likely it is to be fair use. By identifying fanworks as transformative, the OTW lays claim to a powerful narrative of fair use. The term also evokes the contribution of the user's own labor, entitling her to an authorial claim of her own, and also indicating that she isn't interfering with the legitimate scope of rights in the initial, untransformed work. The OTW helped introduce this legal concept into fannish discourse, and it is now common for non-lawyer fans to label their works "transformative" as part of ethical and legal defenses of fandom. Law thus shaped at least part of the community's self-concept in relation to its mainstream legitimacy.

Transformativeness also operates on fans directly: The transformations that fans themselves undergo in discovering themselves as creative actors help them assert their own claims for legitimacy. While lawyers, policymakers, and ordinary citizens are increasingly aware of fan activity—fan fiction even recently entered the *Oxford English Dictionary*—fans have also begun to engage in deliberate activism around copyright reform. *New York Times* best-selling author Naomi Novik, a fan writer and vidder who helped found the OTW, testified before Congress at hearings on fair use. The OTW participated in hearings on the Patent and Trademark Office/National Telecommunications and Information Administration's Green Paper on copyright reform, and submitted comments to the European Commission in its inquiry as to whether current European exceptions and limitations were sufficient. And the OTW is now in its third round of DMCA hearings before the Copyright Office, seeking to renew and expand existing exemptions to §1201's prohibition on circumventing digital rights management technologies in order to make remix videos. Fan video makers provided the bulk of the evidence used to secure the previous remix exemptions, and are on track to continue to do so.

There are other examples of directly fannish activism. The Harry Potter Alliance has promoted explicitly political campaigns to carry out the themes of justice and fairness that fans see in the *Harry Potter* books. The Alliance engaged in both charitable fundraising—a traditional fannish endeavor—and a campaign to pressure Warner Brothers to source the chocolate used for *Harry Potter*–themed candy in ethical ways. Similarly, fans of a boy band in Korea organized around their fandom in protesting U.S. beef imports, resulting in the largest protests in Korea in twenty years.[20]

I find the move from fannish analysis to activism unsurprising. (However, given the stigma often associated with female media fandom, it's been important for people like Novik and me, with economic security and no realistic possibility of being fired for weirdness, to take the lead in speaking up.) Fandom is a training ground that teaches people that they can speak creatively, and that their speech is often welcome. And it's a place where communities of like-minded people meet up and do things together. Political possibility is thus inherent in participatory fandom:

> Scratch an activist and you're apt to find a fan. It's no mystery why: fandom provides a space to explore fabricated worlds that operate according to different norms, laws, and structures than those we experience in our "real" lives. Fandom also necessitates relationships with others: fellow fans with whom to share interests, develop networks and institutions, and create a common culture. This ability to imagine alternatives and build community, not coincidentally, is a basic prerequisite for political activism.[21]

The grassroots aren't just a dead metaphor—they're places where things grow, even if those growing things spend some time underground. For example, Limor Shifman's study of online participation found that videos that generated lots of responses were likely to be user-generated rather than professionally produced.[22] He argues that works by ordinary people inspire others to think that creativity is achievable for them as well and create the feeling of communicating with peers. In addition, repetition in particular is generative: A meme "itself includes a persuasive demonstration of its own replicability and therefore contains encrypted instructions for others' replications," much as fanworks do.[23]

My own fannish engagement happened much as Shifman describes: I discovered fan fiction online, read obsessively for a few weeks, and then thought, 'well, I can write at least as well as some of these folks'— the barriers to entry were low enough that I was willing to take some risks. I'm not unusual in reaching that conclusion. And the great news is that people who intervene in a conversation by making a creative work that comments on the world, or on one part of it, regularly come to understand themselves as creators and actors more generally. Political remix artist Jonathan McIntosh observes of his experiences teaching others to remix, "[a]fter engaging in remix culture, people young and old find it nearly impossible to experience media in a passive or uncritical way. As members of that remix culture even if we never make a remix video ourselves, we can't help but make imaginary mash-ups in our heads when watching television or movies."[24] In the context of student video editing, Professor Christina Spiesel and her colleagues likewise noted that "[a]ll it takes is the experience of lifting a sound track from one clip and attaching it to another for students to know with certainty that everything on film is constructed and that they can be builders in this medium."[25]

Despite these liberating tendencies, the OTW's use of transformative-ness as a specifically legal and legitimizing concept implicates us in more than a legal system. It endorses a certain kind of creativity. Louisa Stein and Kristina Busse challenge the OTW's investment in "transformation," while also acknowledging its merits:

> OTW's emphasis on the transformative properties of fan creativity is strategic: the transformative dimensions of fan works enable them to be included in [the] fair use exemption against copyright violations. OTW's valuation of transformation (and implicitly originality) reflects a legal culture that upholds values of originality, linking originality with idea ownership. However, no matter how strategic the rationale, this turn to language of transformation (and implicitly originality) suggests that even in its cultural embrace of repetition and limitation, media fandom (or at least the parts of it represented by OTW) still remains at least tenu-ously invested in more traditional notions of originality, transformation, uniqueness, and progress.[26]

This criticism is not unfounded, but I believe the OTW exists in pro-ductive tension with more radical elements who would reject concepts of ownership and authorship altogether. Some fans pay very little at-tention to intellectual property, or argue that widespread unauthorized copying of entire movies and books is a way that powerless people can access both knowledge and pleasure.[27] But within fandom's own anti-plagiarism norms and respect for variations are the foundations of a more measured approach, recognizing the interests of both authors and audiences. As Tisha Turk says, "it would be a serious mistake to down-play the legal importance of the language of transformation; it is still a strategy that matters. . . . I'd love to see the legal culture change, but until (or even while) it does, I am disinclined to give up the legal protection and recognition that the language of transformation allows."[28]

We should also pay attention to the interactions between deliberate lawbreaking and operating within the law. Sonia Katyal and Eduardo Peñalver have written persuasively about the role of large-scale and visible violation of property laws as an impetus for law reform: a particular kind of civil disobedience. The OTW's fair use claims offer a middle ground between IP anarchy and IP maximalism; the threat of anarchy doubtless contributes to the appeal of the middle ground (which would otherwise appear to be the extreme of minimalism).

Transgressiveness can also be a value in itself. Theorist Alexis Lothian argues that "fans' appropriative art is not necessarily complicit with legal and economic structures as they stand. It is worth determining who defines the use as fair, and what it might mean to place a value on unfair uses. . . . [M]ashups, vids, and similar arts of juxtaposition challenge the idea that creative legitimacy relies on original ideas that belong only to those who initiate them."[29] For at least some fans, the defiance of cultural and even legal boundaries is part of the thrill of fandom.

Fans are far from unique in their practices of boundary-crossing, going from outlaws to speakers insisting on their free speech rights and back again. For example, Eden Sarid's work on the low-IP world of drag queens notes that operating extralegally has its own value, and that being legalized or governed by laws rather than norms would remove some of the meaning of drag for its current practitioners.[30] Communities examined elsewhere in this volume, such as tattoo artists and graffiti artists, often perceive involvement with the legal system as incompatible with their interests even as owners. Mixing and matching legal compliance is everywhere. People who download full copies of music and movies without authorization are also the most likely to be paying for media.[31] "Hybrid practices (of consuming the same product both illegally and then legally) are not the thoughtless result of rampant criminals, but a considered response to the free market for media users responding to neoliberal discourses of consumer-citizenship, a reaction to its central notion of choice and the call to be a discerning consumer, especially in economically straitened times."[32]

According to fans' self-reports, participating in creative fandom is actually likely to make participants more cognizant of the value of creative labor, and thus more willing to invest financially in creators who are seeking to profit than fans who don't produce their own works. But if creative fans are also "good," paying fans, is that an unqualified positive? Is noncommercial fandom just another way in which ordinary people can be disempowered by elites who reserve all profit for themselves? As the next section explores, subcultures that become visible can be drawn into uncomfortable relationships with capitalism, or even out-and-out exploited, and both have happened to some extent with transformative fandoms.

Noncommercial Creativity and the Market: Not Either/Or But Both/And

The experiments found in fandom can be the source of important and economically significant innovations. Eric von Hippel has tracked the process of user customization in various physical products such as sports equipment, and has found it to be an important source of innovation that ultimately feeds back into the commercial economy.[33] So too with expressive works. As Anne Jamison pointed out, fanworks grow out of desires for variations on what mainstream culture has produced:

> Experimental writing in fanfiction is found and enjoyed by people who share at least one popular taste, a taste that *has* been catered to by mass culture. Many of these readers, however, also have tastes mass culture does *not* satisfy, tastes they may first discover by reading fic. Persuaded by the presence of favorite characters, even the least adventurous readers sometimes embrace stories featuring alternative sexualities and genders or enjoy more stylistically and thematically challenging material than they would otherwise have turned to.[34]

Fifty Shades of Gray almost perfectly fits the pattern von Hippel identifies: A "user" who did not professionally produce the text at issue customized it for her own particular interests (rewriting *Twilight* without supernatural elements and with a lot of explicit sex); the customized version proved popular with other users; and this altered version was then commercialized (during which process some of the rougher edges were smoothed over, as with the innovations von Hippel tracks, although views differ on the value of the result). The example of *Fifty Shades* has led other commercial publishers to seek to satisfy a previously unrecognized market for written erotica that appeals to women, a market they had been unable even to see before a revised fanwork illuminated the demand.

The ability to move into the formal economy is an important part of the innovation cycle. To deem the experimental process infringing, or to force all activity into the formal economy, risks shutting down that generative flow. Just as Uber, Airbnb, and other startups are trying to turn once limited, often freely offered personal interactions into monetized transactions in which a third-party intermediary makes most of the profit, copyright owners dream of monetizing every creative expression related to their works. But to do so would be both futile and potentially deadly to creativity.

True respect for creative variation means accepting the inevitability of an economy that is a hybrid of distanced, market-based interactions and individualized, non-monetary relations.[35] Fanworks were never completely noncommercial. Before the Internet, print zines and fan art sold in small, offline markets. Though fanzines are less visible now in the flood of content online, some fan art continues to be sold in the broader new markets enabled by aggregator sites such as Etsy (crafts and art) and DeviantArt (visual art).[36] The pre-Internet fanzine and fan art economy was largely run within fandom, by people who were fans themselves. By contrast, Etsy, DeviantArt, Wattpad, and Amazon's Write On and Kindle Worlds (specifically for authorized derivative works set within certain fictional "worlds") are all at least in part attempting to use fanworks to build a larger business. Kindle Worlds in particular attempts to harness the energies of fandom by promoting Amazon's platform as a way for fan authors to write non-canonical stories in their favorite "worlds," such as the late lamented show *Gossip Girl* or the ongoing show *Pretty Little Liars*, and to get a share of the revenue generated from selling those stories. Amazon does minimal pre-screening of submissions, and passes a large percentage of sales revenue to the original copyright owners and a smaller share to the fan authors. This development may pose a greater threat to the dynamics of fandom than previous commercial endeavors, insofar as non-fannish businesses may seek to drain fandom of possible economic value rather than letting it thrive on its own.

Along with exploitation, suppression of experiments with content and form is also a substantial risk when economically motivated entities are involved. Amazon's Kindle Worlds, as noted above, has content restrictions foreign to most fandom spaces. Among other things, Amazon bans the popular "crossover" genre, in which characters or settings from one world intersect with another. Although Amazon is coy about the limits of its ban on sexually explicit content—it wouldn't want to lose out on the next *Fifty Shades of Grey*—Amazon retains broad discretion to police the appropriateness of content. It appears that, in light of Amazon's history of suppressing gay and lesbian content and "kinky" content, explicit sexuality is more likely to survive if it is otherwise conventionally heterosexual. Bans on "erotica" and "offensive content" are standard in Kindle Worlds, along with world-specific restrictions, such as a vague requirement that characters be "in-character," along with bans on "profane language," graphic violence, "references to acquiring, using, or being under the influence of illegal drugs," and "wanton disregard for scientific and historical accuracy." In *G.I. Joe* works, the popular character Snake Eyes can't be portrayed as a Yankees fan, possibly because *G.I. Joe*'s corporate owner, Hasbro, comes from the heart of Red Sox country.

Kindle Worlds additionally requires works to be of a certain length, which is understandable for a commercial enterprise but deadly for social practices that thrive on spontaneity, experimentation, and flexibility. Although fannish poetry has a long history, there will be no *Vampire Diaries* sonnets on Amazon celebrating the characters in the popular teen supernatural book series (and later TV show). The formal innovations of noncommercial remix are unlikely to take root in such sanitized soil.

In addition, Amazon requires writers to be at least eighteen years old, excluding the many young people who discover, and benefit so much from, creative fandom. While much fannish energy comes from young people who have a lot of time and not much money of their own, and are therefore an underserved group in the commercial market, Amazon's understandable worries about contracting with minors prevents them from participating in "authorized" fan creativity.

With all these limitations, it's not surprising that Kindle Worlds doesn't seem to be making a big impact in terms of sales or numbers of works available. The main concerns raised by its presence are twofold: (1) newcomers might believe that authorized platforms are the only acceptable spaces in which to create as fans, deterring them from going beyond what is allowed in these walled gardens; or (2) copyright owners might seek to use the existence of authorized spaces as reasons why unauthorized fanworks shouldn't count as transformative or should be deemed to harm the market for authorized works. Given the current easy accessibility of other fannish spaces, the first concern is not yet a problem—though if Amazon manages to control search results sufficiently, it could become so. The second is a doctrinal issue that requires legal analysis.

In other work, I have explored the dangers of assuming that commercial endeavors can replace noncommercial fandom, because of the substantial constraints on content that professional publishers and licensors impose; the dangers of concentrated, monopolized creative industries; and the risks to privacy involved.[37] Commercialization can only be acceptable if it's additive, not subtractive. Moreover, there are other models than that of the outsider intermediary-exploiter. Some new small presses, often run by fans themselves, try to find fan writers and have them publish works that don't qualify as derivative works for copyright purposes. The most famous of these is surely *Fifty Shades of Gray*, discussed above, which was published by a fan-run imprint before being picked up by a major publisher. While many authors have honed their talents in fan fiction communities, rarely have they been as open about it as E. L. James—another sign of fannish visibility and integration into the larger creative economy. But the existence of such monetization plans should not be used to argue that there is no further need for transformative fair use.

Even in a world with easy licensing, creative fandom should still be free. Fandom benefits its participants—it makes them happy—and does not inflict the kinds of harms on others that would justify the regulation of creative speech. But pleasure can be hard to defend in legal terms, even among progressives, who often surrender to the lure of technocracy. "Courts are squeamish about pleasure. Despite the American emphasis on 'life, liberty, and the pursuit of happiness,' you will rarely see a court acknowledge that seeking pleasure can be an important part of pursuing happiness."[38] Moreover, courts have proven largely unwilling to hear free speech arguments for limiting copyright, at least not without a specific political message. Because pleasure and speech are the true drivers of fandom, fans have often sought other ways to explain the good that fannish communities do, and this leads to another way in which noncommercial fannish endeavors interact with commercial economies: fandom as a training ground.

As a strategic move, defenders of fandom often tout fandom's benefits in teaching useful skills in writing, video editing, coding, and other economically significant endeavors.[39] Henry Jenkins called his popular article on *Harry Potter* fandom *Why Heather Can Write*.[40] Rather than simply accepting the pleasure of creating and engaging fannishly, a BBC One documentary on fandom justified it in terms of skill-building: "Through their fandom, fans are developing skills that will make them more employable in the future. . . . Even to build these fanpages and have thousands of followers is learning to market something and build something . . . they can go work for a company and build their social media profile because they know what they're doing and how to do it well."[41] An official UK government report took the same tack, emphasizing twenty-first-century skills acquired because remix made them fun.[42] It's nice not to pathologize fans, but this rather instrumental attitude toward fandom also has its limits, suppressing a lot of what makes fandom pleasurable in the first place. When I'm not trying to convince policymakers of the utilitarian benefits of fandom, I prefer the more artistic terms used above: fanworks, like other forms of copying, are wonderful ways for people to find their own voices.

One can also explain fandom in terms of the labor its production involves, which may be a middle ground between the market and the "frivolous." Terms such as fanworks and the Organization for Transformative Works emphasize the outputs and not the processes (or the pleasures) of fandom. There are benefits to this reframing:

> Calling this work "work" opens up appreciation for the skills involved, much as with feminist insistence on care work as labor. The labor framework provides a powerful way to value what fans are doing, in contrast to the dismissals that have long attended fandom. If industry has not framed fan action as work to avoid payment, then the pleasure framework sells fans short vis-à-vis what they do for each other.[43]

However, we still need to insist on hybrid justifications for legal protection for noncommercial creativity. These justifications do not conflict, but overlap and interact. The instrumental benefits of fandom do exist; the work of making fanworks is real work; *and* pleasure and play are valuable in and of themselves.

Without valorizing play, it is hard to defend creative freedom or to preserve the spaces of experimentation and collision from where new works come. Or to understand why it's a good thing that people see movies and listen to music rather than, say, buy new toasters. If creativity lacks meaning in itself, why would experiencing the output of someone else's creativity matter? Play enriches our lives, even if it doesn't produce anything else. Respect for play can also connect intellectual property with the more progressive aspects of real property law in which, as Carol Rose has explained, there is a history of providing access rights to otherwise privately owned land to the public specifically for pleasure and recreation.[44]

Conclusion

Creative fandom offers a clear illustration of the ways in which there can never be a full separation between gift and market economies, despite rhetorics of separatism. This is another way in which fandom's "answer is always yes"—yes, we are a gift economy; yes, we participate in the market. Creativity emerges from complex, overlapping interactions that are poorly described by abstract "incentive" theories. Intellectual property theory can't just be a theory of law; it needs to engage with practice. Fandom challenges the separation between commercial and noncommercial found in much intellectual property law—not just in copyright's fair use doctrine but in trademark and the right of publicity's willingness to regulate any expression sold for money. Intellectual property law could benefit from greater attention to degrees and types of commerciality, and recognize that the presence of money isn't always a reason for law to intervene—not just because of external First Amendment limits on intellectual property law, but because extending rights can disrupt the very creative endeavors the law hopes to nurture.

One damaging way in which the failure to respect both commercial and noncommercial aspects of work has played out in the past is the devaluation of women's work. There are serious risks of replicating this expropriation in monetization of fandom:

In recent years, media producers have explicitly sought to solicit fan participation as labor for their profits in the form of user-generated content that helps build their brand. Many fans perceive these developments as a desirable legitimation of fan work, but they can also be understood as an inversion in the direction of fannish theft. Rather than fans stealing commodified culture to make works for their own purposes, capital steals their labor—as, we might consider, it stole ideas from the cultural commons and fenced them off in the first place—to add to its surplus.[45]

Fans therefore also need to talk about the way that our pleasures are mobilized in order to keep us providing uncompensated value to copyright owners: After all, we like it. One ongoing goal is therefore to make economic hybridity less repressive and exploitative than the cooptation offered by initiatives such as Kindle Worlds. Many markets are, as Sal Humphreys says, "hybrid market environments where there is no such clear distinction between the social and commercial economies—where instead they co-exist in the same space, and where some people occupy different positions over time within the same markets."[46] Moreover, there are prospects for healthy integration. The question is how to honor the noncommercial elements and preserve their freedom without trying to create (impossibly) separate spheres, and without calcifying a reward scheme structurally biased against women, sexual minorities, people of color, and others who find in fandom a corrective to mainstream productions that ignore or misrepresent them.

Defending hybrid spaces, where relationships matter but commerce is not banned, is important because full marketization represents a loss of freedom and potential.[47] Commercial attempts to muscle out noncommercial spaces will likely pose the biggest challenge, legal and nonlegal, to fans in coming years. As commercial entities move from suppression to cooptation, our legal and practical strategies must change as well. In particular, we should always recognize that the individual and the community, along with the market and the private/gift economy, are often opposed, but they are not (just) opposites. They also interpenetrate. We make our systems, and then our systems make us. Creative fandoms demonstrate this interdependence in the context of modern copyright law, which both shapes and then (through the efforts of activists and advocates) is shaped by fandom. A healthy creative ecosystem, like a well-functioning intellectual property regime, needs this kind of play in the joints. I have faith that fandom can resist the totalizing narrative of full commercialization as it previously resisted IP maximalism.

NOTES

1 Peter Decherney, *Hollywood's Copyright Wars: From Edison to the Internet* (2013), 225.

2 Nele Noppe, *Fandom unbound: Otaku culture in a connected world*, Mizuko Ito, Daisuke Okabe, and Izumi Tsuji, eds. (book review), http://journal.transformativeworks.org.

3 James Gibson, "Risk Aversion and Rights Accretion in Intellectual Property Law," 116 *Yale Law Journal* 882 (2007).

4 Laura A. Heymann, "Naming, Identity, and Trademark Law," 86 *Indiana Law Journal* (2011): 437–442.

5 Kristina Busse and Karen Hellekson, "Identity, Ethics, and Fan Privacy," in *Fan Culture: Theory/Practice*, Katherine Larsen and Lynn Zubernis, eds. (Newcastle: Cambridge Scholars Publishing, 2012), 38.

6 Jessica Silbey, *The Eureka Myth: Creators, Innovators, and Everyday Intellectual Property* (2014).

7 Tisha Turk, "Originality, transformation, repetition" (Mar. 28, 2013), http://tishaturk.dreamwidth.org; see also Larry Lessig, *Remix* 63–64 (arguing that one benefit of remix comes "not so much [from] the quality of the speech it produces, but [from] the effect it has upon the person producing the speech").

8 National Telecommunications and Information Administration, "Request for Comments on Department of Commerce Green Paper, Copyright Policy, Creativity, and Innovation in the Digital Economy, Comments of Organization for Transformative Works ("OTW")" (Nov. 13, 2013), 25, http://www.ntia.doc.gov.

9 Ibid., 34.

10 http://thegeekiary.com.

11 Karen Hellekson, "Making Use Of: The Gift, Commerce, and Fans," 56 *Cinema Journal* 125 (2015): 130–131.

12 Casey Fiesler's dissertation research shows that, of 30 user-generated content sites surveyed including YouTube, Facebook, and Twitter, the AO3's Terms of Service relating to copyright were among the clearest—the AO3 was among the most readable, and survey participants were more accurate in answering questions about its terms than about any other site's terms, though accuracy was still only 85%. Casey Fiesler, *The Role of Copyright on Online Creative Communities: Law, Norms, and Policy.* https://smartech.gatech.edu/bitstream/handle/1853/53937/FIESLER-DISSERTATION-2015.pdf . PhD dissertation, Georgia Institute of Technology, 2015, 88, 97.

13 Interestingly, the operators were able to choose freely in designing site features of this sort because of laws protecting intermediaries from liability for user-posted

content, particularly the Digital Millennium Copyright Act's notice and take-down scheme and the absolute protection against site operator liability for non-intellectual property torts provided by the Communications Decency Act §230.

14 Mel Stanfill, "Fandom, Public, Commons," *Transformative Works and Cultures*, no. 14 (2013), http://dx.doi.org.

15 *Stargate: Atlantis* (2004–2009), a spinoff of the long-running *Stargate: SG1* (1997–2007) franchise, itself a reboot of the movie *Stargate* (1994), was a show on the Sci-Fi (now SyFy) cable channel. Though never a great hit, it had a premise that allowed fans to invent new "alien" cultures and a buddy dynamic between the two main leads that made it highly popular with American slash fans.

16 Mel Stanfill and Megan Condis, "Fandom and/as Labor," 15 *Transformative Works & Cultures* (2014), [4.10], http://journal.transformativeworks.org (suggesting that selling fannish crafts for profit still retains identification with fandom and rein-forces community, whereas "pulled-to-publish" fan fiction whose fannish origins have been hidden distances itself from fandom and "refut[es]" fannish spaces); see also ibid., [5.7] ("Fan fic is published and freely available online; to pull it only to republish it as original fiction suggests an element of dishonesty on the part of the author. In contrast, fan art—particularly in the form of jewelry or clothing—is rarely offered for free elsewhere first. . . . Although fan artists may post their pic-tures and ask for advice or feedback, this is much less common than fan fic writ-ers posting works in progress or using beta readers to review their work. For one person to profit from the work of a community . . . can be seen far more clearly as exploitation.").

17 "Warnings," http://fanlore.org.

18 Lilah Pace's *Asking for It* (2015), for example, contains a prominent "Reader Advi-sory" with further details on the back cover about the role of rape fantasies in the plot; Pace is the pseudonym of a *New York Times*–bestselling author and longtime media fan. Riptide Publishing, a small publisher focused on non-heterosexual science fiction and fantasy, uses a detailed tagging system for various features, including explicitness of sex and explicitness of violence.

19 David Fagundes, "Talk Derby to Me: Intellectual Property Norms Governing Roller Derby Pseudonyms," 90 *Texas Law Review* 1093 (2012): 1145 (footnote omit-ted).

20 Media Literacy and Social Action in a Post-Pokemon World, http://www.itofisher.com. ("[Y]ou should never underestimate the power of peer-to-peer social com-munication and the bonding force of popular culture. Although so much of what kids are doing online may look trivial and frivolous, what they are doing is build-ing the capacity to connect, to communicate, and ultimately, to mobilize.").

21 Henry Jenkins and Sangita Shresthova, "Up, up, and away! The power and poten-tial of fan activism," *Transformative Works and Cultures*, http://journal.transfor-mativeworks.org (quoting Steven Duncombe).

22 Limor Shifman, *Memes in Digital Culture* (2014), 75.

23 Ibid., 83.

24 Henry Jenkins, "DIY Media 2010: Fan Vids (Part Three), Confessions of an Aca-Fan" (Feb. 4, 2011), http://henryjenkins.org.

25 Christina O. Spiesel et al., "Law in the Age of Images: The Challenge of Visual Literacy," in *Contemporary Issues of the Semiotics of Law* 231, Anne Wagner et al., eds. (2005), 252–253.

26 Louisa Stein and Kristina Busse, "Limit Play: Fan Authorship between Source Text, Intertext, and Context," 7 *Popular Communication: The International Journal of Media and Culture*, 192 (2009): 205.

27 For a challenge to devaluation of pure "piracy," see Lawrence Liang, "Piracy, Creativity and Infrastructure: Rethinking Access to Culture," (July 20, 2009), http://papers.ssrn.com.

28 Tisha Turk, "Originality, transformation, repetition" (Mar. 28, 2013), http://tishaturk.dreamwidth.org.

29 Alexis Lothian, "Living in a Den of Thieves: Fan Video and Digital Challenges to Ownership," 48 *Cinema Journal* 130 (2009): 132–133.

30 Eden Sarid, "Don't Be a Drag, Just Be a Queen—How Drag Queens Protect their Intellectual Property without Law," 10 *FIU Law Review* 133 (2014).

31 See, e.g., Bart Cammaerts et al., "Copyright & Creation: A Case for Promoting Inclusive Online Sharing," (Sept. 2013), 10, http://www.lse.ac.uk/media@lse (noting that file sharers spend more on media than non-file sharers).

32 Lee Edwards et al., "'Isn't It Just a Way to Protect Walt Disney's Rights?': Media User Perspectives on Copyright," *New Media & Society* 1 (2013): 10 (citation omitted).

33 Eric von Hippel, *Democratizing Innovation* (2005).

34 Anne Jamison, *Fic: Why Fanfiction Is Taking over the World* (2013), 22.

35 See, e.g., Patryk Galuszka, "New Economy of Fandom," 31 *Popular Music and Society* 1 (2014) (discussing new hybrid economies using both gift and market exchange, including fans as sponsors, stakeholders, co-creators, investors, and filters to discover commercial opportunities).

36 Stanfill and Condis, "Fandom and/as Labor," [4.2] (discussing fannish sales of zines, artwork, and jewelry, as well as fannish sales through newer e-commerce sites that allow individuals to upload designs for production).

37 See ibid.

38 Susan Reid, "Sex, Drugs, and American Jurisprudence: The Medicalization of Pleasure, Gender & Sexuality Law Online," 1 (footnotes omitted), http://blogs.law.columbia.edu.

39 See OTW Submission to NTIA.

40 Henry Jenkins, "Why Heather Can Write," *MIT Technology Review* (Feb. 6, 2004), http://www.technologyreview.com.

41 Claudia Rebaza, "OTW Fannews: Storytelling Platforms" (March 9, 2014), http://transformativeworks.org (quoting documentary, http://www.bbc.co.uk).

42 Ian Hargreaves, "Digital Opportunity: A Review of Intellectual Property and Growth," *UKIPO* (2011): 50 ("Video parody is today becoming part and parcel of

the interactions of private citizens, often via social networking sites, and encourages literacy in multimedia expression in ways that are increasingly essential to the skills base of the economy.").

43 Stanfill and Condis, "Fandom and/as Labor," [3.4] (citations omitted).

44 Carol M. Rose, "The Comedy of the Commons: Commerce, Custom, and Inherently Public Property," 53 *University of Chicago Law Review* 711 (1986); see also Jennifer Rothman, "Copyright, Custom and Lessons from the Common Law," in *Intellectual Property and the Common Law*, Shyamkrishna Balganesh, ed., https:// papers.ssrn.com (analogizing copyright limitations to public access rights to private land for recreational purposes such as dances, horse races, cricket games, and the like; such purposes are "preferred because they support social engagement and connections in a community").

45 Lothian, "Living in a Den of Thieves," 135.

46 Sal M. Humphreys, "The Challenges of Intellectual Property for Users of Social Networking Sites: A Case Study of Ravelry," *Proceedings Mind Trek* (2008), http:// eprints.qut.edu.au.

47 Rebecca Tushnet, "All of This Has Happened Before and All of This Will Happen Again," 29 *Berkeley Technology Law Journal* 1447 (2014).

8

Internet Pornography without Intellectual Property

A Study of the Online Adult Entertainment Industry

KATE DARLING

The Internet is for porn.
—U.S. House Congressional Hearing on the Stop Online
Piracy Act[1]

The magnitude and prevalence of adult entertainment as a business is undeniable. For decades, even centuries, the industry has flourished despite considerable social and legal obstacles. It is often on the forefront of new media adoption, from paperback books to photography, cable television, and home video.[2] Market demand for adult entertainment drives the success and failure of new technologies, and at the same time, technology helps to proliferate adult content. When the World Wide Web launched in the 1990s, there were about ninety adult magazine publications in the United States.[3] By 1997 there were an estimated nine hundred adult websites on the Internet.[4] Today, there are millions. The largest sites dwarf comparable mainstream media websites, hosting more than 100 terabytes of content and clocking in excess of 100 million page views per day.[5] Value estimates for the industry are in the billions.[6] Although no reliable data exist on the exact size, it's evident that the online adult entertainment industry carries considerable economic weight.

While the Internet has created a new world of business for adult entertainment, it has been a double-edged sword for the traditional model of producing and selling content. On the one hand, adult content producers have capitalized on the increased privacy and convenience for consumers, perhaps even more so than their mainstream counterparts in film and music. On the other hand, an Internet architecture specifically designed for copying and sharing digital files has ushered in an era of unprecedented copyright infringement. From individual use, to file-sharing systems, to content aggregation websites, the unauthorized sharing of adult content has become increasingly widespread and difficult to prevent. Content ownership, while protected in theory through the legal system, can often no longer be enforced in a cost-effective way.

For any industry that deals in easily replicated goods, this should pose a problem. Copyright enables content producers to recoup production costs by letting them sell their product exclusively. Economics predicts that without this mechanism, there will be no incentive to produce content. This theory seems to be supported by the stories in the news media that forecast the death of the adult entertainment industry.[7] And there's no doubt that adult content producers are struggling and have taken a substantial financial hit. But is the industry really dying? To this day, content production persists, numerous companies remain in business, and new ones are entering the market. If there is no effective copyright protection for the traditional content of the industry, how is it still being produced? Why do adult entertainment businesses continue to survive in the face of these difficulties?

This study addresses two questions. First, it investigates the hypothesis that copyright enforcement in the online adult entertainment industry is prohibitively difficult. Second, it explores whether and how adult content producers are recouping their investments. Based on qualitative interviews with industry specialists, lawyers, adult entertainment workers, and content producers,[8] it concludes that copyright enforcement is generally not an effective method of recouping costs. As a result, the industry has shifted toward new business models. Rather than focusing only on selling content, the industry is increasingly moving into services and experiences, which are inherently difficult to copy. The production of standard content continues, both as a basis for this secondary market, as well as for marketing purposes.

This chapter also discusses what we can learn from this exploration and to what extent the study's findings may be industry-specific. Given the adult entertainment industry's similarities to mainstream film and music production, it is a particularly useful area of research. The insights from norms-based creative communities are greatly valuable, but close-knit communities are not necessarily comparable to larger, more complex industries. This study is an analysis of a billion-dollar market for entertainment goods with strong parallels to the industries at the center of the copyright debate.

Copyright Infringement of Adult Content

Adult content is loosely defined as the depiction of sexual acts or sexual subject matter through writing or visuals, such as photography, film, and other media, that is specifically designed to arouse sexual interest.[9] So long as this content is an original work and fixed in a tangible medium of expression, it is protected under the United States Copyright Act. While some would argue that certain types of adult entertainment should not be granted copyright protection because they do not promote "progress," U.S. courts have repeatedly determined that copyright law does not discriminate according to the nature of the content.[10] The question of whether or not it is legal to produce or distribute the content is a separate question from whether or not it is copyrightable. If a work meets the very low bar of originality, the Copyright Act grants it the same protection as any other type of copyrightable expression.

When adult entertainment companies first began to distribute content over the Internet, they profited from the increased privacy and convenience for consumers. Making content available online meant that consumers could purchase adult entertainment without leaving the four walls of their homes or dealing with physical objects like magazines, videocassettes, and DVDs. It also meant circumventing local resistance to brick-and-mortar retailers and making content accessible to far more people both domestically and internationally.

The downside to the vast distribution network of the Internet is that it simultaneously facilitates unauthorized use of content. Digital files are easy to copy and share, allowing for copyright infringement on an unprecedented scale. Despite this, the adult industry continued to thrive on selling content for quite some time. In the early days, online copyright infringers were individual users who captured content through scanning or downloading and made it available to others on websites. Industry specialists claim that this type of unauthorized use, while widespread, generally did not negatively impact business. Some companies even used it as a branding opportunity. It wasn't until later that increasing broadband access made peer-to-peer file sharing an efficient and popular way to share and distribute digital content, often without permission from the copyright holder. In 2008, more than 150 million people were using peer-to-peer networks and an estimated 35% of downloads were adult-related material.[11]

While file sharing played a role in undermining the sale of content, the real game changer happened with the development of the video platform YouTube, which ushered in an era of user-uploaded content aggregators ("tube sites"). Similar in design to YouTube, tube sites allow users to view and upload videos. In most cases, unregistered users can access and watch the videos, while only registered users can upload content. But registration is usually anonymous and uploads are unlimited. There is little to prevent anonymous users from uploading content without authorization from the rights holder. Adult industry specialists and producers attribute the death of the copyright business model to the increasing popularity of these sites after 2006.

For adult entertainment consumers, these platforms offer advantages over file-sharing networks because no files are downloaded, and they allow for easy previewing and switching between videos. Compared to other entertainment, adult content consumers may be unique in that their browsing experience is often part of the consumption. While music consumers might visit an online music store to purchase a specific album by the Swiss glam-rock band Bitch Queens, consumers of adult material often prefer to peruse a variety of content. Furthermore, consumers can be comparatively impatient and driven to purchase for immediate use. These factors, plus the anonymity, and finally the lower legal risk of watching user-uploaded and remotely hosted videos make the tube sites an attractive choice for consumers looking for free content.

Free access via file sharing or tube sites also means that no credit card transaction takes place. Online payments are traceable, and users may prefer to create as few records as possible of their consumption. Because unauthorized content is often free, it also protected consumers during the wave of identity theft and scams that plagued the industry in the early days of the Web. When the floodgates to selling adult content online first opened, the lack of regulation and low barriers to entry meant the emergence of scam sites, rife with pop-up ads, "mousetrapping," browser hijacking, and malware. Some adult marketing partners used unlawful practices to promote content. Two popular schemes for subscription websites were credit card "banging"—using a customer's credit card for unauthorized purchases, often only charging a multitude of small amounts—and pre-checked cross sales. Pre-checked cross sales would coax users to sign up for website memberships at a low price or for a free trial version, but include an automatic subscription in the fine print unless cancelled, and additionally include sign-ups to multiple affiliate websites "for free," many of which renewed the subscriptions automatically for a fee after the trial period. Some did not honor customers' subscription cancellations, continuing to charge their credit cards until a potentially embarrassing call was made to the card company. One producer insisted that copyright infringement was far less of a problem than the fact that "the industry destroyed its own business models."

With the bad apples spoiling the bunch, accessing unauthorized content became a more attractive option for consumers worried about becoming victims of scams, having their personal data stolen, and facing potential embarrassment. At the same time that barriers to entry changed and the unsustainable scam businesses began to die out, content was becoming available on the tube sites and could now be consumed both legally and anonymously, leading consumers to flock to the free platforms.

Compared to the less socially stigmatized mainstream entertainment industries, consumers of adult content may display less loyalty toward creators, making it harder for producers to guilt users into financially supporting the content they consume. Industry specialists also pointed out that they are dealing with a new generation of Internet users who are accustomed to an abundance of free material online. In what interviewees described as "the perfect storm," the crash of the economy, a general cultural shift in consumer expectations, users' privacy preferences, a lack of loyalty toward creators, and the erosion of trust through scam proliferation all came together to drive users to file-sharing and tube sites, encouraging pervasive copyright infringement. But since creators are protected from unauthorized uses by law, why aren't the content owners enforcing their legally granted rights?

Copyright Enforcement Difficulties

U.S. copyright law grants authors protection against unauthorized reproduction and distribution of copyrighted content. Adult content owners are thus entitled to legal action against infringers. But the effectiveness of the methods at their disposal is limited. Litigating cases against individual infringers is often economically prohibitive and carries few prospects of recovery. With regard to file sharers, copyright owners first need to identify unauthorized versions of their files and then the Internet Service Provider (ISP) of the infringing user. The ISP is required to hand over the name and address of the individual account owner, but only if subpoenaed by the copyright owner. This requires a so-called John Doe lawsuit to be filed with a court and the subpoena to be approved by a judge. Once the copyright owner has the name and address of the account holder from the ISP, it can pursue a civil lawsuit against the alleged infringer.

In practice, copyright owners will then instead contact the account owner and ask for a settlement amount under the threat of taking them to court. Given the large number of file sharers and the minor scale of infringement, copyright owners have started bundling multiple users into one court action instead of seeking subpoenas in each individual case. Both of these strategies are technically permissible. In fact, they are economically necessary to keep the cost of litigation within an affordable range. If content owners weren't able to collect settlements or bundle their targets, the costs of enforcing their copyrights would be prohibitively high. But these two strategies have posed difficulties for adult content owners.

First of all, courts have not looked kindly on the settlement demands given the sensitive nature of the content. Users may often be overly willing to settle and pay, just to prevent the knowledge of their adult content consumption from becoming public in court. Account owners may even pay up if they are mistakenly targeted, simply to protect their personal reputation. In fact, some lawyers have been accused of using shaming tactics to extort settlements from users.[12] While not all litigants intentionally extort users and some may consciously target large-scale file sharers and ask for reasonable settlements, the fact that people have a privacy incentive to pay up makes it difficult to determine the boundaries of an efficient settlement system. As a result, courts have started to dismiss the cases.[13]

Courts have also been unfriendly toward the bundling model, denying subpoena requests when the file sharers were from different jurisdictions, from different swarms and times, or had potentially different defenses.[14] They have also found that identifying an account owner is not enough evidence to determine who was actually sharing the file over the network.[15] Generally, some of the interviewed lawyers suggested that courts tend to be unsupportive based on the nature of the content. They also suspected that courts were fed up with mass end-user lawsuits, which require significant judicial resources. Weary of the paperwork that the John Doe litigation brings without ever actually reaching a trial, lawyers say that the courts will find any reason within their power to dismiss the cases. A few players have further hindered the cause by falling into bad graces with judges through their tactics, earning themselves hefty fines and negative publicity.[16]

In interviews, both producers and industry lawyers were divided on whether end-user litigation could be an effective part of a business strategy. At the time of this study, only eight companies in the U.S.-based adult entertainment production industry had engaged in legal action against file sharers. Of those interviewed, all of them said they undertook it for some compensation through settlements. But they also stated that it was part of a larger strategy and by no means enough on its own to effectively prevent copyright infringement and recoup costs.

Interestingly, while some industry lawyers encourage their clients to proceed with end-user litigation, which is arguably in the lawyers' financial interests, others have advised their clients against it.[17] Of the producers that do not litigate, most said that they would never go after file sharers as part of their business model. The stated reasons were manifold. Particularly small producers said that it was too expensive. Even if they could afford to hire legal counsel and pay court fees, they felt that the returns were too low and that litigation would never be cost-effective. Others said that they did not believe in "suing customers," claiming that file sharing had expanded their audience and with it the number of potential paying users. They said that some file sharers occasionally purchase content, and that the companies who were fighting the current social norms of file sharing would lose customers as a result. Relatedly, some felt that litigating against this technological disruption was not a long-term solution, stating that they preferred to apply their efforts and resources elsewhere. Finally, some simply said that file sharers could not be convinced to buy content through legal threats, since they were not going to pay for content either way. Rather than try to "go after students who are just going to go get stuff from the tube sites if they can't download it," they thought that companies should focus their efforts on marketing to their actual customers, "people with disposable income."

While the companies that litigate tend to be the larger ones, not all large companies in the business litigate. As mentioned above, producers generally feel that the crux of the copyright infringement problems is the free content on the tube sites. Even if file sharing were completely eliminated, this free material still undermines producers' ability to sell copyrighted content. The individual users who upload stolen content to tube sites are anonymous and prohibitively difficult to track down. But what about the intermediaries, the tube site operators themselves?

Section 512 of the Digital Millennium Copyright Act (DMCA) exempts certain service providers from liability, granting them a "safe harbor" in exchange for their removal of infringing content at the request of copyright holders.[18] This provision protects the tube site owners from being held responsible for copyright infringement through their users.

If a copyright owner notifies the tube site of infringing material, the platform operator must respond "expeditiously" to comply with the takedown notice and remove the content. In practice, "expeditiously" will usually mean within a period of about 24–48 hours, which for the adult tube sites means that the content may have already been viewed millions of times. Furthermore, once the content has been taken down, it will often quickly reappear. While repeat infringers are required to be banned from posting to the site, the content can be uploaded under a different user account, leading to a continuous circle of takedown notices and uploads that producers likened to "cat and mouse games" or "whack-a-mole."

Most producers expressed frustration with the safe harbor provision because it requires right holders to locate all unauthorized uses of their material and to alert the intermediary in order to trigger the law's takedown procedure. Because not all firms have the time and resources to monitor the sites for their material and send notices, some have outsourced this to a cottage industry of external companies that specialize in the task. Others are working on technological solutions to automatically identify their content and send notifications. Both of these solutions are costly and limited in effectiveness. For this reason, many producers are instead exploring partnerships and revenue-sharing models with the tube sites.

Because of the obstacles in copyright enforcement, producers and industry specialists confirm that the industry cannot rely on copyright protection as it is intended to function. In the absence of the economic incentives provided by copyright, the traditional business model of creating and selling content has become a losing strategy.

> You know, in this industry, when we started, you made a movie and you put it out on DVD and that was your income. And anybody that just stuck with that model? They're not around anymore.

According to conventional copyright theory, production will suffer if there are no legal barriers to copying. While underproduction is difficult to measure in practice, industry members do believe that production of adult content has decreased in recent years as a result of copyright infringement. But the interesting question is whether that's the whole story.

Looking at how the industry has weathered previous changes, technological disruptions are always times of struggle. Many companies go out of business, but they clear the way for new market entrants. The companies that have survived and stayed profitable in the long term have been flexible enough to quickly and fundamentally adapt their business models in times of change. If there is one industry that can survive whatever hardship is thrown at it, it is adult entertainment. Part of the industry's flexibility might be because it is historically unable to rely on law enforcement or policy makers when dealing with technological disruption. The socially stigmatized business has little political clout and adult entertainment companies are comparatively weak in lobbying policy makers to represent their interests. Because politics is not an option, these players may be especially quick to accept new environments as a given and figure out how to work within them.

While the digital age has been challenging, the conversations and interviews in this study suggest that the industry is restructuring itself to adapt to this new environment. Companies are shifting toward selling what cannot easily be copied or offered for free and looking for new ways to recoup production costs. Interestingly, it looks like traditional content may still be produced within these new business models.

Services

Ultimately, I think the defense is a good offense. You know, create a good product, have it easily available at a good price point, so people don't want to go around trying to find it.

Whenever there's a new way for people to consume, we'll get there. And we'll get there quick.

While average consumers may be less likely to pay for content that they can find for free elsewhere, consumers are willing to pay for content that is tied to services. Unlike music albums, adult entertainment is often used immediately, and consumers will make purchases quickly and compulsively—a consumption pattern that providers can exploit.

At the most basic service level, providers will invest in the visual aesthetic and usability of their websites. While the material may be available through unauthorized sources shortly after a release, the producer sites are convenient, high-quality, have tailored aesthetics, and are able to cater to individual tastes through reliable and narrow categorization of content.[19] Since browsing is often part of the consumption, well-designed sites offer an added service value to the consumer and ultimately allow producers to sell material that is available for free elsewhere. Many websites still offer subscriptions, tying in users with the promise of continuously updated content that is easily found and immediately available. Although less lucrative than about five to ten years ago, producers report that subscription models continue to attract paying customers and contribute to their income. When asked why users would pay for their service if they can find the same (or similar) films or photos elsewhere, many assume that their customers value not having to navigate or sift through free material to find the content that they want.

Subscription models work particularly well in niche markets. Similar to the way that the music and book industries have been able to expand into less popular areas with online distribution, some producers are now focused on exploiting the long tail of the adult entertainment market. By accommodating narrower customer preferences, producers remain able to create and sell traditional content, because it is difficult to find rare or highly specific interests elsewhere. Sometimes production costs are sufficiently low to allow individual commissions for personalized projects. Unlike for the majority of adult content, niche brands are often able to build a loyal customer base that is interested in financially supporting creators.

Since content is often copied and distributed without authorization, some producers will also license their content non-exclusively at a very low price. This means that websites may offer authorized duplicates of the same content available on other websites, in addition to their own content. What the providers then compete over are distinctions in design, format quality (for example higher resolutions, faster downloads, or streaming video), content curation, search functions, media integration, and other service aspects. In these cases, there appears to be very little investment in the quality of content production—non-exclusively licensed content is among the cheapest produced. But at the same time this model incentivizes higher investments in service.

Companies are constantly playing with new video-on-demand models. Smart TVs and Netflix-like platforms can offer anything from individual films to streaming subscriptions for a monthly fee. Comparable to previous models of adult cable television and video-on-demand in hotel rooms, even the small bit of convenience that these models offer today seems to generate willingness to pay. Low content production costs for adult material could make freemium subscription models (supported by advertisements and premium content upgrades) sustainable. While producing content is still important to producers, many feel that they ultimately compete over "bringing content to the consumer."

Another service area that has grown in size and importance is the mobile market. Adult content providers are quick to innovate in the smartphone and tablet space, despite considerable obstacles.[20] While some stores do not allow adult-themed apps, adult websites were among the pioneers of mobile-friendly web design and there is a thriving app market for less-restrictive device platforms (e.g., Android).[21]

During times when unauthorized files needed to be tediously converted to different formats, producers were quick to offer their content in every possible format and provide instant access and cross-platform streaming to any device (for example from web to mobile devices, but also to Blu-ray players and game consoles like PlayStation). New advances in streaming from cloud and locker services are interesting, because providers could additionally store content libraries for the consumer, reducing the risk of discovery on their hard drive.

> We might not make as much money on DVDs anymore, but now we have all of these other revenue streams, and all added up together, from cable TV to VOD to Internet to all this stuff added up, that creates the revenue that you need in order to make it successful.

But capitalizing on services is not the only way that producers are moving to recoup their investment costs. The main shift in the industry has been toward creating interactive experiences for the user.

Interactive Experience

> [T]he industry is adapting—there's a lot more "live" stuff going on, there's also a lot more gaming, interaction.

> You see more companies dabbling in interactivity with the content. So I think that as an industry, we are evolving.

According to interviewees, the most significant way that adult entertainment is adapting to compete with free content and recoup costs is by focusing on interactive experiences. As an interviewee described one of the challenges:

> There's not another industry in the world that is media that is for a very specific reason. You can go watch a YouTube video for hundreds of thousands of different reasons. To laugh, to cry, to show your friends, to learn to hack, to whatever, it's everything. But pornography is just to get off. That's the only reason to watch it. So how do you monetize it [if content is free]?

Producers are keeping a close eye on developments in immersive technology. Some are playing with concepts of virtual spaces and thinking about ways to create interactive experiences with various kinds of new technologies. For example, some companies have invested in, or recently launched, virtual strip clubs and other digital 3D or virtual reality worlds, where users can watch media and interact with performers and each other. "[I]t's a good way of creating something that's harder for people to replicate, because you're creating an interactive experience."

One of the biggest interactivity trends in adult entertainment is live chat and live camera shows. Adult sites use popup chat windows to engage website visitors. Some are fully automated "bots," others feature an actual person on the other end, and some will begin as an automated conversation and transfer to a person later on. Personal attention through live chat is one of the strategies that pay sites use to set themselves apart from free sites.

Most industry specialists and the majority of producers noted that one of the most lucrative business models in the industry today is live camera shows. Performers establish a direct connection to consumers via webcam, either out of their own homes or from a studio. Live camera platforms provide a personal experience that is significantly different from recorded content. While the content of a live cam can be recorded and the resulting video material distributed without authorization, the recording of someone else's session lacks interactivity. "You can steal the feed, but you can't steal the experience." In fact, distribution of recorded cam content, whether authorized or unauthorized, can serve as marketing for live camera websites and their performers.

Chat and live camera offer advantages over static video in customizability and personal connection. Not only can they cater to a variety of content preferences, but also to more diverse motivations to seek out the entertainment in the first place. For example, one live cam website operator mentioned a customer who spends hours every week playing chess with one of the performers. He said that the "product" had expanded to meet new demands, for example the desire for personal connection.

It's worth noting that many of the mainstream news articles predicting the downfall of the industry use adult entertainment "stars" as an example. They report anecdotes of lower average wages and famous stars struggling to find work. But according to industry specialists, this narrative does not take webcam performers into account. Many of the performers who make money through live camera and chat websites are not interested in being "stars," because it might actually hurt their business. When what they offer is a personal, intimate, exclusive experience, it decreases the value of their service to the consumer if the experience is too obviously shared with many.

> There's the whole porn star thing, but then there's webcam girls. You know, webcam girls don't want to be known. 'Cause then that blows the opportunity of making a lot of money from people who are spending a lot of money. The guys who are spending hundreds of dollars a day to watch them on webcam, they're not gonna spend it if everyone knows who she is. 'Cause they want that exclusivity. More like, "oh this is my girlfriend"-type feeling, as opposed to being star-struck or in awe of the girl. And if you look at how many webcams there are, I think that porn stars are over. It's like novelty, almost. Like the old-school porn is. I think it can always exist, it's just more of a novelty than it is a business that's making a lot of money.

Another area where producers are looking to create immersive interactivity is gaming. The adult industry has previously faced a number of obstacles in the video game market. Not only are adult companies unaccustomed to the large ex-ante investments necessary for quality game production,[22] they have also been restricted from platforms, mainstream advertising, and standard distribution channels. But with fairly recent quality advances in online gaming, distribution channels and cost are less of an issue. And with increasing consolidation in the industry, companies are more able and willing to make long-term investments. Some of the larger producers have been experimenting with games, releasing initial trial versions for free to attract users and then offering paid upgrades or in-game purchases. Producers are also trying to customize the game experience by letting players create their own 3D scenes.

Finally, companies are searching for ways to build not only virtual, but also real-life social communities around their products. Adult communities are restricted from social media platforms like Facebook, word-of-mouth marketing is less practiced, and videos are generally not widely shared among friends and strangers. But not all platforms restrict adult content: Tumblr is host to a lot of curation and community-building around specific preferences, and many people in the adult industry use

Twitter to communicate with and connect to their customers and fans. Building social interaction and community appears to work especially well for niche markets. For example, one of the larger U.S. fetish producers has successfully built a participatory, interactive experience in San Francisco, including public tours of its facilities, allowing people to watch live shows in person or even participate in scenes, and creating a social network and live webcam community.

All of these strategies provide an experience to consumers instead of selling static content. While this shift makes sense given the difficulties of preventing photo and video material from being copied, it doesn't necessarily mean that adult entertainment producers will give up on traditional content production.

Traditional Content Production

To me, I think there's more money to be made in offering some of your content for free than in trying to protect it.

Producing copyrightable content still serves a function if it can be tied to services or experiences, or used for marketing purposes. Producers said that they were continuing to create standard photo and video content. Looking at the history of the online business, giving content away as advertisement is not a new strategy. Playboy adopted this approach in the 1990s when it realized that its images were being copied and shared online.[23] Rather than attempt to enforce its rights, it marked all of its material with its logo, the Playboy bunny, and harnessed the unauthorized distribution for branding purposes, using it to increase traffic to its website and attract new customers. Not stopping there, Playboy began to actively encourage the use of its material, contacting the people who were hosting the images and offering them a business proposition: If the host added a link back to the Playboy website, Playboy would pay $25 or more for any new subscriber directed to them through the link. It even offered the host sites assistance in improving their web pages. So while continuing to produce high-quality images, Playboy started focusing on selling subscriptions—a service for which people were willing to pay.

Today, producers are engaging in similar tactics. Given the high visibility of content on tube sites, producers are able to distribute video clips to a large audience quickly and cheaply. They can disseminate material without having to pay for hosting or bandwidth, which many producers said had become a heavier financial burden than content production itself. The tube sites are able to cover their bandwidth costs through economies of scale and advertising revenue. Many producers now actively place their own content on the tube sites in the form of short, branded video clips. Sometimes this happens as part of a partnership with the site operator. Producers also distribute branded video clips over file-sharing networks: "we seed our own torrents . . . ; when you search for a pirated version, you find us, first."

Some also host free content on their own websites, saying the traffic and subsequent purchases and sign-ups are worth the bandwidth cost.

> People . . . see the value of making a piece of content that can be ripped off easily and giving it away, and then monetizing elsewhere. You know, things that can't be stolen.
>
> I work with musicians and all day long I tell them "give your music away for free." Because of the eyeballs. If you get maybe a couple thousand people buying your music, that's nothing compared to hundreds of thousands of people who will download it if you give it away. And then . . . you get them to buy x, you know, something that you can sell. . . . and I think that's way more valuable than a piece of intellectual property and fighting that.

Producers also confirmed that content is generally substitutable, meaning that sticking to the model of selling content would be undermined by other producers giving content away.

> The desire to have specific content is being completely set aside by the fact that you can just get other stuff.

> With adult, we're facing not just piracy, but also free content.

> The whole thing's a double-edged sword, I mean, you can lock down your website so it would be impossible for people to redistribute the stuff, but then it's really going to affect what people's expectations are. People expect when they come to a website they're gonna see videos, photos, and

if they like the video they can download it and have it. So there's a hunt-ing and gathering on top of a horny desire that causes people to join these sites. And if you take that away from them, then they're unfulfilled. And . . . you have to satisfy the people who are legitimately there, and that also means that there are some people who are going to take advantage of that and redistribute it when they shouldn't.

Once this cycle has started, it is difficult to switch strategies, because producers who do not use content as a loss leader are at a disadvan-tage. Some indicated that the current situation resembled a prisoners' dilemma, in that no company has the incentive to deviate from giving away content, even though the industry might be better off if everyone played by the same rules. But given the difficulties of copyright enforce-ment, it's unlikely that a coordinated strategy would salvage the previous business model.

It's already changed, so why try to stop it? You have to learn what the new business model is to make money with that environment. And, you know, yeah, it's kind of fucked up, but a lot of things are fucked up. And it is a reality, so there's no way to change it.

Currently, the majority of producers continue to produce and give part of their content away for free. A few indicated they did so as part of a win-win business model. The others felt that they simply had little choice in the matter, either because their material was likely to be ap-propriated and distributed through unauthorized sources anyhow, or because their consumers expected free material and would substitute elsewhere if they did not make it available. In producing and giving away content as a loss leader, companies now try to draw attention to their brand, their websites, their services, and paid experiences.

Companies are becoming larger and better organized, incorporating production, marketing, and distribution. While most people have heard of Playboy or Hustler, fewer have heard of a company called Manwin. Yet in recent years, these new players have come to dwarf their more famous predecessors in size and market power, first acquiring networks of tube sites and then production companies. These changes in structure come with rising barriers to entry in the industry. Those able to enter the market and succeed are comparatively professional and strategic companies, with the financial means to invest in a variety of business models as the industry adapts to environmental changes. Consolidation and integration allow firms to cross-subvent their operations, working with content as a loss leader while making other products and services profitable.

As the industry restructures itself to adapt to its low-IP environment, this raises a more general question: How do we evaluate these changes within the economic framework of copyright and innovation policy?

Lessons from the Adult Entertainment Industry

When asked about their predictions for the future of the industry, all of the industry specialists and producers believed that the adult entertainment business would continue, despite its hardships.

> I don't think it's going to kill the porn industry. No way. There's way too much money to be made right now. I mean, webcams are just ridiculous. So it's just people who understand this [the changed world] that are going to do well. [. . .] I don't think piracy is gonna kill this industry.

Contrary to the stories in the press and the basic intuition behind copyright policy, this study suggests that the adult entertainment industry is surviving. Given its robustness in the face of change, it's worth considering whether there are lessons to be learned for innovation policy. Some industry-specific factors may translate to other creative industries on a case-by-case basis, but the shift toward services and interactive experience seems both broadly applicable and fundamentally important to consider in the context of innovation policy. It adds another perspective to the oversimplified debate over what types of creation we as a society want to incentivize and how to best support creators and content makers.

To borrow a modified example from Pine and Gilmore,[24] take coffee. Coffee can be sold to consumers in different ways. One way is to package coffee beans that people purchase as a product. Another way is to provide a service, i.e., selling prepared cups of coffee. In this case, consumers are paying for the product, but also for the service of having it prepared and ready for immediate consumption. Yet another way is to construct an experience around the product, such as a hipster co-working coffeehouse, where people will pay not just for the coffee and the service, but also for the surrounding atmosphere. The interesting thing about this type of market is that the different goods—products, services, experiences—can cross-subvent each other. Even if coffee beans are made available for free, consumers will still be willing to pay for the services and experiences.

Applied to the online adult entertainment industry, coffee can be likened to traditional content—photography, film, etc. In this case, however, content is a non-exclusive, non-rivalrous information good. It can be easily copied once produced, leading to unlimited availability. Since consumers can get content for free, businesses tie content to services and experiences for which consumers are willing to pay. At the same time, they continue to produce and distribute information goods that they can tie to their brand and use to build their reputation. Another difference is that the distribution of information goods is cheap. In fact, the tube sites, the very mechanisms that have undermined producers' ability to sell content, are a highly cost-effective dissemination device. Free material that is distributed through tube sites can get hundreds of millions of views per day. The bandwidth costs for hosting the content are covered by the content aggregator. Producers therefore have continuing incentives to provide traditional content—to feed services and experiences, but also to strengthen their brand.

Our current copyright law is based on a simplified uniform theory, without regard for factors or circumstances that may sustain innovation in practice, or steer investment incentives in new directions rather than eliminate them. If coffee beans are easily replicated, the story goes, producers will have insufficient incentive to invest in coffee production. The market for coffee beans will die. To correct this, limited exclusive rights are created, taking into account that this will also limit access and distribution.

To be clear: One cannot claim an exogenous shock that makes coffee beans available to everyone for free will not cause negative market effects, just as one cannot claim that unauthorized piracy and content aggregators have not caused negative economic effects in the adult entertainment industry. Even if a system of cross-subsidizing various types of goods is sustainable, production may still be at a level below what we as a society desire, both in terms of quality and quantity. It is important to remember, however, that our current copyright system constitutes a tradeoff. Exclusive rights should only be granted to the extent necessary to sustain a socially desirable level of creation.[25] In other words, the social benefit of copyright should be weighed against the costs it imposes. Both sides of the tradeoff are incredibly difficult to measure, but lawmakers and society must rely on the best possible information available when making policy decisions.

Other studies in this book have come to the conclusion that the market failure assumed in the absence of formal IP protection is not always as strong as predicted by traditional theory. Content production in the adult entertainment industry has not disappeared as our simplified theory would suggest. However, one should be hesitant to conclude that a blanket removal of copyright protection would strike the right balance for production. Just because an industry can survive without, or with less, copyright protection does not mean that economic market failure is absent. In the absence of copyright protection, the level of content production may still be lower than economically optimal.

And it is realistic to assume that production of adult content has decreased as a result of copyright enforcement difficulties. But this study demonstrates some persistence of content production, as well as increased investment in other areas. Standard copyright theory does not take into account incentives to produce for secondary markets or branding purposes. As discussed below, this shift is something that other creative industries are experiencing, as well, and it is something that theory and policy need to take into consideration.

One theoretical concern is the reduction of content quality. In the absence of copyright protection, production may focus on cheaper, ephemeral works, with less upfront investment and more immediate gains. This is a legitimate worry for creative industries, and it is here that there may be a significant difference between the adult entertainment industry and some of the other entertainment industries in practice.

Even during the boom of filmmaking in the industry, when producers had the means to invest high amounts in content quality, production costs for adult material steadily remained far lower than those of the major non-adult entertainment film industry. For example, *Pirates*, the most elaborate, expensive adult movie ever produced, cost a total of $1 million,[26] as compared to the $317 million cost of Hollywood block-buster *Pirates of the Caribbean—At World's End*.[27] The majority of adult films are not elaborate and are produced for far less. While high-quality production is undeniably of certain value to some consumers, it would be difficult to argue that the average user of adult content prefers a market with a smaller number of full-length, expensive films to one with very many different films that are short, simple, and inexpensive. Consumer preferences are likely part of the reason that most standard content producers have not invested large sums of money in high-quality plots, creative content, expensive sets, or special effects, focusing instead on short product cycles and high output rates.

The phenomenon of "Gonzo pornography"—professionally produced content that is made to look especially cheap—is a further indication of socially optimal low production costs. In the United States, legal record-keeping requirements create obstacles for homemade amateur-produced adult content,[28] but cheaply made U.S. content labeled as "amateur" has become rampant over the last decade. Interestingly, most of the popular "amateur" material is only portrayed as such and actually professionally produced.

While some might claim that the vast supply of "amateur" content is just cheap to make and doesn't necessarily reflect consumer preferences, many producers feel that amateur films are actually appealing to consumers because of their authentic feel. In fact, the real or perceived popularity of actual amateur adult content in the 1990s is what spawned this type of professionally produced film. Gonzo pornography effectively imitates user-generated content. The style of filming tries to capture the look and feel of a non-professional production, usually omitting scripts, plots, acting, costumes, and expensively groomed stars, and will even use bad lighting, cheap sets, and a shaky camera on purpose. Often, one person will do the directing, filming, and participate in the film all at the same time, which means that the production team can consist of as few as one to three people.

Needless to say, the costs of producing amateur-style content are extremely low. Assuming that some consumers actually do value this type of content more than expensively produced feature films, this means that the costs to produce enough of it to satisfy the market are low. Even when accounting for quantity and other consumer preferences, the overall costs for economically optimal adult content production are significantly lower than for Hollywood studios. In a market where information goods are optimally cheap, the decrease in production caused by loss of copyright may not be as substantial as for other industries.

As discussed in Chris Sprigman's chapter, the absence of IP protection could actually affect the kind of content produced rather than the amount of artistic production.[29] Looking at other studies on markets with low IP protection, many show increased investment in types of content that are more difficult to replicate. For example, French chefs develop intricate recipes that require additional know-how or personal assistance to copy,[30] and tattoo artists will customize and personalize their artwork.[31] This effect need not be negative. Oliar and Sprigman, in their 2008 study on stand-up comedy, argued that the shift they observed from a focus on joke performance to a focus on joke content cannot be easily evaluated in terms of what type of investment is more socially desirable.[32]

While it is difficult to make the case from a purely economic perspective that necessity drives optimal innovation, and while it would be far-fetched to claim that there is no market failure in the traditional sense in the struggling adult industry, the shift toward experience goods may not be quite as forced or suboptimal as assumed. In fact, one of the reasons adult entertainment drives new media formats so strongly could be because of users' continuous demand for novel methods of consuming content. If users tend to seek out ever-newer ways of enhancing their overall experience, they will be particularly responsive to new formats. One producer pointed out that, in succession, all new media formats for adult content have moved toward creating the most immersive experience possible. She postulated that the trend toward selling interactivity and experience was only partially spurned by current copyright protection issues and was essentially a natural development that had less to do with hardship-induced necessity than with what new technologies were available.

With regard to other major entertainment industries, the broad change this study observes in the adult market is by no means unique. Other industries are seeing a parallel shift toward experiences and services. For example, while file sharing is blamed for declining sales in the major music recording industry, it has had a positive impact on complementary markets for live performances,[33] as well as for electronics and communication services.[34] We also see the effects of letting consumers browse free or unauthorized content to help them make informed decisions before purchasing.[35] Amidst these shifts, both the quantity and the quality of music may not suffer as much as traditional theory assumes.

The movie industry, despite declining DVD sales, appears to be reaching a much wider audience through streaming services, capitalizing on the increase in broadband and digital networks, and profiting from more and better-targeted advertising.[36] Independent musicians are giving content away as a loss leader to build their fan base and capitalize on live performances,[37] and independent filmmakers and authors are using crowd sourcing to fund their upfront investments in content production.[38]

While the general trend toward services and experiences is universal, the most effective methods may differ across industries. The adult entertainment market is characterized by low production costs, commodity-type goods, high demand, and somewhat unique consumer needs and preferences. As such, this industry may be in a better position to capitalize on demand-driven traffic, immediacy, and privacy, while other entertainment industries may be better able to capitalize on ancillary markets for merchandise, loyalty toward creators, or crowd-sourced funding. Most important, the costs and benefits to copyright may vary across industries. Even with an enforceable copyright system, the economic costs of protecting adult entertainment content may be lower than for other entertainment goods, because content is more substitutable. This means that the monopoly-like effect of the exclusive rights is lower. But it also means that social welfare may not suffer in absence of copyright if consumers value access more than high-quality content.

It seems overly simplified to argue that the entertainment industries function just as well without copyright, and that our system of exclusive rights should be completely discarded. The general idea behind intellectual property, that it aims to correct a market failure and compensate creators for their investments, can't be cast aside without a better understanding of the involved costs. As the debate about the tradeoffs in current innovation policies evolves, we need more information of the sort that this book provides. Policy makers should consider that in some cases, consumers might prefer access over product quality, and that secondary markets could sustain both production and quality. This study sheds some light on a previously obscured value judgment for policy makers in practice.

Providing detailed, industry-specific insights into the types of investments and entertainment goods that result from changes in law, technology, and consumer expectations is valuable. How these insights are applied more generally depends on what types of goods policy makers want to incentivize. It also depends on whether the aim is to support creators and their incentives, or whether it is to ensure the widest possible distribution of works. Policy debates have brought copyright alternatives to the table, suggesting various ways to compensate creators for their work, while at the same time mitigating the costs of granting exclusive rights.[39] But in order for these debates to be grounded in practical reality, we need to analyze the workings of individual industries in order to better understand the needs of consumers and creators. This chapter shows that studying real-world markets can provide helpful insights to policy discussions as we think about revising our innovation laws in the digital age.

NOTES

This chapter is adapted from research undertaken at the Swiss Federal Institute of Technology and from the previous publication "What Drives IP Without IP? A Study of the Online Adult Entertainment Industry," 17 *Stanford Technology Law Review* 655 (2014).

1 Markup of H.R. 3261: Stop Online Piracy Act: Hearing before the U.S. House of Representatives, Committee on the Judiciary, 112th Cong., 1st sess. Washington, DC (December 15, 2011), p. 312, quoting Robert Lopez and Jeff Marx (Comps.), The Internet Is for Porn, *Avenue Q The Musical*, RCA Victor Broadway (2003).

2 Peter Johnson, "Pornography Drives Technology: Why Not to Censor the Internet," 49 *Federal Communications Law Journal* 217 (1996): 220–221.

3 Ogi Ogas and Sai Gaddam, *A Billion Wicked Thoughts: What the World's Largest Experiment Reveals About Human Desire* (Penguin, 2011), 6.

4 Ibid., 6–7.

5 Sebastian Anthony, "Just How Big Are Porn Sites?" *Extremetech* (April 4, 2012), http://www.extremetech.com.

6 Dan Miller, "Porn Revenues Exceed $5 Billion According to Industry Survey," *Xbiz Newswire* (July 2012), http://newswire.xbiz.com.

7 See for example Louis Theroux, "How the Internet Killed Porn," *The Guardian* (June 6, 2012); Ben Fritz, "Tough Times in the Porn Industry," *Los Angeles*

Times (August 10, 2009); Chris Morris, "Is the Porn Industry Imperiled?" *CNBC* (January 2012), http://www.cnbc.com; Michael Stabile, "End of the Porn Golden Age," *Salon* (March 3, 2012), http://www.salon.com ; David Futrelle, "Sex on the Internet: Sizing Up the Online Smut Economy," *Time Magazine* (April 2012); Joe Garofoli, "Economic Woes Hit Porn Industry," *San Francisco Chronicle* (March 2, 2009), http://www.sfgate.com; "The Trouble With Pornography: Hard Times," *Economist* (September 12, 2009).

8 In 2012, I conducted interviews with industry experts and 21 producers of adult entertainment in the United States. The quotes in this chapter are from the producer interviews.

9 See, for example, *City of Youngstown v. DeLoreto*, 19 Ohio App. 2d 267 (U.S. 1969), 274–275.

10 *Bleistein v. Donaldson Lithographing Company*, 188 U.S. 239 (1903); *Mitchell Bros. Film Group v. Cinema Adult Theater*, 604 F.2d 852 (5ᵗʰ Cir. Tex. 1979); *Jartech, Inc. v. Clancy*, 666 F.2d 403 (9th Cir. 1982).

11 Jerry Ropelato, "P2P Networking—Kids Know! Do Mom & Dad?" *Top Ten Reviews* (2008), http://internet-filter-review.toptenreviews.com.

12 *Malibu Media v. John Does 1–10*, 12C3623 (C.D. Cal. pending).

13 *AF Holdings, LLC v. Comcast Cable Communications, LLC* 12C3516 (N.D. Ill. 2012).

14 *Pacific Century International Ltd., v. Does 1–101*, 11–02533 (N.D. Cal. July 8, 2011); *On The Cheap, LLC v. Does 1–5011*, 10–04472 (N.D. Cal. filed October 4, 2010); Rhett Pardon, "N.Y. Magistrate Judge Tosses 4 Porn BitTorrent Suits," *Xbiz Newswire* (May 7, 2012), http://newswire.xbiz.com.

15 *VPR Internationale v. Does 1–1017* (C.D. Ill. April 29, 2011).

16 *Mick Haig Productions, e.K. v. Does 1–670*, Case No. 3:10-cv-1900-N (N.D. Tex September 2011); Mike Masnick, "Copyright Troll Claims Sanctions Against Him Are 'Bulls**t' and He's Going to Keep Sending Questionable Subpoenas," *Techdirt* (July 16, 2012), https://www.techdirt.com.

17 Greg Piccionelli, "10 Things to Consider Before Engaging a Firm to File a Mass Copyright Infringement Lawsuit," *Xbiz Newswire* (January 2011).

18 Title 17 U.S.C. Section 512—Limitations on liability relating to material online (Implementation of the Online Copyright Infringement Liability Limitation Act of 1998).

19 Hugh Hancock, "Why a Good Porn Site Makes Our Web Show Pages Look Like Crap," *Guerilla Showrunner* (February 25, 2011), http://guerillashowrunner.com.

20 PR Newswire, "Vivid Entertainment Launches 'Vivid Touch—First Browser-Delivered Web App for Apple Smart Phones and Tablets," *PR Newswire* (September 24, 2012), http://www.prnewswire.com.

21 Jason Kincaid, "Android's App Store for Pornography, MiKandi, Adds Support for Paid Applications," *Techcrunch* (November 23, 2010), http://techcrunch.com.

22 A study conducted by M2 Research in 2009 shows average video game development costs of $10M for one platform, and $18–28M for multiple platforms. See

Wanda Meloni, "The Brief—2009 Ups and Downs," *M2 Research* (January 5, 2010), http://m2research.com.

23 John Schwartz, "The Pornography Industry vs. Digital Pirates," *New York Times* (February 8, 2004), sec. 3, col. 2; Money and Business/Financial Desk: 1.

24 B. Joseph Pine and James H. Gilmore, "Welcome to the Experience Economy," 76 *Harvard Business Review* 97 (1998): 97–105.

25 Paul Goldstein, *Goldstein On Copyright*, 3rd edition (Aspen Publishers, 2010), §1.14 ("Economic Foundations of Copyright").

26 Dana Harris and Thalia Ron, "'Pirates' Pic Unbuckled," *Variety* (September 15, 2005), http://www.highbeam.com/doc.

27 Jenny Aluning, "Top Ten Most Expensive Movies of All Time," *Star Central* (January 17, 2010), http://www.starcentralmagazine.com.

28 For example, in June 2005, the 18 U.S.C. §2257 recordkeeping requirements were extended to site hosts as "secondary producers," which is defined as anyone who "inserts on a computer site or service a digital image of, or otherwise manages the sexually explicit content of a computer site or service that contains a visual depiction of, an actual human being engaged in actual or simulated sexually explicit conduct." See 73 *Fed. Reg.* at 77, 468.

29 See the Conclusion to this volume, by Chris Sprigman.

30 See chapter 1 of this volume, "Norms-Based Intellectual Property Systems," by Emmanuelle Fauchart and Eric von Hippel.

31 See chapter 4, "Owning the Body," by Aaron Perzanowski.

32 Dotan Oliar and Christopher Sprigman, "There's No Free Laugh (Anymore): The Emergence of Intellectual Property Norms and the Transformation of Stand-Up Comedy," 94 *Virginia Law Review* 1787 (2008): 1847–1850.

33 Alan Krueger, "The Economics of Real Superstars: The Market for Concerts in the Material World," 23 *Journal of Labor Economics* 1 (2005): 1–30.

34 Felix Oberholzer-Gee and Kohleman Strumpf, "File Sharing and Copyright," in *Innovation Policy And The Economy*, vol. 10, Josh Lerner and Scott Stern, eds. (University of Chicago Press, 2010), 19–20, 44–45.

35 Birgitte Andersen and Marion Frenz, "Don't Blame the P2P File-Sharers: The Impact of Free Music Downloads on the Purchase of Music CDs in Canada," 20 *Journal of Evolutionary Economics* 715 (2010).

36 Michael D. Smith and Rahul Telang, "Piracy or Promotion? The Impact of the Broadband Internet Penetration on DVD Sales," 22 *Information Economics and Policy* 289 (2010): 289–298.

37 Yochai Benkler, *The Wealth of Networks: How Social Production Transforms Markets and Freedom* (Yale University Press, 2006), 421, 426; Kal Raustialia and Christopher Sprigman, *The Knockoff Economy—How Imitation Sparks Innovation* (Oxford University Press, 2012), 179–184.

38 Inge Ejbye Sorensen, "Crowdsourcing and Outsourcing: The Impact of Online Funding and Distribution on the Documentary Film Industry in the UK," 34 *Media, Culture & Society* 726 (2012): 726–743; Alison Flood, "Kickstarter Becomes

Fourth Biggest Publisher of Graphic Novels," *The Guardian* (July 11, 2012), Online UK ed., http://www.guardian.co.uk.

39 Neil Netanel, "Impose a Noncommercial Use Levy to Allow Free Peer-to-Peer File Sharing," 17 *Harvard Journal of Law and Technology* 1 (2003): 1–84; Christian Engstrom Mep and Rick Falkvinge, "The Case for Copyright Reform" (2012), http://www.copyrightreform.eu/.

9

Nollywood

Pirates and Nigerian Cinema

OLUFUNMILAYO B. AREWA

Nollywood—the film industry of Nigeria—reflects an important aspect of many creative landscapes: The emergence of new artistic movements, at times seemingly from nowhere, that have an enormous impact on cultural production. Over the course of little more than two decades, Nollywood has become the second largest producer of films in the world, just behind Bollywood, and the world's leading producer of digital video films.[1] During this period, Nollywood has matured and become a part of a broader Nigerian film industry that some refer to as New Nigerian Cinema. Notably, Nollywood achieved this success without the presence of strong copyright protection, contrary to dominant expectations about IP. Nigerian cinema, in both its early and more mature varieties, demonstrates that creativity may derive from unforeseen sources. Nollywood also reflects significant digital era trends in both the creation and distribution of cultural products. It demonstrates that conceptions of intellectual property must take greater account of a potentially broad spectrum of creativity. This chapter discusses Nollywood and Nigerian cinema within the context of broader digital era divides, business and cultural practices, and contemporary creative landscapes.

Nollywood and Digital Era Divides

Nigerian filmmaking, which enjoyed a golden age in the 1980s, was largely moribund by the end of the decade.[2] But in the early 1990s, Nigeria started on a path that has led it to out-produce, in terms of numbers of films released, most major film producers in the world, including

Britain, Italy, Spain, Germany, France, China, Japan, and the United States.[3] Nollywood films have become pervasive and "wildly popular" in Africa, as well as among African diasporic communities.[4]

Nigeria is an unlikely locale for the development of a major film industry. Although Nigeria has fairly comprehensive copyright laws,[5] enforcement has traditionally been weak.[6] In addition, there are a number of infrastructural and institutional challenges, including the absence of formal distribution and marketing networks, a lack of production, distribution, and exhibition chains, insufficient funding sources and venture capital, inadequate skills and training, and industry fragmentation.[7] More general concerns, such as chronic electricity shortages and inadequate roads, stall Nollywood production and distribution.

Nonetheless, Nollywood has thrived. It has become a fast-growing sector of the Nigerian economy,[8] generating an estimated US$ 250 million annually,[9] which makes Nollywood the second largest export sector in Nigeria after oil.[10] Lagos, the commercial capital of Nigeria, is the center of Nigerian filmmaking and distribution. Nollywood may refer to distinct video film industry segments. It includes English-language films, often produced in southeastern Nigeria, with principal production and marketing occurring in cities such as Enugu, Onitsha, and Aba, and film distribution that is integrated with the Lagos-based film marketing system. It also encompasses production of films in local languages, including Hausa-language films produced in Kano (Kannywood) and Yoruba-language films produced in Lagos. Although early Nollywood films were typically direct-to-video, films are increasingly shown in the growing number of movie theaters in Nigeria.[11]

Many trace the origins of Nollywood to the success of *Living in Bondage*, an Igbo-language film released in 1992, which sold hundreds of thousands of copies.[12] *Living in Bondage* was written and produced by Kenneth Nnebue, an electronics dealer and film promoter, who had previously produced Yoruba-language films. Nnebue wrote and produced *Living in Bondage*, the story of a man of power and wealth who kills his wife in a ritualistic murder but repents when she haunts him, in order to sell a large stock of blank videocassettes.[13] Like *Living in Bondage*, Nollywood films are often quite melodramatic and borrow style and texture from existing television and film traditions, including American soap operas, B-movies, and Bollywood films.

In its earliest days, directors in Nollywood were largely self-taught, and Nollywood has incorporated institutional structures facilitated by digital technologies.[14] Nollywood reflects broader access to technological tools of cultural production, which in turn has led to significant democratization of access to culture.[15] In contrast, during the colonial era, filmmaking in Nigeria and elsewhere in Africa was largely reserved for European directors and producers because films were thought to be too complex for Africans to produce or understand.[16]

Viewers attribute the appeal of Nollywood films to a number of factors. For many in Africa and in the African diaspora, these films provide characters and stories with which they can identify and that show a cultural connection to issues relevant in Nigeria and elsewhere in Africa.[17] Nollywood films are also highly commercial. The most successful are melodramas "filled with adultery, bribery and elements of local mysticism."[18] Because of their commercial appeal, Nollywood films may compete with Hollywood films in Nigeria and elsewhere in Africa.[19] Nollywood films are watched throughout Africa, and African immigrant communities in Europe and the United States have played an important role in the rise of Nollywood, as well. A number of Nollywood films draw attention to the Nigerian diaspora.[20]

The development of the industry is a complex story that may be told on multiple levels. Nollywood simultaneously reflects varied and at times contradictory narratives about disruptive technologies, diaspora, the democratization of culture, entrepreneurship, and development. In part, the story of Nollywood is one of directors and producers actively utilizing technological innovations, particularly technologies of digital video production. The rise of Nollywood illustrates the revolutionary potential of digital technologies in Africa. In particular, it reflects technology leapfrogging—the skipping over of intermediate, transitional technologies—that is increasingly prominent in Africa today. Because it adopted digital film production and distribution without first developing a traditional film industry infrastructure, Nigeria has not had to undergo the same transition to digital now occurring in Hollywood and elsewhere.[21] Nollywood came of age during the digital era and gives testimony to the potential democratizing cultural and business impact of digital technologies. It also demonstrates important cultural and business consequences of disruptive technologies. Nollywood then gives evidence of a changing global terrain of digital-era cultural and business practices and is likely a harbinger of things to come.

As digital-era business contexts challenge participants in the creative industries, many industry players have increasingly sought to bolster their business fortunes through reliance on copyright law enforcement. This increasing focus on copyright law has influenced legislative activity and has been evident in stronger formal and informal copyright enforcement. Conflicts about how creative works should be produced, consumed, and disseminated continue in varied contexts and geographic locations, underscoring the pervasive contestation that has come to characterize significant portions of digital life. Full understanding of such disputes requires greater attention to changing cultural and business practices and how such changes relate to dominant assumptions about copyright.

Copyright is based on implicit yet often incomplete, and at times even incorrect, assumptions about human behavior. On the creation side, the typical incentive story is at best incomplete in depicting creative practices in a number of contexts. As a result, how people create, why people create, and the factors that motivate creation are often not well understood. By providing widespread access to technological means of creating professional-quality content, the digital era has contributed to disruption in creative activities that even prior to the digital era did not exactly conform to dominant copyright assumptions about creativity. Nollywood draws attention to the ways in which context impacts acts of creation, and it further demonstrates how significant creativity can occur without effective intellectual property protection.

Nollywood also draws attention to digital-era disruption on the distribution side. In the past, copyright did not overtly touch on everyday practices and ordinary people. Although copyright has long served as a gatekeeper for determining availability and access to cultural material, technological realities meant that dominant pre-digital era business models relied on control of access to technologies of reproduction and dissemination. Ordinary users' access and use of materials was circumscribed to a significant degree. Thus, if an average user wanted to make a copy of a record album, for example, available technologies meant that the user's copy would likely be of significantly lesser quality than the original. This also made such copies unlikely to compete with the original. An appropriate analogy here might be handheld recordings of movies shot from the back of a theater that were made available on the streets of New York and other urban areas. Although a market might exist for such products, it is not likely one that creates serious competition. The fabric of meaning and implications of such copying have changed in the digital era, largely as a result of the convergence of digital technologies that enable near perfect copying with Internet distribution. The movies available on the street today are often high-quality verbatim copies.

Whereas Hollywood would understandably view the distribution of such copies as a threat to its business model, Nollywood gained prominence in large part due to pervasive unauthorized distribution of its films. Although such unauthorized distribution is often referred to as *piracy*, that word tends to diminish and ignore the topography of unauthorized uses, which may be both complex and multifaceted. Understanding these varied meanings in Nollywood requires embracing underlying complexity and delving into factors that drive unauthorized uses.

Nollywood without Intellectual Property

Nollywood developed in a legal and business environment without strong intellectual property protection.[22] Although Nigeria has comprehensive copyright laws, they are outdated and do not correspond well with digital-era cultural and business realities. In addition, Nigerian copyright enforcement has traditionally been weak.[23] Nigerian law provides for civil and criminal liability for copyright violations,[24] while remedies for copyright owners in Nigeria include damages, injunctions, accounting of profits, and delivery of copies or materials used to make copies.[25] Past lack of copyright enforcement in Nigeria has been due to a variety of factors, including a traditional lack of domestic copyright constituencies. Weak enforcement may be at least in part a legacy of technology leapfrogging in Nigeria, which essentially skipped the "film" stage of the film production business by going directly to digital video production. This leapfrogging means that industry structures based on centralized distribution and control that promote and enforce particular intellectual property configurations simply did not develop in Nigeria as they did in Hollywood, where the film industry exerts considerable influence over intellectual property policy. These differences in institutional structures make it difficult for Nollywood participants to assert control over Nollywood distribution. In addition to limited copyright enforcement, infrastructural and institutional limitations in Nigeria make the accomplishments of Nollywood participants surprising. Although Nollywood developed to a significant degree within the informal sector,[26] it now involves a complex mix of more than 30 unions, distributors, and other players.[27]

Given this legal milieu, Nollywood can be seen as a natural experiment for the types of creativity that may arise in the absence of strong intellectual property protection. This experiment reflects the actions of varied and at times overlapping roles, including creators, entrepreneurs, and infringers, all of whom have contributed to the growth of Nollywood and its distribution networks. The Nollywood example suggests the need for more nuanced understanding of the interaction between intellectual property and cultural production and greater recognition of the potentially varied ways that intellectual property may influence the shape of cultural production. Nollywood creativity thus has direct relevance to ongoing debates about appropriate levels of intellectual property protection and what creations might arise and be disseminated under weak intellectual property frameworks.

As has been the case elsewhere in the world, digital technology gives people access to tools that can be used to create content. The lower cost of digital video productions in Nigeria is thought by many to have broadened participation on the creation side. Technology has enabled the widespread distribution and consumption of such films worldwide, as well as in Nigeria. Digital technology enabled Nollywood to develop without infrastructure like large studios, projectors, screens, and film reels that would have been required in the pre-digital era.[28] Dominant Nollywood business strategies in the early days of the industry involved high-volume production of films of relatively low technical quality. These strategies reflected a Nollywood business environment characterized by a lack of formal government or private film financing and widespread unauthorized distribution of Nollywood films. Although reliable figures about Nollywood are difficult to obtain, existing data from the mid-2000s suggest that Nollywood films cost approximately US$ 15,000 to US$ 40,000 to make, were often financed by friends and family, and had an average production time of approximately 7 days. A

Nollywood film could thus be shot, edited, and packaged for sale in a matter of weeks.[29]

The viral spread of Nollywood films was a key element of early Nollywood successes. Despite extensive physical distribution of Nollywood films in Africa, Nollywood distribution networks as a whole have attributes that make them more akin to decentralized digital distribution networks of virtual works than traditional pre-digital physical distribution networks for content. Nollywood films are often shared and are available in communal settings in Nigeria, which gives even those with limited financial resources access to the films. An estimated 67 percent of homes in Nigerian urban areas have either VHS or VCD players.[30] Even those without video players at home are able to watch Nollywood films in informal video parlors for less than US$ 0.25, as well as in communal locations such as street stalls, hair salons, shops, bars, and other small businesses.[31]

The cost of content is an issue highly relevant in developing countries such as Nigeria, particularly because cost appears to be a major factor underlying media piracy.[32] Although Nollywood films have traditionally been distributed within Africa largely through sale of physical discs, Nollywood films are increasingly available on YouTube and other Internet sites at no cost, as well as through platforms such as iROKOtv, referred to by some as the Netflix of Africa, that offer Nigerian films on demand.[33] Nollywood production and distribution models have significant implications for unauthorized distribution of films,[34] and the lack of industry control over distribution has facilitated the viral spread of Nollywood films within Africa and among diasporic communities, giving Nollywood a large global footprint in Africa, Europe, and the United States.[35]

Other historical examples suggest that flexible application of intellectual property frameworks may serve as an effective development strategy. German industrial development in the nineteenth century may be attributable at least in part to a lack of comprehensive national copyright protection, which led to a proliferation of books and knowledge that was the basis for German industrial power.[36] The flexible approach of the United States in the nineteenth century with respect to global rights frameworks contributed to its economic development.[37] Similarly, a number of countries in Asia have followed a strategy of weak intellectual property as a mechanism for facilitating the adaptation and imitation of foreign technologies, which was used to develop technological, scientific, and commercial capacity.[38] The U.S. development model represents an important one for developing countries today. In the copyright arena, for example, the United States followed a developing-country approach toward intellectual property enforcement that took account of the needs of the local context with respect to access to knowledge and considered widespread copyright piracy of foreign authors to be international fair use.[39]

Similarly, emerging businesses sectors may benefit from flexibility in the application of copyright. As Nollywood illustrates, businesses in early development stages may actually gain brand recognition and market share as a result of low levels of intellectual property protection. As an emerging industry sector in the earliest years of its development, Nollywood likely benefited from widespread unauthorized distribution of Nollywood productions. Widespread unauthorized distribution enabled viewers to sample Nollywood films and helped solidify recognition of Nollywood products among a wide network of Africans on the continent and in the diaspora.[40] In the early days of Nollywood's market penetration, losses from sales were likely ameliorated by increases in the intangible value of the Nollywood brand.

Nollywood's path to date has led some to suggest that it may represent an alternative model for the development of cultural industry businesses.[41] The ability of Nollywood participants to create robust and sustainable business models will be a key issue in any assessment of the future of Nollywood. The market-driven Nollywood approach is, however, less costly than existing models of film production and distribution and may in fact offer a new model for developing countries that wish to develop domestic film industries. But the model Nollywood has come to represent is at odds with the dominant way of thinking about the interaction between cultural production and intellectual property.

The Digital Era, Intellectual Property, and Business

Intangibles like intellectual property have become a key source of economic growth and business value on a global scale in the digital era. The increasing utility of intellectual property is amplified by the value that markets increasingly attribute to the creation and exploitation of such resources. That market response, in turn, has been a significant factor in widespread adoption of business models that treat cultural products as valuable assets. Markets for creative products protected by intellectual property and market responses to uses of intellectual property resources underpin and reinforce the dynamics created by this valuable asset model. The increasing importance of intellectual property flows over into the political arena as business interests play a prominent role in shaping intellectual property discourse and doctrine.

Valuable asset business models entail the exploitation of cultural products from a value maximization perspective. Valuable asset practices typically involve extensive use of control mechanisms to extract maximum profits from all possible uses of cultural material. The potential for control in the digital era contrasts significantly with prior eras when copyright gave greater space for noncommercial uses like private personal use.[42] Value maximization business models have tended to lead to greater assertions of control and less acceptance of uncompensated uses than might have been tolerated in the past.

At least two concurrent forces in the digital era have contributed to the appeal of value maximization models that exploit cultural products as valuable assets. One key factor is the growth and globalization of markets for entertainment goods and services. Second, investors increasingly recognize the market value of intellectual property assets,[43] creating trading markets for intellectual property. Players have emerged, for example, that specifically focus on creating liquid markets for intellectual property assets such as patents[44] and securitized royalty streams from copyrighted works.[45]

The creation of active markets for intellectual property assets has intensified existing pressures to make intellectual property rights stronger. Valuable asset approaches may, however, also have cultural consequences that should be more closely scrutinized. The cultural material protected by intellectual property is often far more than a valuable asset, may serve important cultural functions, and may play a role in vibrant traditions and creativity more generally. Valuable asset models may also have a significant impact on investment decisions made by existing industry participants. Participants that focus on maximizing value may be less likely to invest in creative products that are perceived to be riskier and that might involve significant unknowns. Such trends are evident in the movie industry, where the high-profit blockbuster movie increasingly defines industry centers such as Hollywood.[46]

These trends also mean that creative endeavors that involve significant uncertainty, such as those undertaken in the early days of Nollywood, may be less likely to be initiated under increasingly dominant valuable asset approaches. The landscape of creativity could thus potentially be significantly affected as a result of investment decisions that embed assumptions of valuable asset models. Such decisions may have a significant impact on creativity itself, particularly since creative movements outside of dominant normative assumptions about creativity have long been an important source of creativity. Underlying assumptions about appropriate types of cultural products may thus have an impact on diversification of cultural products and types of cultural products favored by mainstream industry participants.

Business and cultural models profoundly shape conceptions of creation and visions of the broader creativity spectrum that encompasses various modalities of creation. Valuable asset models typically assume that intellectual property resources exist largely to enable protection of revenue streams for the copyright owner and are for the most part consistent with incentive-based theories of copyright. Valuable asset visions of intellectual property often thus focus on ways that owners of copyrighted works can protect and control their property. The vision of creativity implicit in such models is inherently limited. Valuable asset models often treat intellectual property assets much like museum pieces to which access and authority to use and modify should be tightly controlled. Such treatment has significant implications for the capacity of others to use such works. Valuable asset models embed a limited vision of creativity that gives priority to certain types of creativity, particularly professional activity under the rubric of established industries. This vision of creativity is limited and may not sufficiently incorporate varied modalities of creation. Varied and potentially changing norms and practices that may distinguish participants within and among artistic traditions may also not receive sufficient acknowledgment under valuable asset approaches.

Nollywood and the Construction of Digital-Era Piracy

As Nollywood has matured, its relationship to valuable asset models has grown more complex. Technological and institutional discontinuities in Nollywood have played an important role in the development and enforcement of Nigerian copyright laws. After decades of relatively weak copyright enforcement, the Nigerian Copyright Commission has in recent years undertaken more active enforcement efforts as a result of the impact of Nollywood and an increasingly visible domestic Nigerian copyright constituency.[47]

As the industry has grown into a global presence, its poor distribution systems have contributed to endemic unauthorized distribution, and some argue that related losses of revenue are an impediment to Nollywood's continued growth.[48] Intellectual property laws in countries such as the United States reflect a legacy of centralized industry structures that have promoted and enforced particular intellectual property configurations. The lack of control over distribution of cultural products that has become increasingly apparent in the digital era was evident in Nigeria even in the era of physical distribution. The general lack of control over Nollywood distribution reflects the increasing convergence between Nollywood distribution and digital-era distribution patterns more generally.

Nollywood creators suffer from at least two types of distinguishable yet related unauthorized copying and distribution. First, counterfeiters duplicate popular films and resell them, directly depriving Nollywood creators and distributors of revenue. Second, retail distributors sell or rent films that come from counterfeit sources but may also copy and distribute videos themselves. The first type of unauthorized copying can be addressed to a significant degree by copyright enforcement strategies. The second type of unauthorized copyright also implicates copyright but is also closely connected to industry organization and manners of doing business. Counterfeiting of Nollywood films has been facilitated by the low price point and quality of early Nollywood videos, which gives distributors little flexibility in pricing. Some suggest that audiences are not willing to pay greater amounts for improved quality.[49] As Nollywood matures and achieves greater scale, lost revenues from unauthorized distribution are an increasing problem that requires both legal and business solutions.

This is in part a result of a changing topography of film production in Nigeria that is particularly evident in the more expensive films associated with what some refer to as New Nigerian Cinema. Industry segmentation in Nollywood is evident in multiple levels of film quality and, with some films showing in cinemas, in higher costs associated with some emerging industry segments. The return of cinemas to Nigeria has led to the creation of films shot in 35-millimeter for viewing on large theater screens, such as the 2008 Nollywood release, *Amazing Grace*. Further, some of these films are pushing Nollywood into new genres and production techniques. In 2010, for example, *Kajola*, a Nollywood science fiction film, premiered in theaters in Nigeria but was pulled from cinemas in Lagos after customer complaints. The manner of *Kajola*'s withdrawal from theaters also draws attention to questions of formality and compliance with contracts in Nollywood. As Nigerian cinema expands from its origins in Nollywood video films, varied approaches to filmmaking and varied business models have arisen, including lauded releases such as Kenneth Gyang's *Confusion Na Wa*, Eric Aghimien's *A Mile from Home*, and Daniel Oriahi's *Misfit*, as well as Mahmood Ali-Balogun's *Tango with Me*.[50]

Conventional solutions, however, should not be applied in Nollywood and elsewhere without significant attention to context. Available evidence highlights the variable role that intellectual property laws may play in the development of cultural industry sectors such as Nollywood. The Nollywood case draws attention to the potential benefits of low levels of intellectual property protection, particularly in the case of emerging industry sectors. Nollywood now has significant brand value and is distinguished from video film production elsewhere in Africa by virtue of its brand. Low levels of copyright protection were an important factor in the early widespread dissemination of Nollywood films. Unauthorized distribution of Nollywood films has led to calls in recent years for greater intellectual property enforcement against Nollywood pirates. Discussions that attempt to place events in Nollywood within a broader global discourse about piracy may significantly oversimplify the role of unauthorized uses in Nollywood. Further, low levels of copyright protection that existed in the earliest stages of Nollywood development may be instructive in considering what constitutes optimum levels of intellectual property both in instances of developing business sectors, as well as in developing countries generally.

As Nollywood has matured and industry segmentation has increased, some industry participants consider piracy to be the biggest constraint on the future development of Nollywood.[51] Nollywood has likely reached a point where higher levels of copyright enforcement might be beneficial to further development of at least some segments of Nollywood. Recent discussions of Nollywood draw attention to the losses that its producers suffer from varied types of unauthorized uses that make it harder for at least some Nollywood films to recoup costs and make a profit, which many believe will further circumscribe the ability of Nollywood directors and producers to get financing.[52] As has been the case in other arenas such as music in the digital era, many may assert that intellectual property enforcement can help solve the problems of unauthorized distribution. As is the case in those other arenas, hopes about the potential of intellectual property enforcement to make up for fundamental problems with business models may constitute a mirage that misses other potentially lucrative sources of value for certain types of content. Nollywood underscores the potential benefits of thinking about levels of intellectual property protection in a flexible manner that takes account of the stage of development of the industry and country.[53]

Although unauthorized distribution of Nollywood films has facilitated Nollywood brand recognition, unauthorized distribution has also likely reduced short-term proceeds to producers, directors, and distributors of Nollywood films and thus may also serve as a harbinger of future limitations of existing Nollywood distribution and business models. Current Nollywood business practices result in production of more content than will likely be successful. The potential risks of this strategy are at least partially ameliorated because of the relatively low cost of many early Nollywood films. In the early days of its development, Nollywood creators typically did not invest extra money in increasing the quality of films, but rather quickly released movies to see which ones would become popular. The pressure for quick releases may thus itself be a business response to piracy.

Some producers and distributors cannot meet or accurately predict demand for hit films, which leads to significant copying and revenue losses to many Nollywood producers. Popular Nollywood films are often rapidly copied, at times by marketers entrusted with distributing the film. The inability of producers to keep up with demand may provide an opening to bootleggers who can meet such demand.[54] Nollywood business models already embed mechanisms to deal with the problem of unauthorized distribution. In addition to relying on speed and lead time, Nollywood creators often stay ahead of pirates by relying on remakes and multiple sequels.[55] Remakes and multiple sequels can be seen as yet another business mechanism for dealing with problems of unauthorized distribution because they enable better prediction of potential demand for particular movies.

Discussions of piracy in Nollywood demonstrate the need for finer distinctions in discussions of unauthorized copying and distribution more generally and greater focus on types of unauthorized distribution that represent the biggest business threats. More fine-grained analysis is needed because the success of Nollywood is likely attributable at least in part to rampant unauthorized global distribution of Nollywood films. The Nollywood story may not fully conform to dominant assumptions about incentives often made in intellectual property discourse about the relationship between intellectual property protection and cultural production. This example suggests the need for more nuanced understanding of the interaction between intellectual property and cultural production and greater recognition of potentially varied ways in which intellectual property may influence the shape of cultural production.

Future Paths for Nigerian Cinema

Unauthorized distribution of Nollywood films is part of a wider pattern in the digital era. Widespread unauthorized copying has led to pervasive labeling of all types of unauthorized copying as piracy. Although some Nollywood films continue to be distributed in physical format in Africa, unauthorized distribution of Nollywood films underscores the pricing consequences of loss of control over distribution networks that have become pervasive in the digital era more generally.

The informal structure of Nollywood distribution makes unauthorized distribution of Nollywood films fairly easy to do. Although Nigeria has a copyright law that protects Nollywood creators and a Nigerian Copyright Commission that visibly and prominently focuses on preventing piracy, significant counterfeiting occurs in Nigeria.[56] However, a 2010 raid and seizure of more than 10,000 counterfeit Nollywood DVDs in Brooklyn may give indications of greater future Nigerian copyright vigilance, which may benefit Nollywood creators.[57]

Addressing Nollywood's challenges requires multiple strategies that seek to simultaneously reduce and monetize piracy. Pre-digital cultural industry distribution models outside of Nigeria could impose pricing that in part reflected the value of effective control of the distribution network. Digital-era business and cultural realities have shifted many cultural industry participants along the control continuum in a direction of less control. A content control continuum might have no control at one extreme, which would encourage widespread distribution of content and might lead to dense networks of distribution that may be nonlinear and difficult to predict. The content owner would likely have little control over pricing, which suggests that the volume of distribution would be higher than if the owner could impose a higher price. Absolute control over distribution would be on the opposite extreme of this continuum and would enable a content owner to control all uses of content, with commensurate reductions in volume.

Intellectual property rights permit exertion of high levels of control over content in theory. However, digital-era technologies may effectively nullify or considerably reduce any ability for such control, particularly on the distribution side. This represents a significant digital-era shift with which cultural industry participants are still grappling. Pre-digital era technologies and industry business practices in the United States, for example, reinforced and gave teeth to the control rights granted under copyright laws. The Internet has compromised effective control over a broad range of cultural industry distribution networks, making control over content increasingly difficult for many content owners. Control over content would make the composition of the network highly predictable and likely less dense, assuming that the content owner could completely control the network and all uses of the content.

The digital era has in many instances moved creators of content closer to the no control side of the content control spectrum. Given the lesser control over the composition of distribution networks that this move entails, creators in Nollywood and elsewhere should seek to develop new models that will garner greater value from the distribution network itself and other sources of value related to content, rather than the content itself. For example, through varied advertising strategies, creators could confound pirates by giving away the content for free. A number of mechanisms could be used to monetize Nollywood networks, including embedded advertising, product placement within Nollywood videos, and sponsorship deals. Such strategies would of course require that the content owner be able to harvest other sources of revenue from the distribution network or other uses of content. Nollywood creators could, for example, focus on striking deals that leverage the value of Nollywood distribution networks by utilizing technologies that will enable them to sign deals that entail receiving upfront compensation based on distribution through sales of individual films or portfolios of films.

Discussions about arenas, such as Nollywood, in which unauthorized uses may be evident or even widespread should seek to move beyond copyright and piracy to fundamental reconsideration of a broader range of business and legal issues. Digital-era cultural industry outcomes in a number of arenas reflect fundamental failures of extant business models that may be best addressed through attention to the failed models rather than stronger copyright law frameworks.

Nollywood business models would also benefit from greater attention to intellectual property rights other than copyright, including trademark and branding strategies. In addition to focusing on trademarks and branding, Nollywood producers should continue to professionalize distribution networks and improve industry responses to supply and demand signals so as to anticipate and meet the demand for hit films. As part of Nollywood network revenue harvesting, Nollywood producers could, for example, attempt to develop greater understanding about Nollywood consumers globally through surveys and use of prizes to give consumers incentives to provide information. Information concerning Nollywood consumers could be used as a basis for determining the best courses of action for developing pre-production revenue sources.

Nollywood reflects important aspects of the landscape of creation and distribution of cultural products. Nollywood also highlights the potentially varied role of copyright frameworks in actual contexts of creation. Examining the dynamics of creative communities such as Nollywood can draw attention to the operation of copyright in practice and the extent to which dominant assumptions about copyright creation and distribution may be incomplete or even inaccurate in some instances. Copyright operates in a shifting landscape of cultural production that must give sufficient flexibility to enable a broad range of creative approaches. Copyright applied in an inflexible and decontextualized manner has significant potential to hinder creativity rather than incentivize it. Close examination of contexts of creation such as Nollywood can thus shed light on the operation of copyright more generally.

NOTES

1 Will Connors, "Nollywood Babylon," *Wall Street Journal* (May 22, 2009), http://online.wsj.com; "Nigeria Surpasses Hollywood as World's Second Largest Film Producer," *UN News Center* (May 5, 2009), http://www.un.org.

2 Akin Adesokan, "Practising 'Democracy' in Nigerian Films," 108 *African Affairs* (2009): 1, 7, 10.

3 David Parkinson, "Hooray for Nollywood," *Film in Focus* (Dec. 8, 2009): 1, http://www.filminfocus.com.

4 Ajibade Babson, "From Lagos to Douala: The Video Film and Its Spaces of Seeing," *Postcolonial Text* 3 (2007): 1; Eno Akpabio and Kayode Mustapha-Lambe, "Nollywood Films and the Cultural Imperialism Hypothesis," *Perspectives on Global Technology and Development* 7 (2008): 266, 269.

5 Remedies for copyright owners in Nigeria include damages, injunctions, accounting of profits, and delivery of copies or materials used to make copies. Nigerian Copyright Act, §§16, 18, 19. Nigerian copyright law also provides for criminal liability. Nigerian Copyright Act, §18.

6 Connors, "Nollywood Babylon."

7 United Nations Conference on Trade and Development (Unctad), *Creative Economy Report 2008: The Challenge of Assessing the Creative Economy Towards Informed Policy-Making* (2008), 9; Ismail Radwan, "Nollywood Has Talent!" *Nazikiliza World Bank Blog* (Aug. 5, 2011), http://blogs.worldbank.org (noting that major obstacles to future Nollywood growth include: "rampant piracy, no venture capital, lack of a distribution and marketing network, lack of film studios and poor production techniques").

8 UNESCO, "Nollywood Rivals Bollywood in Film/Video Production," *Institute For Statistics* (Nov. 3, 2009), http://www.uis.unesco.org; Emmanuel Cocq with Florence Lévy, "The Audiovisual Markets in Developing Countries Statistical Assessment Centred on 11 Countries," *UNESCO Working Paper* 59, http://www.unescobkk.org (noting lack of organized government support for Nigerian film industry).

9 Connors, "Nollywood Babylon"; Adedayo Ladigbolu Abah, "One Step Forward, Two Steps Backward: African Women in Nigerian Video-Film," 1 *Communication Culture & Critique* 335 (2008): 335 (noting that Nigerian video film industry has reached nearly US$ 300 million a year).

10 Connors, "Nollywood Babylon."

11 Jonathan Haynes, "Nollywood in Lagos, Lagos in Nollywood Films," *Africa Today* 54 (2007): 134; Abdalla Uba Adamu, "Currying Favour: Eastern Media Influences

and the Hausa Video Film," *Film International* 5 (2007): 77; Oris Aigbokhaevbolo, "Nollywood: A House Divided and Standing," *The Africa Report* (June 2015).

12 Haynes, "Nollywood in Lagos, Lagos in Nollywood Films," 132.

13 "Nigeria's Film Industry," *Economist* (July 27, 2006), http://www.economist.com.

14 Parkinson, "Hooray for Nollywood."

15 Akin Adesokan, "Loud in Lagos: Nollywood Videos," 19 *Wasafiri* 43 (2004): 45, 46 (describing Nollywood as reflecting "a revolution from below" growing out of music video bootlegging and soap opera cannibalization, and the remnants of "Nigerian cinema's golden era").

16 Lizelle Bisschoff, "Sub-Saharan African Cinema in the Context of FESPACO: Close-Ups on Francophone West Africa and Anglophone South Africa," 45 *Forum for Modern Language Study* 441 (2009): 443 (discussing limitations on film production by Africans in francophone countries); Matthew E. Sauer, "Nigeria and India: The Use of Film for Development-Whispers in a Crowd," 6 *African Media Review* 25 (1992): 29 (noting that film production in pre-independence Nigeria was reserved for white directors and producers).

17 Ogova Ondego, "Kenya & Nollywood: A State of Dependence," in *Nollywood: The Video Phenomenon in Nigeria*, 114, Pierre Barrot, ed. (Bloomington: Indiana University Press, 2008), 114–117 (noting impact of Nollywood films in Kenya and criticisms about film quality); Barrot, "Audacity, Scandal & Censorship," in *Nollywood: The Video Phenomenon in Nigeria*, 43 (discussing impact of Nollywood films in Zambia); Ibbo Daddy Abdoulaye, "Niger & Nollywood: The New Romantics," in *Nollywood: The Video Phenomenon in Nigeria*, 97–103 (noting that thousands of Nollywood videos find their way across the border to Niger); Steven Gray, "Nigeria On-Screen: 'Nollywood Films' Popularity Rising Among Emigres," *Washington Post* (Nov. 8, 2008): E01, http://www.washingtonpost.com; Emma D. Sapong, "African Immigrants Find Connection in 'Nollywood' Films," *Punch* (Oct. 8, 2007), http://odili.net; Egbe Osifo-Dawodu, "WIFV-DC Member Promotes the Nigerian Film Industry in the U.S.," *Women in Film and Television International* (Feb. 8, 2007), www.wifti.org; Frank Bures, "Nigerians Thrill to Their Own Stories," *Los Angeles Times* (May 21, 2006), http://www.latimes.com; "Nollywood Dreams," *Telegraph* (July 31, 2004), http://www.theage.com.au.

18 Connors, "Nollywood Babylon"; Jonathan Haynes, "Introduction," in *Nigerian Video Films* 1 (Jonathan Haynes, ed., 2000), 22–24.

19 "Nollywood," *African Movie Channel*, http://www.africanmoviechannel.com; "Film Profile No. 2: Osuofia in London [Parts I and II]," directed by Kingsley Ogoro, in *Nollywood: The Video Phenomenon in Nigeria*, 22, 23 (noting that the first public screening of *Osuofia* in London in front of 2,000 people brought in more money than the *Lord of the Rings* on the day of its simultaneous release in cinemas in Nairobi); Gbemisola Adeoti, "Home Video Films and the Democratic Imperative in Contemporary Nigeria," 1 *Journal of African Cinema* 35 (2009): 37 ("Its phenomenal growth has, therefore, resulted in the successful displacement of Indian films and their romantic duets, the cowboy exploits of American films as

well as Chinese films with combative legs and arms flying in the air at the slightest provocation.").

20 Akin Adesokan, "Excess Luggage: Nigerian Films and the World of Immigrants," in *The New African Diaspora* 401 (Isidore Okpewho and Nkiru Nzegwu, eds., 2009), 402–403.

21 Tom Rosso, "Movies 2.0: Digital Effects Magic Explained," *Popular Mechanics* (Jan. 2007), http://www.popularmechanics.com ("The impact of digital technology on Hollywood has been gradual but all-encompassing. Today, a movie can be shot, edited and distributed—from camera to theater and beyond—without involving a single frame of film. The transformation is at least as sweeping as the introduction of sound or color in the early 20th century, and it is changing both the business and the art form of cinema"); Nyay Bhushan, "Bollywood Billions: Indian Distribution and Production Change with the Times," *International Film Journal* (Dec. 1, 2008) (discussing the transition to digital cinema production in Bollywood); Edward Jay Epstein, *The Hollywood Economist: The Hidden Financial Reality Behind The Movies* (2010), 47–48 (discussing the economics of distribution of film prints that may in the future lead to a full transition to digital distribution of films to theaters).

22 Connors, "Nollywood Babylon"; Copyright Act, (Consolidation Ch. 68), 1988 (1999), No. 47 (No. 42), as amended by the Copyright Amendment Decree No. 98 of 1992 and the Copyright (Amendment) Decree of 1999; C. M. Adelowo, A. A. Egbetokun, I. Olunyi, D. A. Abolaji and W. O. Siyanbola, "The Management of Copyright in the Creative Country Industry in Nigeria: Nollywood Experience" (2010), http://umconference.um.edu.

23 Connors, "Nollywood Babylon."

24 Nigerian Copyright Act, §§16, 17, 18, 19, 20; Adebambo Adewopo, *Nigerian Copyright System: Principles and Perspectives* (Abuja: Odade Publishers, 2012), 29–35.

25 John Asein, *Nigerian Copyright Law & Practice* (Abuja: Books & Gavel Publishing, 2012), 301–333.

26 Jonathan Haynes, "'Nollywood': What's in a Name?" *The Guardian* (July 3, 2005), 134, http://www.odili.net.

27 Organizations involved in the Nollywood industry include the recently formed Audio-Visual Rights Society of Nigeria, a collective rights organization, the Filmmakers Cooperative of Nigeria, which has developed its own distribution outlet in Surulere Market in Lagos and established committees to improve the quality of Nollywood films, the Association of Core Nollywood Producers (ANCOP), Motion Picture Practitioners of Nigeria, the Actors Guild of Nigeria, the Nigerian National Film Corporation, and the National Film and Video Censors Board. Audio-Visual Rights Society of Nigeria, http://avrsnigeria.com/; David Parkinson, "Hooray for Nollywood," *Film in Focus* (Dec. 8, 2009), 5, http://www.filminfocus.com; Alex Eyengho, "Some Associations and Guilds in Nollywood," Post, *Association of Core Nollywood Producers (ANCOP)* (October 21, 2013), http://www.nollywoodancop.org.

28 Pierre Barrot, "The Italians of Africa," in *Nollywood: The Video Phenomenon in Nigeria*, Pierre Barrot, ed. (Bloomington: Indiana University Press, 2008), 15–16.

29 Connors, "Nollywood Babylon"; Sallie A. Marston, Keith Woodward, and John Paul Jones, III, "Flattening Ontologies of Globalization: The Nollywood Case," *Globalizations* 4 (2007): 54.

30 Barrot, "Italians of Africa," 15–16.

31 Ramon Lobato, "Creative Industries and Informal Economies: The Case of Nigerian Video," *International Journal of Cultural Studies* 13 (2010).

32 Social Science Research Council, *Media Piracy in Emerging Economies* (2011), http://piracy.americanassembly.org: i–iv.

33 Mfonobong Nsehe, "Nigerian Internet Millionaire Raises $2 Million More for 'Netflix of Africa,'" *Forbes* (July 17, 2012), http://www.forbes.com.

34 "Kelani Cries Piracy as Arugba Goes on General Release," *Nigeriadailynews.com* (June 5, 2010), http://ndn.nigeriadailynews.com.

35 Connors, "Nollywood Babylon"; Matthias Krings and Onookome Okome, eds., *Global Nollywood: The Transnational Dimensions of an African Video Film Industry* (Bloomington: Indiana University Press, 2013).

36 Frank Thadeusz, "No Copyright: The Real Reason for Germany's Industrial Expansion?" *Spiegel Online International* (August 18, 2010), http://www.spiegel.de/international.

37 Zorina B. Khan, *The Democratization of Invention: Patents and Copyrights in American Economic Development, 1790–1920* (New York: Cambridge University Press, 2005), 309.

38 Linsu Kim, *Learning and Innovation in Economic Development* (London: Elgar, 1999).

39 Nagesh Kumar, *Intellectual Property Rights, Technology and Economic Development: Experiences of Asian Countries, Study Paper 1b* (London: Commission on Intellectual Property Rights, 2002), 28, http://unpan1.un.org/intradoc/groups/public/documents/apcity/unpan017422.pdf.

40 Brian Larkin, "Degraded Images, Distorted Sounds: Nigerian Video and the Infrastructure of Piracy," *Public Culture* 16 (2004).

41 United Nations Conference on Trade and Development (UNCTAD), *Creative Economy Report 2008: The Challenge of Assessing the Creative Economy Towards Informed Policy-Making* (UNCTAD 2008), 125.

42 Jessica Litman, "Lawful Personal Use," *Texas Law Review* 85 (2007): 1872–73.

43 Ocean Tomo, "Ocean Tomo Indexes," at http://www.oceantomo.com/indexes.html; General Electric, *2006 Annual Report* (2007), 6; Viacom, *2006 Annual Report* (2007), 4.

44 Joff Wild, "Introduction: Exciting Times for IP Market Makers," *IP Value 2009* (2009), http://www.iam-magazine.com.

45 Keith Medansky, "Considering Intellectual Property Securitisation," *IP Value 2005* (2005), http://www.dlapiper.com; Mark Steyn, "Bowie Bonds," *Slate.com* (May 8, 1997), http://www.slate.com; Justin Rohrlick, "David Bowie's Role in the Credit

Crisis," *Minyanville.com* (September 30, 2009), http://www.minyanville.com; Duff and Phelps Credit Rating Agency, "Special Report Asset Backed Securities: DCR Comments on Music Royalty Securitizations" (September 1999), http://people. stern.nyu.edu.

46 Howard Jay Epstein, *The Hollywood Economist 2.0* (Brooklyn: Melville House, 2012), 35–36.

47 Afam Ezekude, "Nigeria's Anti-Piracy Drive Yields Results," *WIPO Magazine* (June 2012), http://www.wipo.int.

48 Uzoma Esonwanne, "Interviews with Amaka Igwe, Tunde Kelani, and Kenneth Nnebue," *Research in African Literatures* 39 (2008): 38.

49 Enyonam Osei-Hwere and Patrick Osei-Hwere, "International Flow of Nigerian Video Films, Paper Submitted to the 2008 Conference of the International Communication Association," Montreal, Canada (May 22–26, 2008), 8, http://www. allacademic.com.

50 Aigbokhaevbolo, "Nollywood," 84–85.

51 Jonathan Haynes and Onookome Okome, "Evolving Popular Media: Nigerian Video Films," in *Nigerian Video Films*, Jonathan Haynes, ed. (Athens, Ohio University Press, 2000), 69; United Nations Educational, Scientific & Cultural Organization (UNESCO), "Information Sheet No. 2, 2009: Analysis of the UIS International Survey on Feature Film Statistics" (January 2009), 2, www.uis.unesco. org.

52 Haynes and Okome, "Evolving Popular Media," 69.

53 Eno Akpabio, "Nigerian Home Video Films As a Catalyst for National Development," *Journal of Sustainable Development* (2004).

54 Haynes and Okome, "Evolving Popular Media," 69; Connors, "Nollywood Babylon."

55 Pierre Barrot, "Film Profile No. 4, Dangerous Twins (Parts I, II and III)," in *Nollywood: The Video Phenomenon in Nigeria*, Pierre Barrot, ed. (Bloomington: Indiana University Press, 2008), 43.

56 International Intellectual Property Association (IIPA), *2009 Special 301 Report on Copyright Protection and Enforcement: Nigeria* 2009, www.iipa.com.

57 Kareem Fahim, "Pirated Films from Nigeria Are Seized in Brooklyn," *New York Times* (November 4, 2010), http://www.nytimes.com; African Artists Collaborative, *Public Interest IP Case Study Series, Copyright Protection: A Nollywood Anti-Piracy Strategy*, http://gallery.mailchimp.com.

Conclusion

Some Positive Thoughts about IP's Negative Space

CHRISTOPHER JON SPRIGMAN

To start, let's transport ourselves back to 1995. And let's imagine a conversation about, of all things, the future of encyclopedias. I'll start the conversation with a passage from Daniel Pink's terrific 2009 book, *Drive*,[1] describing two new encyclopedias that are about to hit the market.

> The first encyclopedia comes from Microsoft. As you know, Microsoft is already a large and profitable company. And with this year's introduction of Windows 95, it's about to become an era-defining colossus. Microsoft will fund this encyclopedia. It will pay professional writers and editors to craft articles on thousands of topics. Well-compensated managers will oversee the project to ensure it's completed on budget and on time. Then Microsoft will sell the encyclopedia on CD-ROMs and later online.
>
> The second encyclopedia won't come from a company. It will be created by tens of thousands of people who write and edit articles for fun. These hobbyists won't need any special qualifications to participate. And nobody will be paid a dollar or a euro or a yen to write or edit articles. Participants will have to contribute their labor—sometimes twenty and thirty hours per week—for free. The encyclopedia itself, which will exist online, will also be free—no charge for anyone who wants to use it.[2]

Pink then says that in fifteen years—that is, in 2010—one of these two will be the biggest and most widely used encyclopedia in the world, and the other will no longer exist. Which is which?

You already know the answer. Microsoft shuttered its proprietary encyclopedia in 2009, the same year Pink's book was published. Meanwhile, the all-volunteer, open-source Wikipedia has grown like kudzu. At its peak, Encarta had entries on approximately 62,000 subjects. Wikipedia currently has nearly 35 *million* entries in 288 different languages, all of them written and edited collaboratively by more than 69,000 volunteer contributors around the world. It is estimated that Wikipedia receives almost 500 million unique page views every month.[3] It is not just the world's leading encyclopedia. It is, for anyone under thirty, practically the only reference source that matters.

In 1995, of course, virtually no one would have predicted the stunning success of Wikipedia. Most people would have assumed that Microsoft's encyclopedia, backed by millions of dollars of investment from one of the world's largest companies and protected by copyright—facts are outside copyright's domain, but copyright does protect the particular way in which an encyclopedia entry is written—would win out over a start-up enterprise that seemed pretty flaky and even vaguely communist.

Wikipedia doesn't charge for access, doesn't pay contributors, and doesn't take advertising. It relies on voluntary contributions. And, most importantly, Wikipedia invites people to copy and to edit the content that their volunteers create—the Wikimedia Foundation licenses, free of charge, all Wikipedia content to whomever wants it via a Creative Commons license. In exchange, users must agree to give Wikipedia credit if they publish that content, and to allow others to share whatever they take, including any content they've adapted, according to the same conditions.[4] Yet Wikipedia beat one of the world's most successful firms, Microsoft, at a game Microsoft was determined to win. And now Encarta lives on mostly as an entry in Wikipedia that comes across as a bit of Wikipedia triumphalism.

So that's the story of the competition between Microsoft's copyrighted encyclopedia, and Wikipedia's open source alternative. Wikipedia is significant here because it's a big and important example of how a creative activity can be provoked and sustained with very little use of IP.

But when most of us think about intellectual property, we don't think about Wikipedia. We think about books, films, music, and maybe software—creative fields in which IP plays a significant role in shaping creative incentives, and the behavior of market participants generally. For years, when we thought about IP, we didn't think about other creative fields like fashion design, or cuisine, or creative cocktails, or Nollywood movies, or pornography, or surgical procedures, or football, or roller derby, or fan fiction, or financial services, or graffiti, or tattoos, or perfume, or stand-up comedy. Those fields traditionally did not generate much IP-focused discussion, because the creative work done in those fields relied less, if at all, on formal IP rights.

About a decade ago, that began to change.[5] Scholars in law, sociology, anthropology, economics, and other disciplines began to explore what Kal Raustiala and I labeled IP's negative space.[6]

The Concept of IP's "Negative Space"

When we started talking about IP's negative space,[7] Kal and I meant to identify creative activities and industries to which IP rules could apply, but which for some reason entirely or mostly escape this type of regulation. We also meant to launch a claim that these creative spaces had something to teach us about the effect of IP rules on creative incentives.

Kal and I were thinking about the concept of negative space as it exists in art, where part of the impact of an art work is made by the space that the work *does not* fill. Here's a humble but apt example—the logo of the UK Guild of Food Writers.[8] Even without the text, the logo tells a reasonably percipient viewer that both writing and food are referenced; the image's negative space does the work of conveying the second point.

Kal and I used the concept of negative space in art as a way to motivate a related thought about IP—if the space that an art work doesn't fill can tell us something about that work, then perhaps the space that IP law doesn't fill can tell us something about IP. In particular, we were interested in how well IP's incentives story—that restraints on copying are necessary to motivate creativity—holds up in the real world. And we reasoned that one way of knowing whether the story made sense was

Logo of the UK Guild of Food Writers.

to look for areas of creative work that, for some reason—an accident of history, or doctrine, or as a result of the norms of a particular creative community—was removed from IP's focus.

Did we see healthy innovation in that low-IP segment of the creative economy? If so, why? If not, why not? We hoped that by looking at a sufficient number of low-IP creative areas, we would be able to understand the various ways in which innovation incentives can succeed or fail. And perhaps ultimately we could say something more general about the strength and breadth of IP's incentives justification.

As the chapters in this volume illustrate, that work is now well under way, but there is a lot more to do for the negative space scholarship to achieve its potential. The journey will be long in part because we started at the beginning. What falls within and what falls without IP's domain remains largely unexplained in the literature; we have some theories but not a lot of empirical evidence that explains why certain creative endeavors are granted IP rights and others not, and that can tell us where IP rules should be tightened or relaxed. And, to be frank, despite some early attempts,[9] the negative space literature has similarly failed as yet to provide a coherent account of why IP pervades some creative endeavors and barely touches others.

What the negative space literature has given us so far is a clutch of fascinating case studies. Studies of the fashion industry,[10] creative cuisine,[11] fan fiction,[12] pornography,[13] nineteenth-century U.S. commercial publishing,[14] video games featuring significant user-generated content,[15] stand-up comedy,[16] roller derby,[17] software,[18] jam bands,[19] tattoos,[20] magic,[21] and the flu vaccine[22] show the ways in which creative production can flourish with little IP, or with a degree of IP protection far short of the maximal propertization the law can provide.[23] Related studies of scientific innovation document communal practices that emphasize sharing and resist the full potential for propertization of research.[24] And, as Eric von Hippel and others have shown, a lot of innovation is generated by users, in contexts as varied as extreme sports, surgery, library science, and commercial high-tech manufacturing, who work mostly in the absence of IP incentives, and who often share the fruits of their creativity.[25]

Taken together, these studies suggest that IP incentives are not as central to innovation, across a wide range of different sorts of creative environments, as an enthusiast for the traditional incentives justification would have expected. Some have noted that low-IP equilibria can be unstable, and that they can also lead to a variety of non-optimal outcomes, including inefficient non-IP strategies for maintaining competitive advantage, and exploitation of knowledge workers.[26] But the negative space literature has nonetheless succeeded, I believe, in displacing what previously was far too automatic an association between innovation incentives and intellectual property rules.

The explanations for how low-IP creative communities maintain innovation incentives vary. Sometimes creative incentives coexist relatively easily with copying, because copying sets trends that drive consumption of the creative good. This is the story in the fashion industry, and also, in part, helps explain the dynamic in Nollywood movies. Sometimes social norms step in to regulate appropriation. We see this in stand-up comedy, tattoos, roller derby, surgical procedures, graffiti, fan fiction, and to an extent in creative cuisine. Sometimes creative incentives depend on first-mover advantage. This dynamic is found in many instances; for example, aspects of the financial services industry depend on it, and it also explains part of the story in Nollywood movies.[27] Sometimes creative incentives are established and maintained by firms taking advantage of market power unrelated to formal IP. This also helps to explain the large amount of innovation without IP in the financial services industry, and perhaps also explains part of how innovation happens in creative cocktails.[28] Sometimes industries preserve creative incentives by shifting away from forms of creativity that are easily copied, and focusing business models on other forms of creativity that are resistant to appropriation. Examples can be found in the pornography industry, and in the music industry as well.[29]

All of these mechanisms are interesting in themselves. But are there broader points that we can take away from the negative space scholarship thus far? Yes, there are.

Negative Space Scholarship and the Ellicksonian Pushback Against Legal Centralism

It's important to acknowledge the intellectual foundation of the negative space work. I and many others consider Bob Ellickson's work—and especially *Order Without Law*, Ellickson's book on the ranchers of Shasta County, California[30]—as the source for much of the work that has been done in the growing negative space literature.

In the most widely read academic work that led to *Order Without Law*, Ellickson showed that Shasta County cattle ranchers, a community that one would predict would be aware of and would rely upon formal rules of property—cattle stray, and, when they do, damage fences and crops—actually didn't behave, for the most part, as if the formal property rules were relevant. Instead, the ranchers developed and enforced a set of social norms regarding responsibility for straying cattle. Some of these norms looked efficient relative to the formal property rules they displaced, some did not. The most important point that I and others took from Ellison's work was that particular communities had achieved order using social norms rather than formal law.

Ellickson's work has guided the negative space scholarship in both a narrow and broad sense. Some of the negative space work is a direct outgrowth of Ellickson's work—that is, the segment of the negative space literature that documents the displacement of formal law by the social norms of a particular creative community. My work with Dotan Oliar on the anti-joke-stealing norms of stand-up comedians is in this vein, as is Dave Fagundes' study of roller derby names, and Aaron Perzanowski's work on tattoo artists. And then there is Bob Spoo's terrific book, *Without Copyrights*. Spoo tells the story of the nineteenth-century American publishing industry, which operated in a legal regime where foreign works essentially didn't get copyright and were free to be copied.

The ideology of copyright predicts that in the low-IP environment Spoo describes, there will be chaos, a kind of free-for-all that provides no return to foreign authors and publishers. What we see instead is quite a bit of order without law. Spoo describes a quite detailed and fluid system of "trade currency" under which American publishers made what looked like purely gratuitous payments to foreign publishers and foreign authors, and agreed among themselves to a sort of "first-among-pirates" rule governing distribution of foreign works in the United States. So the norms of the U.S. publishing industry provided a good deal of order without law—a degree of order which, if you credit the incentive thesis, provided some return to foreign authors for the U.S. publication of their works.

I would note that the low-IP regime in the United States for foreign works coincided with an amazing growth of literacy in the United States. I suspect that the two are related. A recent empirical study about literacy in continental Europe suggests that Germany's comparatively lax copyright regime during the period led to an increase in both literary output and literacy among Germans.[31] So the efficacy of low-IP regimes is not just of academic interest; it has real-life policy implications.

Other work in the emerging negative space literature takes guidance from Ellickson at a higher level of generality. For example, my work with Kal Raustiala on the fashion industry leans on Ellickson in a broader, and, I think particularly crucial, way. Ellickson's work was the first sustained attack that I had experienced within the legal academy on what I'll refer to as legal centralism—the idea (very popular among lawyers and legal academics) that the law that is made by the state, i.e., the formal law of statutes and regulations and court decisions, is the law that matters.[32] And our work on the fashion industry is a story that, like Ellickson's account of the Shasta ranchers, pushes back against legal centralism and reminds lawyers that the world isn't all about them.

Kal and I didn't find the fashion industry to be relying principally on social norms—although I would not be surprised if fashion designers do have norms or at least widely recognized practices that regulate appropriation to some degree, not least because occasionally we have been told as much. Rather, we argue that imitation is not harmful to innovation in fashion—and indeed, might be helpful—because of the way that consumers behave.

The fashion industry is rife with knockoffs. Knockoffs are everywhere; they're part of the ecosystem in fashion. Take the women's clothing store chain Forever 21, which is a multi-billion-dollar retailer that is growing here in the United States and now also in Europe. Forever 21's entire business model is based on knockoffs.

So there's nothing unusual about knocking off. As an empirical matter, that's just how the fashion industry operates—both in the United States and in Europe. What's interesting for lawyers is how rampant knocking off fails—at least visibly—to drive down the level of creativity and creative production in this industry.

Why do fashion knockoffs not destroy the industry's incentives to create new designs? The canonical justification for intellectual property protection, in the United States at least, is that unless we restrain competition from copyists, creators will not create. If you talk with members of Congress, that's the sort of story you'll always hear. If you check the U.S. Constitution, that's the reason given by the Framers. That's been the reason, throughout American history, for IP protection: to incentivize creative work.

The fashion industry simply doesn't follow that logic. What we found, in looking at this industry, was that the freedom to copy not only did not destroy the creative impulse; it actually incentivized and accelerated it. We found, moreover, that the relatively friendly coexistence of imitation and innovation in fashion was wired into the industry at its deepest level. Copying is, we found, a basic element of the industry's trend-driven business model. We saw that time and again, as designers came up with a new design, those designs were adopted by others as soon as there was some (often very early) evidence of their appeal. What emerges from this process is something that's familiar to all of us—a trend.

Trends are the centerpiece of the fashion world. And what are trends but a series of things that look alike? This ability to copy and to create a trend is really what has fed the fashion industry. We all know that things come into fashion and they go out of fashion. Imitation accelerates that process; it provides a way for consumers who care about fashion to say, "hey, I want that look," or "I want that item." Copying first helps to set or identify trends, and to anchor consumers' expectations about what is in style at a given moment, which benefits the fashion industry by lowering consumers' information costs and easing the decision about what to wear. That, in turn, of course encourages more apparel purchases by lowering the risk of purchase. And then, as copying spreads, it helps to kill the trend that it birthed. As a design becomes very widely copied, its cachet with the fashion-forward falls. Those consumers jump off the aging trend for a new one that copying is helping to establish. Copying is, in short, the engine that drives the fashion cycle.

To be clear, while copyright law doesn't apply to most fashion designs and design patent and trade dress law have, thus far, been at most a sideshow in the industry, trademark law does at least protect brands if not designs. Trademark is very important for the industry, because it helps to maintain the distinctiveness and value of fashion industry brands.

But it plays a minor role, at best, in regulating the copying of fashion designs.

This brings us back to Bob Ellickson's relevance to the negative space literature. There is no formal law preventing the copying of most fashion designs, but it doesn't matter much. The law is not central to the industry's innovation incentives. In contrast, in Europe there is a lot of formal law that, at least nominally, prohibits the copying of most fashion designs. And yet there is in Europe, as in the United States, an awful lot of knocking off. In the United States, the industry thrives with relatively little law. In the European Union, the industry thrives despite the presence of a lot of law, which it largely ignores. In both jurisdictions, law is not central.

What Kal and I found in the fashion industry spurred us to think more about how this kind of economic success and ordering could develop despite the lack of IP protection. One way to think about it is that this negative space that we talked about turns out to be pretty positive from an economic point of view, at least in some industries. The fact that IP protections don't exist for fashion designs doesn't destroy the incentive to make designs; it actually spurs it. That is, itself, an interesting finding, but I think it's also a pretty powerful statement about our IP system, because it gets at the core of this very idea that, but for IP protection, we will not see creative work. That is a thread, or a through line, in the negative space literature thus far.

I'll conclude this section by admitting my surprise, and disappointment (mostly in myself) that the concept of IP's negative space didn't come earlier. The story that IP tells about itself is a legal centralist story writ large. "No one but a blockhead," Samuel Johnson said, "writes but for money." IP has taken that statement to heart. Without property rights, creativity will fail—that is the heart of IP's justification and the motivating force behind IP law.

It's a perfectly sensible theory about how the world works, but like a lot of perfectly sensible theories, when you look at the world, reality is a lot more messy and interesting and subtle. It took a long time, I think, for IP lawyers to start looking around them because the theory was so comforting and sensible and affirming of the importance of what IP lawyers do. IP lawyers were used to presuming that IP laws play a central role in spurring creativity. They were interested mostly in explaining how IP law accomplished that. They were not particularly interested in looking at places where there was no IP.

That was a mistake. In particular, it was mistaking the means for the end. The means are intellectual property rules; the ends we're seeking are innovation and creativity. IP lawyers should think more like *innovation lawyers*. That is, they should care more about innovation, and treat the tools we are employing to provoke it as sometimes expedient, rather than invariably necessary.

The Negative Space Literature and the Law's Unintended Consequences

The negative space literature has begun to explore another facet of IP's effect on real-world creativity that could turn out to be very important. The principal justification for IP protection, at least in the United States, has to do with the question of "how much?" That is, how much creative work will be produced in a particular setting. In a world without restraints on copying, IP theory tells us to expect too little creativity—i.e., an amount less than the social optimum. A lot of the negative space literature calls into question the idea that IP protection is about how much, because we see creativity occurring seemingly unimpeded in a range of low-IP settings. But in some of the studies we do see a different effect—an effect on *what kind* of creative work is produced. So in other words, legal rules can affect the *type* of innovations we see. We might get certain kinds of creative work versus other kinds depending on whether we have a lot of IP protection, a little bit, or none.

We see this effect in my work with Dotan Oliar on stand-up comedians.[33] In that paper, Dotan and I trace the development of stand-up comedy through two eras: the post-vaudeville era of joke slingers like Henny Youngman, Milton Berle, Jack Benny, Bob Hope, and Phyllis Diller, and the modern age of personalized comedy which started with people like Lenny Bruce and Mort Sahl and Dick Gregory and is today represented by comedians as diverse as Sarah Silverman, Zach Galifianakis, Amy Schumer, Aziz Ansari, Louis C.K., and Trevor Noah.

In the post-vaudeville era when Henny Youngman was young, comedians stole what they could steal. Comedians had no apparent norms, back in the day, against stealing jokes. In fact, they joked about something that they called the "Corn Exchange," which reflected the fact that jokes were essentially public property; stand-ups bought them, sold them, stole them, adapted them. Jokes were part of a commons that comedians could access. You could see reflections of that fact in a great Milton Berle joke: Berle would come up on stage and say, "You know, the guy who came on before me was so funny I dropped my pad and pencil."

So in the post-vaudeville era, comics operated on a norm of open access to other comedians' jokes. It's important to acknowledge that this situation was never universally beloved; comics did sometimes sling insults at joke thieves—Milton Berle, for example, was sometimes dismissed as the "Thief of Bad Gags." But despite a lot of appropriation, there were no lawsuits among comedians for stealing jokes.

In comedy's second period, which began in the mid- to late 1960s, the situation changed pretty dramatically. Beginning at this time was a generation of comedians—Lenny Bruce, Mort Sahl, Dick Gregory, and others—who took comedy in the direction that so much popular culture was taking through the 1960s; i.e., more individualized, more political. Comedy became less of an enterprise of collecting and slinging jokes at people, and more about self-exploration, individualized narrative, and the development of individualized persona.

At about the same time that comedy changed in this way, the nature of the rules governing joke-stealing also changed. Comedians still did not sue one another over joke theft. You might have occasionally found a comedian suing a t-shirt company, or a book publisher—i.e., a person or firm outside the community who had taken a joke without permission. But if you look for lawsuits between rival comedians during that time, you will not find them.

So what's changed? Starting in the late '60s and very much strengthening in the '80s and continuing today, comedians developed a set of social norms about joke stealing: A norm against stealing jokes; norms about how comedians recognize ownership of jokes that are co-authored; norms about how comedians recognize the transfer of jokes from one comedian to another. And these norms are backed by a stiff regime of community sanctions. Comedians spend a lot of time in each other's company, in comedy clubs around the country, they see each other's material, they have a sense of the pedigree of particular jokes, bits, and routines, and when they detect stealing, they often report it to the originator.

What happens next is hard to predict in any particular case, but matters tend to follow a few well-trodden paths. The parties often will first try to work things out; but if working out is not in the cards, then the originator and his or her allies will retaliate. Retaliation comes in a few forms. The most common is simple bad-mouthing. That may not sound like much, but keep in mind that comedians are, as a group, pretty good at bad-mouthing. Take the case of the late Robin Williams, who had a really bad reputation as a joke thief. There's an interview with Williams in *Playboy* magazine, where he says, "you know, at a certain point I stopped going into comedy clubs—I stopped doing standup and I stopped going into comedy clubs. Why is that? Because I couldn't stand the bad-mouthing, I couldn't stand the looks that I got from people."

Or take the case of Carlos Mencia, another rather famous alleged joke thief. In 2007, Mencia was confronted angrily by a fellow comedian named Joe Rogan at a comedy club in L.A. The videotaped confrontation where Rogan accused Mencia of joke-stealing, which included threats of violence and eventually audience side-taking, was posted on YouTube, and went viral. Carlos Mencia has since been lampooned by the guys on *South Park*, in an episode where he's beaten to death by a cartoon Kanye West for stealing a joke. Which stands as a pretty extreme form of bad-mouthing—but again, comics are nothing if not inventive.

There are other forms of retaliation. Sometimes comedians will engage cooperatively in group boycotts—i.e., agreements not to work with recalcitrant joke thieves. Sometimes comedians will threaten violence, or even carry out actual physical violence. I don't mean to condone violence. Nor do I mean to uncritically valorize comedians' system of community justice. There's no guarantee that the informal law will reach the right results in joke-stealing disputes that are unclear (of course, the formal law may err as well). And there are aspects of the informal system (the absence of any sort of fair use norm; the lack of an appeal mechanism) that should give us pause. But at a general level, comedians' norms appear to achieve an important end. They restrain joke thievery enough that incentives to invest in the creation of new comedic material remain robust.

What do we take from this? As has been noted above, the typical dialogue about IP protection can be characterized as "more vs. less." That is, if we have more IP, we'll get more creativity, and if we have less IP, we'll get less. Dotan and I didn't really see any evidence for that in the very creative world of stand-up comedians. We don't see any evidence that there was a dearth of comedic production before the norm system took hold in comedy. We see lots of jokes during the era of the Henny Youngman-type joke-slinger. After the norms system takes hold, what we see is not *more* material; what we see is *different* material. We see material that is more personalized, that is more narrative, that is more tailored to individual comedians, that represents a higher level of creative investment.

The idea that IP is not a simple question of more vs. less shouldn't be surprising, but it has profound implications. Seen in this light, IP raises difficult normative questions about what kind of culture we want. You can approach this question using our findings in the comedy paper. In the old comedic community, with its comedic commons, we got the kinds of jokes that were perhaps not amazingly original, but they were the kinds of jokes that you'd tell to your friends. They were the kinds of jokes you'd tell to your mother. If you think of comedy as serving as a social lubricant—the thing that, along with alcohol, makes family gatherings tolerable—then you probably like the kind of comedy that the post–vaudeville era produced, and you probably like the free-appropriation regime that went along with it.

If, on the other hand, you think of comedy as a platform for political statements or individual artistic exploration—i.e., the kind of deeply original, individualized, diverse, richly narrative, and persona-driven comedy we get today—you probably like the informal regime of anti-stealing norms that accompanies this sort of comedic work, that grew up alongside it, that helped to cement it into place.

And, unlike the typical IP discussion about how much creativity we will get, which primarily raises questions that are the terrain of lawyers and economists, questions about what sort of creativity we actually value should involve all of us. These are democratic questions.

We see this effect again in Kate Darling's work on the online pornography industry.[34] Kate's work describes how online piracy, most notably through the ubiquitous porn tube sites,[35] has affected the industry's output. Not primarily by reducing it (although because Kate's study doesn't measure production, that is possible, even if it doesn't appear likely), but by shifting it.

Kate provides evidence, based on interviews of industry participants, that production in the industry has shifted away from pornographic feature films and toward cheaper scenes designed to be viewed on the tube sites, which have entered into deals with many producers to split ad revenue. Kate also documents the rise of the so-called cam girls—i.e., women (and men) who perform live using webcams. Clients pay to join these performances, and the revenue stream that results is resistant to piracy for much the same reason that live music performances are— there is usually no recording, and, even if there is, it's far from a perfect substitute for the live experience. This is true even when the performance is made over an Internet connection, because a feature of these performances is interactivity—ask (and pay) for the performer to engage in a particular sex act, and you might receive it.

What Kate sees in online pornography is a lot like what Kal and I wrote about in *The Knockoff Economy* regarding the music industry's recent history. Online music piracy hasn't reduced the quantity of music produced, or indeed its quality, as a series of studies by Joel Waldfogel demonstrates.[36] But it has reduced revenues from recorded music— according to RIAA figures, revenues are down more than 60%, adjusted for inflation, since 1999, which was Napster's breakout year.

What has happened as the music industry has slipped into low-IP status, involuntarily and with a great deal of kicking and screaming, again raises the question whether the primary real-world effect of IP rights is to regulate "how much?" or "what kind?" The music industry's story suggests it's the latter. Overall output of recorded music doesn't seem to have been affected, perhaps because recorded music is linked to revenues from live musical performances, which are growing smartly. But the industry has shifted its product mix from something that's easily pirated (recordings) to something that is not (concerts). The latter is growing, faster than it probably otherwise would if the former were not comparatively vulnerable to piracy.

The music industry's shift, is, of course, pretty messy. There are winners (the firms that control live performance, such as Live Nation), and losers (the major record companies). And there is the appearance of crisis, not least because the losers have a big megaphone, and, from their narrow perspective, things have gone straight to hell.

But from a broader social perspective, music seems to be doing pretty well as a low-IP industry. We can argue about whether the industry's renewed focus on live performances is a good thing—especially if it comes at the expense of investment in great recordings. I don't see any evidence yet that the two are opposed in some sort of zero-sum game. Great recordings fill the seats for live performances, and live shows make money. That is the new music industry math. Actually, it's not even that. It's more like a return to traditional music industry math, because the heyday of revenues from recorded music didn't last very long, and, for most of the history of the music industry, live performance loomed large as a revenue source. What's old is new again.

The Negative Space Literature and the Question of What (and Who) Is Innovation For?

I'll end by raising one other sort of unintended consequence of the IP law that the negative space scholarship should explore. When Kal and I wrote our first fashion paper, we spent a lot of time looking through registered designs. Way too much time. And, as it turns out, very few fashion designs are registered. There are lots of t-shirt designs and designs for jeans pocket stitching in the European design registry. But surprisingly few entries exist for designs that anyone would describe as relating to "fashion."

On the other hand, there are a surprisingly large number of designs for the outer casings of portable generators—a product that, prior to my tour through the European design registry, I never considered to be particularly "designy."

I wanted to know why companies would register generator casing designs—remember, these registrations don't cover anything functional about the generators, but rather relate solely to their outward appearance—so I made phone calls to a few Japanese companies that made portable generators and asked. I finally was able to get on the phone with an English-speaking Japanese lawyer at one of the companies. What he told me was very interesting. He said that portable generators were a mature technology. They all basically work the same, they are all about as good as one another, they all cost about the same per watt of power generated, and it is difficult and expensive to make significant functional improvements. As a result, the market for portable generators is very competitive.

So, the Japanese lawyer said, we have a problem. We have to differentiate our product, or else we'll be stuck competing mostly on price. So how do we differentiate our product? By making it *look* different.

The purpose of the European design protection system, and of the related American design patent system, is to promote "innovation" in design. It's a branch of the canonical IP story. But "innovation" to what end?

Our American picture of IP is that the sort of innovation it provokes is progressive—that is, innovation improves social welfare, and is therefore something we are right to promote. But the link between "innovation" and social welfare isn't simple. There's a lot of innovation that may be privately beneficial, but nonetheless socially wasteful. The portable generator design protection story I just related is an example. The most optimistic take on the story is that these portable generators look different because different generator casing designs are satisfying different consumer preferences for the appearance of generator casings. If that's true, then the heterogeneous tastes of diverse consumers are being satisfied through product differentiation. And that's a version of the story in which design protection is leading to "innovation" that improves social welfare.

The problem is that this optimist's version seems, at least to me, palpably ridiculous. The Japanese lawyer wasn't a naïf about the meaning of the story, and I see no reason why anyone else should be, either. The truth is that portable generators are basically commodity items. There is (or was) sharp price competition in the market for these products, and consumers benefit from that. Design "innovation" is, in this instance, the producers creating meaningless aesthetic distinctions using IP.

The producers' hope is that by introducing aesthetic distinctions, and advertising them, the producers will create consumer demand for aesthetic content in generators where none had existed before. And that allows the producers to escape from sharp textbook competition for the friendlier (to them) terrain of market power–based competition—aka, oligopoly competition. The effect of the producers' design "innovations" is just to transfer wealth from consumers to producers. That isn't the sort of innovation we think of IP producing. And yet it is often precisely the sort of innovation that IP in fact does produce.

Now, I must acknowledge that a lot of economists will shake their heads at this. To the economics profession as a whole, a preference is a preference, and, if a preference is satisfied, that is unambiguously good. Treating all preferences alike is certainly a very useful simplifying assumption if you're doing economic modeling. And our commitment to free speech likely makes us reluctant to limit producers' attempts to convince consumers that they should value and pay more for aspects of differentiation that were, like the design of portable generator casings, previously meaningless to them. But it's one thing to refrain from interfering, on free speech grounds. It's quite another to *encourage* this process, which is what we're doing when we put design protection systems in place that prevent competitors from imitating these meaningless differentiators.

This is an important set of questions that the negative space literature should explore. How much of the "innovation" produced by IP can be meaningfully characterized as "progressive"? How much cannot? And, in industries where we find less IP, do we find less of both sorts of innovation? Or, perhaps, only less of the meaningless sort?

IP Lawyers → Innovation Lawyers

Let me wrap this up with a more meta observation about what the negative space literature means for people who study and work in the field of IP. Even at this early stage of its development, the negative space literature raises a basic question about what exactly our field is, and what we care about. The negative space literature suggests that the field is *innovation*. And that IP is a sub-field. In other words, that IP is a tool, useful in some instances more than in others. And it is exerting effects that are complex and contingent. The legal centralism story that Bob Ellickson helped undermine in the property context isn't sensible in the intellectual property context, either. This is not to say that the formal law doesn't matter. It appears to matter a lot in pharmaceuticals, and in blockbuster movies. But in a range of other creative industries—some very economically important—it matters far less.

So how do we move away from the ideology that holds that at the root of innovation we invariably should find IP? How do we deal with a culture of IP academics and IP lawyers that imagine there's an IP solution for every innovation problem? This is not just a rhetorical or ideological question; it has real world consequences. We *need* the progressive sort of innovation. It is the single most salient thing that human beings do that over time tends to make life better, and less brutish, nasty, and short. We should care about fostering the conditions that lead to it, and the persistence of legal centralism in this field is likely to lead us astray. Seen in its best light, the negative space scholarship is a call for suspending ideology in favor of opening our eyes, re-engaging in the hard work of empirical study, looking very carefully at the creative communities around us, and getting down and a little bit dirty to figure out how they work.

NOTES

I would like to thank the Filomen D'Agostino and Max E. Greenberg Research Fund for a grant that supported this work. Dedicated to the memory of Greg Lastowka, who was a friend and mentor to many of the scholars discussed and cited here.

1 Daniel H. Pink, *Drive: The Surprising Truth About What Motivates Us* (Riverhead, 2009).

2 Ibid., 13–14.

3 See the Wikipedia entry on "Wikipedia," https://en.wikipedia.org.

4 See Wikimedia Foundation, "Wikipedia Terms of Use," https://wikimediafoundation.org.

5 It's important to acknowledge that Jessica Litman was characteristically prescient in identifying low-IP areas of creativity as potentially valuable objects of study. In her excellent 2001 book *Digital Copyright* (Prometheus, 2001), Litman pointed out that copyright's incentives justification was contestable, and that there were apparent counterexamples. "Of course, we don't give copyright protection to fashions or food," Litman wrote. "We never have."

6 See Kal Raustiala and Christopher Jon Sprigman, "The Piracy Paradox: Innovation and Intellectual Property in Fashion Design," 92 *Virginia Law Review* 1687 (2006): 1764.

7 See generally Raustiala and Sprigman, "The Piracy Paradox."

8 http://www.gfw.co.uk/.

9 See, e.g., Kal Raustiala and Christopher Jon Sprigman, *The Knockoff Economy: How Imitation Sparks Innovation* (Oxford, 2012); Elizabeth Rosenblatt, "A Theory of IP's Negative Space," 34 *Columbia Journal of Law & Arts* 317 (2011).

10 Jonathan Barnett, "Shopping for Gucci on Canal Street: Reflections on Status Consumption, Intellectual Property, and the Incentive Thesis," 91 *Virginia Law*

Review 1381 (2005); Raustiala and Sprigman, "The Piracy Paradox"; C. Scott Hemphill and Jeannie Suk, "The Law, Culture, and Economics of Fashion," 61 *Stanford Law Review* 1147 (2009); Kal Raustiala and Christopher Jon Sprigman, "The Piracy Paradox Revisited," 61 *Stanford Law Review* 1201 (2009); Jonathan M. Barnett, Gilles Grolleau, and Sana El Harbi, "The Fashion Lottery: Cooperative Innovation in Stochastic Markets," 39 *Journal of Legal Studies* 159 (2010); C. Scott Hemphill and Jeannie C. Suk, "The Fashion Originators' Guild of America: Self-Help at the Edge of IP and Antitrust," in *Intellectual Property at the Edge*, Rochelle Dreyfuss and Jane Ginsburg, eds. (Oxford, 2014).

11 See chapter 1 of this volume, Emmanuelle Fauchart and Eric von Hippel's "Norms-Based Intellectual Proprty Systems"; Christopher J. Buccafusco, "On the Legal Consequences of Sauces: Should Thomas Keller's Recipes Be per se Copyrightable?" 24 *Cardozo Arts & Entertainment Law Journal* 1121 (2007);

12 See Rebecca Tushnet's work in chapter 7 of this volume, "Architecture and Morality"; Rebecca Tushnet, "Economics of Desire: Fair Use and Marketplace Assumptions," 51 *William & Mary Law Review* 513 (2009).

13 See chapter 8 of this volume, "Internet Pornography," by Kate Darling; Kate Darling, "IP Without IP? A Study of the Online Adult Entertainment Industry," 17 *Stanford Technology Law Review* 655 (2014).

14 Robert Spoo, *Without Copyrights: Piracy, Publishing, and the Public Domain* (Oxford, 2013).

15 Greg Lastowka, "Minecraft as Web 2.0: Amateur Creativity & Digital Games" (October 5, 2014), http://papers.ssrn.com.

16 Dotan Oliar and Christopher Jon Sprigman, "There's No Free Laugh (Anymore): The Emergence of Intellectual Property Norms and the Transformation of Stand-Up Comedy," 94 *Virginia Law Review* 1787 (2008).

17 See Dave Fagundes' work in chapter 6 of this volume, "Subcultural Change and Dynamic Norms"; David Fagundes, "Talk Derby to Me: Intellectual Property Norms Governing Roller Derby Pseudonyms," 90 *Texas Law Review* 1093 (2012). See also Gerard N. Magliocca, "Patenting the Curve Ball: Business Methods and Industry Norms," *BYU Law Review* 875 (2009) (discussing industry norms against patenting and arguing that business method patents should not be expanded to cover industries where such norms exist).

18 Yochai Benkler, *The Wealth of Networks: How Social Production Transforms Markets and Freedom* (Yale, 2007); Jon M. Garon, "Wiki Authorship, Social Media, and the Curatorial Audience," 1 *Harvard Journal of Sports & Entertainment Law* 95 (2010); Catherine L. Fisk, "Credit Where It's Due: The Law and Norms of Attribution," 95 *Georgetown Law Journal* 49 (2006); Josh Lerner and Jean Tirole, "The Economics of Technology Sharing: Open Source and Beyond," *Journal of Economic Perspectives* 99 (2005).

19 Mark F. Schultz, "Fear and Norms and Rock & Roll: What Jambands Can Teach About Persuading People to Comply with Copyright Law," 21 *Berkeley Technology Law Journal* 651 (2006).

20 See Aaron Perzanowski's work in this volume, chapter 4, "Owning the Body"; Aaron Perzanowski, "Tattoos and IP Norms," 98 *Minnesota Law Review* 511 (2013).

21 Jacob Loshin, "Secrets Revealed: Protecting Magicians' Intellectual Property Without Law," in *Law and Magic: A Collection of Essays* 123, Christine Corcos, ed. (Carolina Academic Press, 2010).

22 Amy Kapczynski, "Order Without Intellectual Property Law: The Flu Network as a Case Study in Open Science" (unpublished working draft on file with author).

23 See also the collection of essays in *Making and Unmaking Intellectual Property*, Mario Biagioli, Peter Jaszi, and Martha Woodmansee, eds. (University of Chicago, 2011).

24 See chapter 3 of this volume, "Derogatory to Professional Character?" by Katherine Strandburg; Katherine J. Strandburg, "Curiosity-Driven Research and University Technology Transfer," in *University Entrepreneurship and Technology Transfer: Process, Design, and Intellectual Property* 93, Advances in the Study of Entrepreneurship, Innovation and Economic Growth, Vol. 16, Gary D. Libecap, ed. (2005); Fiona Murray et al., "Of Mice and Academics: Examining the Effect of Openness on Innovation," *National Bureau of Economic Research*, Working Paper No. 14819 (2009), http://www.nber.org.

25 Eric Von Hippel, *Democratizing Innovation* (2005); Jeroen P.J. de Jong and Eric von Hippel, "Transfers of User Process Innovations to Process Equipment Producers: A Study of Dutch High-Tech Firms," 38 *Research Policy* 1181 (2009); Fred Gault and Eric von Hippel, "The Prevalence of User Innovation and Free Innovation Transfers: Implications for Statistical Indicators and Innovation Policy," MIT Sloan School of Management Research Paper No. 4722–09 (2009), http://papers.ssrn.com.

26 See, e.g., Rochelle Cooper Dreyfuss, "Does IP Need IP? Accommodating Intellectual Production Outside the Intellectual Property Paradigm," 31 *Cardozo Law Review* 1437 (2010).

27 See Raustiala and Sprigman, *The Knockoff Economy*, 155–161.

28 Ibid.

29 See Darling, "IP Without IP." See also Raustiala and Sprigman, *The Knockoff Economy*, 179–184.

30 Robert Ellickson, *Order Without Law: How Neighbors Settle Disputes* (Harvard, 1994).

31 See Frank Thadeuscz, "No Copyright Law: The Real Reason for Germany's Industrial Expansion?" *Spiegel Online International* (Aug. 18, 2010), http://www.spiegel.de.

32 See John Griffiths, "What Is Legal Pluralism," 24 *Journal of Legal Pluralism* 1 (1986).

33 Oliar and Sprigman, "There's No Free Laugh."

34 See Darling, "IP Without IP."

35 Websites, such as pornhub.com, redtube.com, and xvideos.com, that offer clips of pornographic content in a format similar to the way non-pornographic content is offered by YouTube.

36 See Joel Waldfogel, "Bye, Bye, Miss American Pie? The Supply of New Recorded Music Since Napster," NBER Working Paper No. w16882 (March 2011), http://papers.ssrn.com; Joel Waldfogel, "And the Bands Played On: Digital Disintermediation and the Quality of New Recorded Music" (July 2012), http://papers.ssrn.com.

ABOUT THE CONTRIBUTORS

Olufunmilayo B. Arewa is Professor of Law and Anthropology at the University of California, Irvine.

Kate Darling is a Research Specialist at the Massachusetts Institute of Technology (MIT) Media Lab and a Fellow at the Harvard Berkman Center for Internet and Society.

David Fagundes is Professor of Law at the University of Houston Law Center.

Emmanuelle Fauchart is Faculty of Economics and Management at the University of Strasbourg.

Eric von Hippel is Professor of Technological Innovation in the MIT Sloan School of Management and the author of *Democratizing Innovation*.

Marta Iljadica is Lecturer of Law at the School of Law at the University of Southampton. She is the author of *Copyright beyond Law: Regulating Creativity in the Graffiti Subculture*.

Aaron Perzanowski is Professor of Law at Case Western Reserve University School of Law and author of *The End of Ownership: Personal Property in the Digital Economy*.

Matthew Schruers is Vice President for Law & Policy at the Computer & Communications Industry Association. He is also an adjunct professor at Georgetown and American University, where he teaches courses on intellectual property and Internet law.

Christopher Jon Sprigman is Professor of Law at New York University School of Law and co-author of *The Knockoff Economy: How Imitation Sparks Innovation.*

Katherine J. Strandburg is Alfred B. Engelberg Professor of Law at New York University School of Law. She is the co-editor of *Governing Knowledge Commons.*

Rebecca Tushnet is Professor of Law at Georgetown University. With Eric Goldman, she publishes a casebook on advertising and marketing law, and has a forthcoming book on images in intellectual property law. She helped found the Organization for Transformative Works, a non-profit dedicated to supporting and promoting fanworks.

INDEX